COMPUTER HARDW
UBUNTU LINUX
WINDOWS 10
INTERNET INTRODUCTIONS

COMPUTER HARDWARE UBUNTU LINUX WINDOWS 10 INTERNET INTRODUCTIONS

LEARN COMPUTER BASIC HARDWARE, LINUX, WINDOW 10, INTERNET & SHORT OFFICE 2016 INTRODUCTION IN THIS BOOK

Lalit Mali

Notion Press

Old No. 38, New No. 6
McNichols Road, Chetpet
Chennai - 600 031

First Published by Notion Press 2017
Copyright © Lalit Mali 2017
All Rights Reserved.

ISBN 978-1-946869-02-9

This book dedicated to my heavenly father

My inspiration, with my lovely daughter

Siddhi!

Know about Author

Whole book design concept idea of Mr. Lalit kumar mali student of information technology past 16 year, he done "o" "a" level complete from nielit formally called (doeacc) "b" level in term include msc/cs done in computer science along graduate, author interested in different field of information technology include computer science subject name windows, linux, mac os, android, several kind programming with computer advance additional concept, now author working as stock broker past 3 year successfully, even continuing write new books concept on field of information technology.

Thank you
Lalit Mali

Acknowledgements

- SURESH PARMAR
  MBA, SMEP -IIM – AHMEDABAD
  SHREE BALAJI PUBLICATION
  PARTNER.

- I want to thanks Notion press team to publish this book with its default structure with its key points. Special thanks to those author books that I have been reading during my information technology education/career past several years along internet various website, I am continuing improving my skill to offer something great information technology experience to its audience.

Detail Content of Computer Basic Book

- ⮊ Computer basic introduction.
- ⮊ Number system, type of number system.
- ⮊ Computer hardware & its component.
- ⮊ Assembling & disassembling personal computer.
- ⮊ Know about operating system & its features.
- ⮊ Disk operating system & its internal or external command.
- ⮊ Windows accessories apps.
- ⮊ Notepad, word pad, ms paint, power shell, fax and scan.
- ⮊ Linux overview and introduction.
- ⮊ Installing ubuntu linux step by step.
- ⮊ Linux file structure, linux console/terminal command.
- ⮊ Ubuntu linux desktop interface.
- ⮊ Information technology and society.
- ⮊ Application of information technology.
- ⮊ Importance of information technology.
- ⮊ Introduction to internet technology.
- ⮊ Internet protocol.
- ⮊ Internet connectivity.
- ⮊ Internet network.
- ⮊ Service of internet.
- ⮊ Electronic mail.
- ⮊ Short introduction about microsoft office 2016.
- ⮊ Explaining office 2016 menu, tab and dialog window.

Table of Contents

TOPIC 01

Introduction to Computer

- Computer definition.
- Types of computer.
- About personal computer and its component.
- Number system.
- Computer motherboard and its component.
- Type of computer memory.
- Primary memory.
- Secondary memory.
- Types of microprocessor.
- Input devices.
- Output devices.
- Computer assembling step.
- Computer disassemble step.
- Multimedia.
- Complier.
- Interrupter.
- Computer languages.
- Windows 7 desktop elements.
- Windows 10 installation.
- Microsoft office 2013 installation.
- Windows 10 desktop.
- Windows 10 start screen.
- Windows 10 start menu.
- Windows 10 charm bar.
- Windows 10 metro style apps.
- Windows control settings.
- Control panel.
- Task bar & start menu properties.
- System properties.
- Search.
- Personalize.
- This pc/my computer element.
- Windows 10 right click elements.
- Personalize windows.
- This pc hard drive properties.
- Windows 10 start menu properties.
- Microsoft disk operating system (command prompt/cmd).
- About Microsoft dos.
- All dos internal and external command.

Computer Appreciation

Today's modern industrial competitive market where everyone need to extra – ordinary knowledge to get something advance to achieve in their professional and business life for huge business success must need to introduce to her/himself to recognize the technology that help to him/her to build her carrier for tremendous job in sector of information technology computer use across the all world to communicate business it change traditional business communication style with modern technique through information technology.

Most of organization industry business adopts information technology to get new business opportunity to grow business level with world best fast information technology.

Computer modern machine used to done all routine business commercial non- commercial task, for human made condition now days' computer play dual role to perform generate solution & problem output simply computer works in many different sectors to control or handle different task world first computer named by eniac designed by charles babbage.

Computer – is combination of different peripheral attach connect together with cpu(cabinet) rear panel different port all the component create computer machine that done routine all task with the help of computer software instruction.

Computer – is an electronic mechanism that combine multiple input output processing storage device operation, it done routine mathematical, static, conditional, logical, algebraic, trigonometric, ordinary, routine task performer.

Types of computer (traditional)

🖥 Micro computer	🖥 Mini computer
🖥 Main frame computer	🖥 Super computer

Types of computer (use)

🖥 Desktop computer	🖥 Laptop computer
🖥 Notebook computer	🖥 Palm top computer
🖥 Tablet computer	🖥 Ultra-book
🖥 Smart phone	

Type of computer according to use

Desktop computer – desktop computer is category of computer device which consist crt/led/lcd monitor, mouse, keyboard, cabinet, and cabinet component, speaker, definition of desktop computer, all those computers they are fixed at their location and can't move easier, desktop computer come in category of personal computer that used

and operated by dedicated client, for performing and manipulating user created generated task and event easier with help of installed program called software.

Laptop computer – laptop computer are versatile machine which enable you to travel laptop component across worldwide laptop very handy device use anywhere, it may home, office, company, school, building, organization and many more other places laptop do everything just like desktop computer, each laptop consist battery that supply power where electricity not available, sit and relax do your job in comfortable sitting down position, install all required application software in laptop just similar desktop, laptop computer contain all similar devices like desktop it consist lcd/led display, keyboard, touchpad (replace with mouse) all com, ps/2, usb, lpt, ethernet port, hdmi, vga, card reader slot and many port, laptop available in 14" 15" 18" size and more size but they don't have portability.

Notebook – notebook computer are smaller in size and weight than laptop computer, notebook do function all similar like laptop you can pack notebook in your bag and move anywhere wherever you want to be go, install necessary application software in notebook computer, notebook computer capable to do everything that can do desktop and laptop computer major difference between desktop laptop and notebook is notebook computer very handy device use it while you travel in different country and continent, notebook battery provide electricity while notebook electricity charger unplug.

Palmtop computer – palmtop computer small in size you can keep it in your palm or pocket very handy small computer device similar to smart phone size, palmtop design with limited functionality some basic function application installed with palmtop computer you can play game view date make call, calculate numeric, and other telecommunication and information technology activities can be easier to perform, in palmtop you got pen, keyboard, touch screen for input any command and process, in palmtop you can browse web content play multimedia object and other official task easily perform, they small in size less weight minimum power consume charging battery installed etc.

Ultra-book computer – ultra book computer new generation category of laptop and notebook very slim notebook computer with high processor memory battery backup new port and features than previous edition of laptop and notebook computer, now days company developed slim 18mm or lesser ultra-book computer according to customer use, ultra-book got all new features function, eligibility, faster processing, reliability, security, new generation hardware and software capability for processing data and manipulating information.

 **Tablet computer** – tablet computer are new generation of computer device which enable you to do use all computer and cellphone function together at same or place, tablet computer consist computing, telecommunication, voice chatting, video conference, digital camera function, notebook function, internet browsing, calculation, multimedia function, audio video capture recording function availability, in tablet computer you manually input through pen, touch screen keyboard, hand finger, or voice command, tablet computer bigger in size form smart cellphone but lesser than notebook or laptop computer, every table consist a single battery with connect charge pin, similar like notebook, laptop, ultra - book tablet are movable its allow complete portability with robust features, its use mostly during travelling by salesman, business man, student and other one.

Types of computer (technique)

📺 Analog computer   📺 Digital computer   📺 Hybrid computer

Type of operating system developed by individual company/organization World most popular operating system listed below

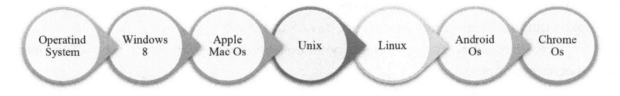

 # Note – all above describe o/s (operating system) struggling in public market for better performance and latest development in public area for better understanding customer requirement and market need everyday life with global changes need.

We now individually explore them step by step

Mac os – mac o/s(operating system) developed and maintain by apple company world most strong platform complete advanced developer commercial look like operating system, mac o/s more popular o/s(operating system) in worldwide among developer, designer, engineer, scientist, even also ordinary computer client, it looks lovely fantastic and glorious appearance first site love environment, it dialog picture control application control option looks very commercial and different from routine o/s(operating system) lineup in these category, company continuing introduce new concept, features, and advance technology to glorify it features worldwide among its user/client.

Listed different mac o/s version below

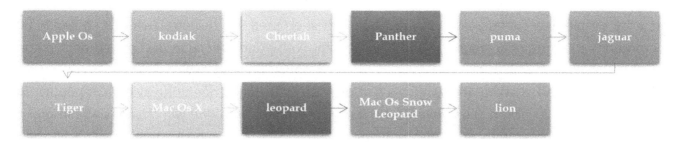

Linux – now days linux will became more popular between in customer, client, server, and developer level, its many reason behind work them are describe them because linux is open source free gpl(general public license)and most of foss (free open source software)application mean you no need to pay use linux commercial and client level, but in some case/condition when use linux o/s commercial for industry organization company then need to buy license linux o/s purchase linux build across the world because its open source so list of online worldwide developer who are regular dedicated to improvement for linux o/s version from world developer community different region, country and continent.

List of popular linux distribution world wide

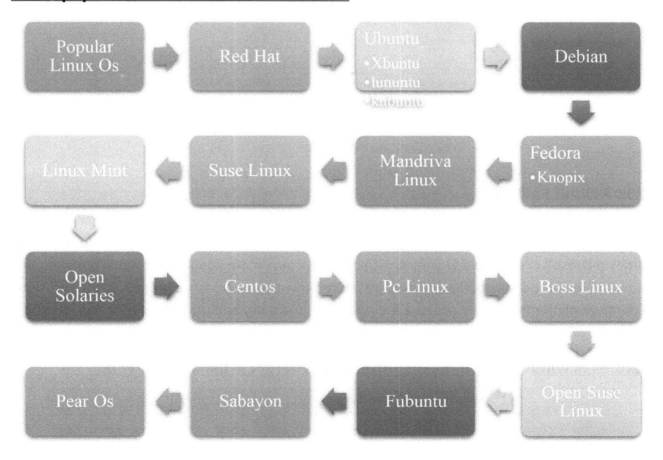

Windows – windows operating most of commercially used and famous in between customer and client level, include business commercial and non- commercial, main usb of windows o/s is use its easy simple user friendly and easy to learn with short step last but not least it is spread in all community their regional language and environment with huge collection of required application microsoft company who pride to developed windows operating system world most 90% computer hold windows market share and windows platform based installed operating system, it popular in commercial business even client level also microsoft company continue will changes add improve feedback of customer with regular improvement for making operating system that full fill their customer routing requirement.

Most popular flavor of microsoft operating system in world

Project about windows

Windows project started by microsoft company since 1986 company started owner mr. Bill gates and his partner, project started for all type of desktop and server client operating system, after long journey microsoft o/s create and launch them it will became more popular and stable o/s(operating system) in list of today's popular operating system now days microsoft o/s used across the globe on different platform machine because it easy simple and gui(graphical user interface)environment provided along easy environment, full fill customer need and feedback.

Features of windows o/s it makes better and different in list of popular o/s

Easy to use	Easy to learn	Multi-purpose	Multi user
Global access	Sharable resource	Network control	Policy management
Graphical	Multi-tasking	Low skill	Easy to install
Dialogue guide	Low maintenance	Connectivity	Liberty

Windows 98 – windows 98 o/s popular in year 1998 this release by microsoft organization cover almost of it market across the world, windows 98 combine many built features and hardware control for windows operation windows 98 have great features and hardware tools for all client and other thing it is a stable plug and play o/s support and cover run install almost platform.

Windows xp – windows xp release after windows 98, me windows 2000 windows xp operating system first time looking great appearance and environment, windows xp is completely graphical, multi user, multi-tasking, multi-threading, o/s, designed for completely level client user windows xp based on winnows 98 windows xp popular and stable version for long time without produce any error, debug, and client issue, best support of windows xp it is totally designed on concept of previous windows release best part of its that microsoft company release windows xp different version name windows xp service pack 1, service pack 2, service pack 3 last release, for supporting and provide greater features and environment for its user to making some stable and advanced need operating system.

Windows vista – windows vista release after windows xp operating system windows vista highly graphical and strong restriction group policy provide software which is totally designed on concept of stop piracy copy or misuse of source code by illegal user, windows vista don't break software restriction and group policy settings generally, it allow only genuine software and hardware support tools, windows vista control, dialog, windows button, title, and other features completely differ from previous release by microsoft company, windows vista add new generation tools and control for new environment with easily access and reduce software piracy and misuse of legal resource even strong windows client and server based restriction policy environment.

Window 7 – windows 7 operating system launch after windows vista successfully working in market, windows 7 operating system advance or upgrade version of windows vista os, windows 7 launched in october 2009 but windows 7 provide and smoother user interface with upgrade software hardware booting kernel instruction then windows vista os, company add new web browser, windows media player, personalization, better security environment, new control panel, networking support, device attachment liberty and many newer concepts add these are included in any version of previous windows operating system.

Windows 8 – windows 8 release by microsoft organization after windows 7 windows 8 foundation designed based or constructed on windows 7 operating system, windows 8 include most of similar features configuration windows foundation but new idea or new concept identity of microsoft company for always create new thing and control for microsoft o/s user windows 8 add many new features control and environment company create new.

Input – input meaning facility that provide by input device manufacturer company build computer hardware that allow us to enter direct data and information into computer machine, now we describe list of computer inputting many more device design for inputting information like mouse, keyboard, joystick, scanner, touch pad, light pen, and other category many more devices here input allow to enter specific raw data in computer for making meaningful result, we always remember no possible to direct enter data and information into computer without attaching any input device with main computer component.

Output – output device that are specially design for producing result on input data, generally output device play of role as confirmation device that are confirm your results on input data, most of commercial popular output device are lcd monitor, speaker, printer, plotter, television etc. These output devices produce result of computer process information and data in shape of output device technique.

Storage units – storage unit are computer secondary storage device which used as container for store computer data, file, folder, image, graphic, text, audio, video, animation, document spreadsheet, program, movie, database, web resources and many more any type of computer generated and processed data and information contain by secondary storage device these are listed below hard disk, floppy disk, zip disk, cd/dvd disk, pen drive, memory card, magnetic tape and chip are common type of secondary storage device, here describe important role of storage unit is these device capable for storing, retrieving and manipulating user enter process data during computer operation.

Cpu– we know about microprocessor and its component but we describe again it a microprocessor and cpu both single component of computer device, cpu contain alu(arithmetic logic unit), cu(control unit), register/memory(temporary storage unit), every raw and process computer data and information control, manipulated, and solve by microprocessor device, microprocessor cpu main component in computer without cpu socket and cpu all computer processing never be easier, microprocessor hold in cpu socket, insert hardly pin cpu in hole of pga(pin grid array)370 p3 socket, in p4 or lga(land grid arrays) 1156 place microprocessor on pin less cpu socket, now drag cpu socket lever till then it would be zero orientation, cpu socket create relation between microprocessor and other mother board component, now turn on computer and open bios view installed processor information and confirm installation of microprocessor, if any problem during cpu socket installation check list all process manually follow during microprocessor installation.

Computer system

Introduction to pc – pc stand personal computer very handy electronic device, reduce human effort before several decades all task technical non- technical task perform by human manually, but after 1960 starting and introduce computer device developed by charles babbage, and some common use software introduce by many developer, and year after year people sociologist know what is a importance of machine technology in human life, now days computer famous between computer developer, designer, operator, and analyst, in different format/shape it may be desktop, laptop, palmtop, notebook, ultra-book, tablet etc. Personal computer now use by many organization, industry, company, firm, departmental store, bank, reservation system at railway, airport, shopping mall, internet use, networking and many more individual purpose generally computer device combine four different element include led, cabinet(cpu), mouse, keyboard and other optional component like printer, scanner, modem, speaker and other required device in this category, computer perform task versatile most of windows multipurpose multitasking application done many task at a same time.

Pc component

Traditional computer   **Now day's computer**

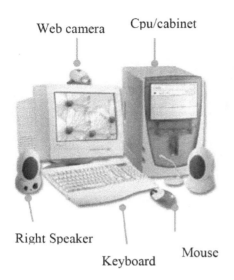

Web camera   Cpu/cabinet

Right Speaker
Keyboard   Mouse

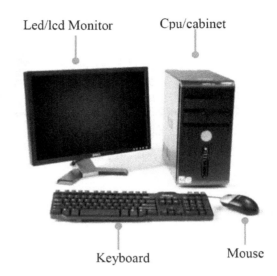

Led/lcd Monitor   Cpu/cabinet

Keyboard   Mouse

Cabinet
Front panel of cpu/cabinet

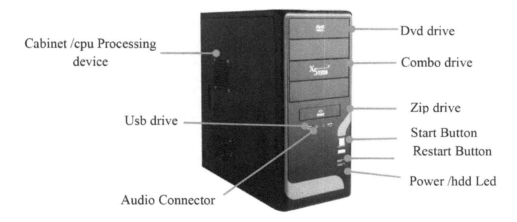

Cabinet /cpu Processing
device

Usb drive

Audio Connector

Dvd drive

Combo drive

Zip drive

Start Button
Restart Button

Power /hdd Led

Rear panel of CPU

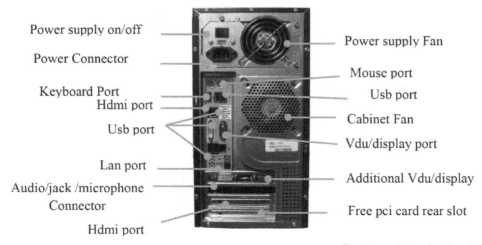

Power supply on/off

Power Connector

Keyboard Port
Hdmi port

Usb port

Lan port

Audio/jack /microphone
Connector

Hdmi port

Power supply Fan

Mouse port
Usb port

Cabinet Fan

Vdu/display port

Additional Vdu/display

Free pci card rear slot

Mother board component description

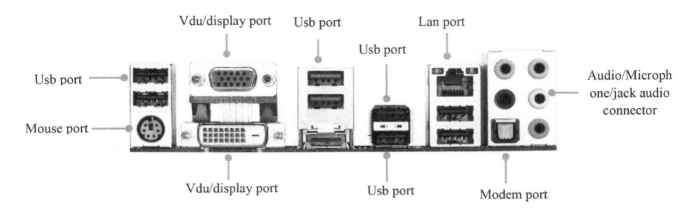

Vdu/display port · Usb port · Lan port

Usb port

Usb port

Mouse port

Audio/Microph one/jack audio connector

Vdu/display port · Usb port · Modem port

Cabinet and its internal component

Smps Connector

Smps rear fan

Dvd drive screw up

Rear panel of cpu

Front panel of cpu

Ports and connector

Heat sink

Start/restart /hdd/power connector

Motherboard component · Motherboard

Bits – bit used in computer for represent data and information, bit represent information in two number is (0, 1) knows and binary number, each and every computer input/output information used in shape of bits.

Number system – number system series of computer keyboard letter, alphabet, symbol, numeric, special character, function keys, combination, while we press any keyboard key/character number system computer converts them equivalent binary code/machine language, machine language directly understand by computer, machine language representation (0,1) form information, computer convert all input keyboard character into equivalent machine code, decimal number system processed by human for routine mathematic/numeric calculation, default computer work on four kind of number system technique and the name is binary, decimal, octal, and hexadecimal number system.

Type of number system

- ➲ Binary number system.
- ➲ Decimal number system.
- ➲ Octal number system.
- ➲ Hexadecimal number system.

Binary number system – binary number system consists base 2 and digit (0,1), binary number system directly understood by computer circuit or register, by default computer representation or process all information in binary shape/form, computer convert any given any number system in equivalent binary number system for processing and computing digital information system.

Ex – $(10111)_2$

Binary to decimal conversion

- ➲ $(100000)_2$
- ➲ $(1000001)_2$
- ➲ $(1850)_2$
- ➲ $(100000)_2 = (32)_{10}$

  $= 1^*2^5 + 0^*2^4 + 0^*2^3 + 0^*2^2 + 0^*2^1 + 0^*2^0$

- ➲ $(1000001)_2 = (65)_{10}$

  $= 1^*2^6 + 0^*2^5 + 0^*2^4 + 0^*2^3 + 0^*2^2 + 0^*2^1 + 1^*2^0$

- ➲ $(11100111010)_2 = (1850)_{10}$

  $= 1^*2^{10} + 1^*2^9 + 1^*2^8 + 0^*2^7 + 0^*2^6 + 1^*2^5 + 1^*2^4 + 1^*2^3 + 0^*2^2 + 1^*2^1 + 0^*2^0$

Decimal number system – decimal number system process by human for routine calculation like addition, subtraction, multiply, division, mathematic calculation etc. Decimal number system consist digit from 0 to 9 (0,1,2,3,4,5,6,7,8,9) and base/radix 10, decimal number process by mathematic student for many math calculations.

Ex – $(154)_{10}$

Conversion decimal to binary

- ➲ $(32)_{10}$
- ➲ $(65)_{10}$
- ➲ $(1850)_{10}$

2	32	0
2	16	0
2	8	0
2	4	0
2	2	0
2	1	1

2	65	1
2	32	0
2	16	0
2	8	0
2	4	0
2	2	0
2	1	1

2	1850	1
2	925	1
2	462	1
2	231	0
2	115	0
2	57	1
2	28	1
2	14	1
2	7	0
2	3	1
2	2	0
2	1	

Octal number system – octal number system also processes by computer for processing computer based generated information and data, default in octal number system it consists digit from 0 to 7 (0,1,2,3,4,5,6,7) and base is 8, octal number easily convert by computer in binary form while creating and manipulating system information.

Ex – $(87)_8$

Hexadecimal number system – hexadecimal number system combination of digit and alphabet, in hexadecimal number 10 digit and 6 alphabets, digit consist 10 integer are (0,1,2,3,4,5,6,7,8,9,) and six alphabet are (a, b, c, d, e, f) letters starting from a=10, b=11, c=12, d=13, e=14, f=15 all digit and alphabet make 16 base of hexadecimal number system, you must to know hexadecimal number system also use to calculate and processed computer based generated information during working on computer data and information.

Ex – $(5a6b)_{16}$

Ascii code – asciii stand as (american standard code for information interchange) used widely character recognize/conversion method followed by computer keyboard, while user hit any key ascii convert alphabet equivalent binary code, ascii developed and design by american, used worldwide for character recognition, asciii cover all keyboard digit 0 to 9 alphabet a to z, a to z symbol, special character, ascii 7-bit pattern of representation process.

Ascii code.

$$X^7 x^6 x^5 x^4 x^3 x^2 x^1$$

Iscii code – iscii abbreviated as (indian standard/script code for information interchange) character reorganization pattern used in indian script, iscii support indian traditional local language like devanagari, kannada, malayalam, oriya, telgu, gujarati, bengali etc. Iscii is 8-bit encoding pattern.

Unicode – unicode standard industry character text representation method follow globe wise by character text information presentation, nowadays modern operating system web browser follow unicode character conversion method.

Ebcdic code – ebdic code stand (extended binary code decimal interchange) used with punch card used in ibm (international business management) company, ebcdic code follow 8-bit pattern for information representation. Ebcdic developed by ibm for their main frame computer, ebcdic working similar ascii unicode and iscii, it converts character alphabet, numeric, symbol, special character etc. Modern computer easily understands ebcdi code.

Bytes – bytes represent computer information, bytes consist 8 bit, 8bit equal to 1 byte, every information in computer process and generated in shape of bytes.

Motherboard slots

- ➲ Pci slots.
- ➲ Pci express slot.
- ➲ Agp slot.
- ➲ Isa slot.
- ➲ Ram slot.
- ➲ Cpu slot.

Explanation of motherboard slots

Pci slots – pci slot abbreviated as (peripheral component interconnect) slot come with new buy brand or old computer desktop server motherboard, these type of computer card increase/expand computer limit for adding some new and old card component, it allow computer user to add additional computer hardware component in pci slot, you can push or install additional sound card, game card, video card, tv tuner card, printer card, scanner card, lan/ethernet card, mode card, device even some other pci supported hardware can be added in empty available motherboard pci slot common pci slot range between 133 megabytes to in pci 2.0 range is up to 128 giga byte, but modern mother board manufacturer provide less quantity of pci slots because todays design motherboard contain all essential motherboard hardware component onboard, so no need to install additional hardware component on it.

Pci express slot – pci express slot extend version of previous discuss pci slot more speed accuracy and transfer speed of data, it is similar to pci slot but commercially pcie slot specially design for higher graphic system supporting function.

Agp slot – agp slot abbreviated as accelerated graphic port, it is a type of computer expansion slot that increase computer motherboard capability, generally it is commercially design for computer high speed resolution graphic card (3d graphic) performance, we say that agp slot advanced slot version of previous pci slot these slot inbuilt on computer motherboard while it manufacturer in company, a common speed of data transfer in agp slot is 264 megabyte to 528 megabyte in some higher agp slot version, intel company design it for motherboard.

Isa slot – isa abbreviated as industry standard architecture computer slot that enable us to add additional hardware card on ibm compatible computer motherboard, it is design for 8 - bit or 16 - bit bus computer motherboard, isa slot used in traditional computer but now day's it is replaced with pci/pcie agp or other memory slots.

Ram slot – ram slot abbreviated as random memory access slot available on computer motherboard, they allow you to insert various category of available ram like sdram, ddr ram, sodimm ram or other type, company provides you two or four ram or more in server board slot for inserting computer memory on computer motherboard, commercially ram slot used in computer to do function of processing and storing computer input/output data and information.

Cpu slot – cpu slot or cpu socket or slot that contain reside microprocessor in it computer motherboard, cpu is brain or nervous system of computer that deal with all computer logical, static, and ordinary job, cpu slot available in any category of computer motherboard manufacturer company, it may be pga 370/pga 470 slot or lga 775 new generation cpu slot, you can easier to install microprocessor in it, when microprocessor properly installed in it then you able to process data and information easier according to its user need.

Motherboard card name

- ➲ Sound card.
- ➲ Vga card.
- ➲ Graphic card.
- ➲ Mouse/keyboard card.
- ➲ Lan card.
- ➲ Wi-fi card.
- ➲ Printer card.

Explanation of motherboard card

Sound card – sound card are type of sound generate system that capable to read or decode sound signal or produce equivalent it in sound form, sound card available in market in various category function or features choose external sound card from available category that meet your requirement, some sound play analog input and stereo output connection some sound provide additional port and cable for increasing sound capability, common install external or built in sound card produce speaker/microphone sound system output. Sound card easier to install on computer pci slot with the help of its guideline.

Vga card – vga card abbreviated as visual graphic array/adapter, popular card used in computer to connect lcd monitor with computer cabinet, first introduced and developed by ibm company, vga card externally used in computer motherboard it provide additional display on one or more computer, buy fresh vga card open computer case see empty pci/vga slot and properly insert it into pci slot, now install vga manufacturer hardware software and connect with monitor/lcd/tft for producing display of computer processing .

Graphic card – graphic card known as video card capable to display high resolution 3 - dimension graphic play high resolution game manages virtual reality world object easier with graphic card, generally graphic card used to control high speed graphical task like animation, 3d multimedia object, vector graphic and similar task easier to perform and control with graphic card in personal and professional computer.

Mouse/keyboard card – mouse/keyboard or mouse or keyboard individual or combined pci card use in second or third generation computer, these card help use while internally mouse keyboard motherboard damage or out of order/service, anyone can by new pci mouse keyboard pci card it gives you two mouse or keyboard individual port even some old mouse keyboard port, now open computer cabinet case see empty pci slot and properly insert mouse keyboard pci card into pci slot start computer and wait if mouse/keyboard card are plug and play then automatically driver installed otherwise need to be manually install it, finally plug mouse or keyboard port into mouse keyboard pci card and access function of mouse and keyboard properly.

Lan card – lan card/lan adapter/ethernet card are a small interface communication card that enable network user to create connectivity sharing resource communicate online or accessing internet intranet or extranet features, lan card essential hardware device in networking buy any lan card open computer cabinet case wait see empty pci slot on computer motherboard now properly insert/install ethernet card into pci slot install ethernet card hardware software, now put computer in start mode wait if ethernet card led blinking or in windows control panel in networking and sharing option show you proper installation of lan, it mean installation is in proper mode, now connect your machine with another computer with local area network or share valuable resources data and information, manage remote connection, view online status with chatting or communicate online/offline mode according to need.

Wi-fi card – wi-fi card or wireless adapter allow you to connecting your desktop, laptop, notebook, ultra-book, even smart phone to connecting wireless service, wi-fi card available in market on depending customer need you can buy internal/pci slot or external/usb port suitable wi-fi adapter even modern ultra-book, laptop or desktop built in facility with wi-fi connectivity, according to buy wi-fi adapter if internal wi-fi card then you need to manually install on computer cabinet empty pci slot, if external than insert into laptop pcmcia laptop slot even easier plug into external usb port, finally proper installation of wi-fi adapter you can able to connect wireless your pda devices like desktop, laptop, or other electronic gadgets that contain wireless connectivity capability, share wireless network resources between connected network component internet intranet and many other online/offline network service with wireless network connectivity, all modern device include smart cellphone laptop, desktop, palmtop, notebook, ultra-book, computer even other pda (personal digital assistance) or gadgets contain wi-fi features inbuilt with connectivity, but in some older gadgets need manually setup of wi-fi adapter service.

Printer card – printer card belong to printing service while internally printer port will became out of order even damage some reason than you need to buy printer card from many printer card manufacturer vendor, now open computer case install printer card on pci slot install printer card hardware software if not plug & play device then manually perform it, finally proper installation of printer card now plug printer port into new printer card and start printing, remember these printer card play same role like existing inbuilt motherboard printer port does.

Smps/power supply – smps(switch mode power supply) main electrical component in computer cabinet, smps supply electricity to mother board component and other hardware device include cd rom, dvd rom, floppy drive, hdd sata connector, zip drive and other remaining component, smps get power from main supply convert it according computer each hardware need and supply it, smps attach many connector 24 pin atx connector for main board supply, ide sata connector for hard disk dvd rom or floppy connector, 4 pin 12 volt cpu connector, cpu heat sink connector etc. Smps convert electricity from analog converter to digital converter.

Smps connector

24 pin smps connector – 24 pin mother board connector connect smps (power supply) with mother board socket, plug easier in motherboard 24 pin socket leave socket lever easily to connect proper installation of installed 24 pin power connector, these connector supply some additional electric power to installed computer mother board device.

4 pin 12 volt p4 connector – 4 pin 12 volt p4 standard power connector use for providing direct computer power voltage microprocessor, it supplies +12 volts into cpu to regulate its function normally, these connectors located separate on new buying or old computer motherboard location, just pug these connectors to provide required power requirement installed computer mother board.

Ide power connector – ide 4 pin power connector specially used to supply electric power to installed computer storage device, optical device, connect and provide main electricity to attach computer component, connect ide power with computer hard drive, video card, installed cd rom, dvd rom, internal hard drive, and other supported

computer peripheral device, this connector known 4 pin molex power connector, these connector connected with red, black, and yellow color wire to provide electricity.

Floppy drive connector – floppy drive connector using to connecting floppy drive in old computer, but now days floppy drives completely outdated it replace with memory card or pen drives, but in pentium and celeron computer days floppy most popular storage between computer user, here 3.5 and 5.1/4 size floppy available in market they store data in both side, floppy drive device that capable to read and write floppy device information, floppy drive power connector 4 pin

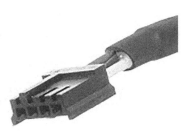

power connector used to connect and supply power to floppy device, these cable plug into floppy device and supply required power to proper function floppy drive function, default 4 electric wire 2 black one red and 1 yellow provide electric current to floppy device.

Sata connector – sata connector upgrade version of ide called pata cable connector, modern computer hardware device use sata connector to connect computer device, sata cable connecting computer optical device, storage device, these cable using to supply component power or data carry device to transfer data and information between source or path, connecting these devices with sata data and power connector.

Motherboard cable

Keyboard cable – keyboard cable connect keyboard from computer cabinet contain motherboard, keyboard cable may be com port, ps/2 port, usb port or wireless port it depend on how much old your buy keyboard version or computer motherboard, but now days company manufacturer build ps/2 usb and wireless common port as using connecting keyboard with computer main board, common used ps/2 keyboard contain six pin connector keyboard design company fix purple color for ps/2 keyboard cable connector where for mouse fix green color, you can easier to connect keyboard cable to computer motherboard port.

Mouse cable – mouse cable connector connect mouse with mother board mouse port, mouse connector cable contains 6 pin port that connect ps/2 mouse from peripheral device, company fix mouse port color green, you can easily plug in it with computer cabinet motherboard rear part and control pointing device button for daily computer operation name selecting, controlling, editing, and commanding with mouse/pointing device.

Ide hdd cable – ide cable use for cd rom, dvd rom, combo drive, hard disk cable, floppy cable, zip disk cable and more other device for connecting with computer motherboard device, ide stand integrated drive electronic and ibm disc electronics ide cable connect from any direction from motherboard and peripheral device, generally plug front port in optical device, or hdd disk rear pert other side of ide cable easier plug in motherboard placed ide master and salve connector, ide cable

come in size 40 pin and 80pin connector, 80 pin pata cable move and carry data and information faster than 40 pin ide cable, pata cable my two or three connector you can connect two optical or hdd device at a same time.

Sata cable – sata cable easier replacement of old pata cable, sata stand(serial advance technology attachment) and pata (parallel advance technology attachment), sata cable have less space thinner and easier to install even faster data transfer rate then pata cable, where pata cable transfer data at 100 mbps but sata cable transfer data at 1.5 gbps to 3.2 gbps and more in newer version, you can connect only single device with sata connector, pata/ide and sata are common data bus that carry information between optical device and secondary storage device with other motherboard component.

Fdd ide cable – fdd stand floppy disk drive cable which connect floppy disk drive with mother board placed fdd connector, now day's company stop making production of floppy drive because floppy in larger in size storage in smaller and easier to damage destroy by any one, today's floppy replace with smart card and pen drive small in size but store more very handy device, fdd connector connect two or more floppy drive zip drive from mother board connector, floppy invented by ibm after year 1965 in those days floppy became reliable storage media that can store share and allow data portability between one or more portable device, a normal fdd cable consist 34 pin ribbon cable connector.

Dvd rom ide cable – dvd rom ide cable connect optical device from motherboard ide master or slave connector established on motherboard, pata/ide connector common used for both hdd and optical drive connector, 40 pin and 80pin ide cable connector common in used, dvd rom ide connector carry information and data between computer motherboard and optical device, read write burn data and information from optical device with easier ide cable, but now days it replaced with sata cable.

Dvd rom sata cable – dvd serial ata (serial advanced technology attachment) cable common used for hdd and optical drive include cd, dvd, and combo drive device, dvd sata cable is thinner ins size more capable to handle large volume of data and information moving and easier it install between motherboard and optical device, sata performance greater than pata dvd, cd rom cable.

Mother board panel connector – motherboard panel connector connects motherboard front panel connection with motherboard placed panel connection, connect start, restart, hdd led, power led, connect from main motherboard panel connection, each panel connector used for specific

purpose while press star button it starts machine, while press restart button it indicate machine in reboot mode, and other common led (light emitting diode) led indicate mean device in working order, these led light shows in red and green light, so user know about system in process mode.

Power cable – power cable is common port that supply main electricity in various computer component, generally two common power cable used in computer for led monitor and computer cabinet for supplying main power in electrical computer component, other use of power cable in computer connect printer, scanner, additional monitor and other device, front end of power cable plug in main  electricity switch and rear end connector plug in monitor and cabinet smps port switch plug.

Vga cable – vga stand (video graphic arrays/visual graphic adapter) are common cable device used in computer to connect led, lcd, tft monitor, projector television and other output media, common vga port contain 15 pin connector module, normal vga cable two front and rear male female connector which connect led monitor with computer cabinet, vga cable carry analog signal, and three color contain in it red, green and blue horizontal synchronization and vertical synchronization.

Usb cable – usb stands (universal serial bus) common usb cable transfer data at 12 mbps rate now days 5 gbps and more in new devices, connect usb supported peripheral up to 127 devices, a common usb supported device are listed here mouse, keyboard, printer, scanner, joystick, bar code reader, pen drive, card reader, cellphone, external hard drive, digital camera, handy cam, web cam and more other device, common usb version in market available is usb 1.0 usb 2.0 and usb 3.0.

 **Hdmi cable** – hdmi abbreviated as (high definition multimedia interface)cable that transmitting multimedia include audio video signal with better resolution higher performance than ordinary multimedia cable, the major impact of hdmi port using in computer television for transmitting highest todays transmit sound, audio, video, image, processing capability, hdmi connect with set top box, a/v receiver, dvd player, blue ray player, gaming console, television, it transmit uncompressed audio video format standard hdmi cable transmit 1080x720 video resolution performance.

Lan/ethernet cable – ethernet cable common cable in networking for connecting local area network device, connect terminal, switch, router, and other network device, two popular categories available of ethernet cable is cat 5 or cat 6, ethernet cable create networking

of office, building, universities, home, company, campus and local area, rj45 connector connect ethernet port in rear panel of computer cabinet and other side port push in switch rear side socket.

Audio cable – audio cable installed on motherboard to connecting a multimedia devices like speaker, headphone, microphone, jack and other multimedia device with your computer system, you just have audio device to plug and play these services, now days all modern motherboard manufacture build onboard sound hardware control, but in year before 2003 and earlier manually need to install sound card and plug in sound connectors pin to produce sound in output form.

Printer lpt/usb cable – printer cable used to connect printer with computer cabinet, generally printer is common output print media that produce soft copy into hard copy, it depend what kind or quality of printer you buy, but generally every computer manually connected with computer through printer cable old computer use parallel lpt port to connect printer device.

Speaker cable – speaker cable using to connecting speaker device with computer motherboard rear audio connection, common speaker cable contain two common cable these are first one in audio connector that connect or produce output voice for computer device, second speaker cable are using to connect for connecting microphone device with main computer cable, it depend on your computer motherboard hardware speaker may be different according to given hardware, common speaker cable play role to connecting medium between computer cabinet motherboard to speaker device.

Rj 11 telephone cable – rj 11 telephone cable using in computer to connecting computer modem device with telephone device with internet service, rj11 connector between telephone device rear component to computer mother board installed rj 11 connector, these cable don't interrupt telephone service while communicate or using worldwide web service through internet connection.

Mouse – mouse is essential component of computer used as pointing device for selecting dialog, windows, control, click and pull down menu handle application software menu function and other control, mouse recognize as input or pointing device, popularly world widely, mouse moving on flat surface or mouse pad, user drag mouse across application windows and perform desire task, now day's mouse consist three button namely left button, scroll button, right button with using left button form select and drag windows click open save print and many more operation scroll button moving application windows between top and bottom direction continuously, right button preview application shortcut menu application control etc.

Type of mouse

- ➲ Mechanical mouse.
- ➲ Optical mouse.
- ➲ Bluetooth/infrared/wireless mouse.
- ➲ Trackball mouse.

Mouse description

Usb/ps/2 mouse cable

Scroll ring/button

Right button

Left button

Mouse surface

Wired Mouse

Type of mouse

Mechanical mouse – mechanical mouse used to move on flat surface rotating inside hard rubber ball, while rubber ball moving mouse sensor activate and control user click pointing operation, with mouse device similar other mouse component use three mechanical mouse button for controlling mouse operation while dealing and controlling computer various operation.

Optical mouse – optical mouse using laser sensor technology activate and control mouse operation, manage by mouse operator, optical mouse contains three button for controlling on the base of lese sensor technology for controlling installed window application and function.

Bluetooth/ir/wireless mouse – bluetooth mouse used wireless sensor to receive bluetooth mouse movement, bluetooth sensor receiver receive wireless signal, infrared mouse working and moving with ultraviolet sensor, wireless mouse using wireless sensor between receiver and sender device component that plug behind rear panel in motherboard component, similar another mouse its working technique different but button operation is very common user all these three button for controlling and managing its operation with left, scroll and right button in windows.

Keyboard

Type of keyboard

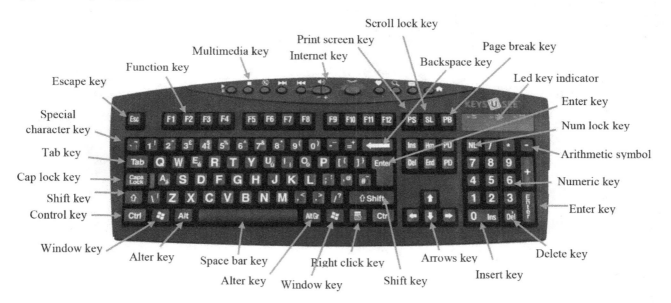

Keyboard key

Multimedia key – multimedia key used to control multimedia operation, like direct play movie audio video play, pause, next, previous, stop increase decrease multimedia application sound volume, even mute it multimedia object directly without using application software.

Internet key – internet key launch internet web browser move on home page search desire text e-mail directly required client and many control other internet operation with internet browsing standard.

Esc key – esc key abort or terminate abnormally process, like escape any operation dialog windows and similar operation perform with esc key.

Function key – function key used to perform specific function in computer world, generally any computer keyboard have 12 functions key from f1 to f12, each key dedicated one or more task in computer field, function keys in software application windows, control cui application, and many other task.

Describe individual function key

F1 function key – used in all windows application as help providing tool, press f1 key in any windows application or software it will mouse you online or offline help application to know more about installed application.

F2 function key – used in c programming, or tally used to control tally button bar operation, other graphical application of software, use f2 simple use of renaming document file name in windows explorer.

F3 function key – using f3 function key to control windows multimedia application, installed tally application, programming application control and operation easier to select and control through f3 function key.

F4 function key – f4 function key using for immediate shutdown computer with alt + f4, include other windows installed application name programming, database, accounting and multimedia control direct operated through f4 key in windows.

F5 function key – using f5 key computer to refresh computer desktop pending or working task, include other installed application shortcut control and features manage through f5 key in window.

F6 function key – using f6 function key to save files in dos, control tally, multimedia, installed office application task with easier these shortcut key.

F7 function key – use in tally, windows media player, microsoft word, and other installed application package allows to using f7 key to control application control.

F8 function key – using f8 function key in window to control multimedia, tally account vouchers, programming control and dialog easier include other various application features.

F9 function key – control multimedia application volume, handle multiple tally accounting vouchers, using in other windows application and control when user need.

F10 function key – use in microsoft word, windows media player, tally, programming, installed database services and operating system control through f10 function key in windows.

F11 function key – use in tally accounting software, programming, office application, internet, database and various other field of application where you able to apply these function key.

F12 function key – using f12 function key to control window operation, multimedia file control, tally control and window key, use in microsoft office or various other use of f12 function key.

Alphabet key – alphabet key are 26 letter from a to z, create paragraph sentence text document letter fax memorandum any query with alphabet key.

Numeric key – numeric key start from 0 to 9, use of numeric key to manipulate math operation number calculation like addition, multiplication, subtraction, division write table and number between 0 and 9. On num lock key before using number key.

Special character key – special character keys include ~! @ # $ % ^ & * () _ +I keys, using special character to performing some special electronic document operation.

~ - tilde.

! - not equal, exclamation mark, run, negation.

@ - at the rate sign.

- hash sign/number sign.

$ - dollar sign.

% - percent sign.

^ - caret sign.

& - address/and sign symbol.

* - multiplication symbol.

(- open parenthesis.

) - closed parenthesis.

_ - underscore.

+ - plus sign.

I - or sign.

Tab key – tab key allow to add tab between windows character space, default tab moving 0.5 in application software windows.

Cap lock key – cap lock key change windows character in from uppercase to lowercase, on cap lock to convert character lower case to upper case.

Shift key – shift key used with toggle operation, allow multiple key combinational use two or more key to joint operation.

Control key – control used as also combination toggle operation key, use control key with other key for mutual operation.

Windows key – windows key used open windows start menu, click on windows key and open windows operating system start menu.

Alt key – alt key also used for mutual combination key operation, open menu, apply many shortcuts with alt key in windows operating system operation.

Space bar key – space bar key used to add space between paragraph, text, document, and content, press space bar key and add space at required location in current document.

Up down left right arrow key – up down left right arrows key moves you windows application in all side all direction, you can play game control game operation with up down arrows key.

Print screen key – print screen key allow you to take or capture windows screen, dialog, graphic, and finally paste in it in bitmap application software.

Scroll lock key – scroll lock key lock windows application scroll moving in both directions, with scroll you can move in left right top bottom direction easily.

Pause break – pause break key pause ms dos command operation, pause windows operation sufficiently where you use it in application.

Insert key – insert key allow to insert text content at required location in cui or gui based application software.

Delete key – delete key delete selected text document folder and other selected content in browse window, or application windows.

Home key – home key moving your location at top in current document windows, if you area at bottom of application click home button to reach at top page.

End key – moves you at bottom page in current application software, if you are in ms word top page position press end key to move bottom of page.

Page up key – page up key moves you one by one page in up position continuously, if your page position is 5 press pages up key you will be reach at top page one by one.

Page down key – page down key move your page location continuously down, if your ms word document current location is one and you want to reach at page 10 press page sown button to continuously reach at bottom page.

Motherboard

Pentium 3 motherboard

Now day's motherboard

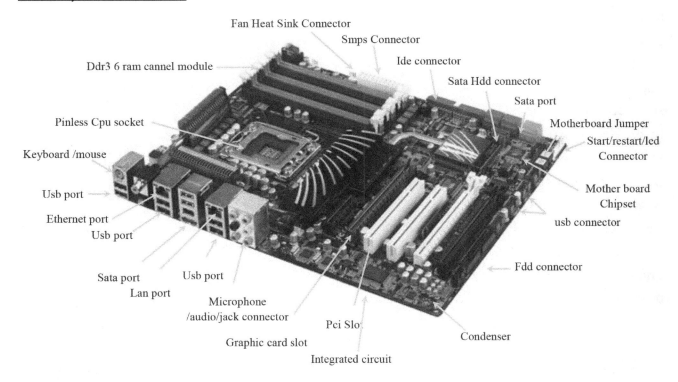

Fan Heat Sink Connector

Smps Connector

Ide connector

Sata Hdd connector

Sata port

Motherboard Jumper

Start/restart/led Connector

Mother board Chipset

usb connector

Fdd connector

Condenser

Integrated circuit

Pci Slot

Graphic card slot

Microphone /audio/jack connector

Lan port

Usb port

Sata port

Usb port

Usb port

Ethernet port

Keyboard /mouse

Pinless Cpu socket

Ddr3 6 ram cannel module

Mother board component

Microprocessor cpu socket – microprocessor cpu main component in computer without cpu socket and cpu all computer processing never be easier or done, microprocessor hold in cpu socket, insert hardly pin cpu in hole of pga(pin grid array)370 p3 socket, in p4 or lga(land grid arrays) 1156 place microprocessor on pin less cpu socket now drag cpu socket lever till then it would be zero orientation, cpu socket create relation between microprocessor and other mother board component, now turn on computer and open bios view installed processor information and confirm installation of microprocessor, if any problem during cpu socket installation check list all process manually follow during microprocessor installation

Pin(pga) cpu socket – pga (pin grid array) microprocessor developed and design by intel company in year 1998, pentium 3, or pentium 4 processor socket computer mother board hold pga cpu socket, in pga socket you need to pus pin processor hardly press from notch side, now press it till then it will properly installed, now pull down pga 370 cpu socket level from 90 degree to 0 degree insertion force orientation, now drop some heat sink liquid on microprocessor installed cpu aluminum heat sink along heat sink fan it make cool cpu while it work long, even it control cpu temperature and voltage
level, finally start computer open bios view processor information if all information correct and cpu display it mean all the step correct during follow cpu installation, now days company stop making

production of pentium 3 pga socket it replace with new lga 1156 socket used in intel core i3, i5, i7 processor and modern one design microprocessor cpu socket.

Pin less (lga) cpu socket – pin less microprocessor socket invented by intel company and design for new generation intel mother board lga(land grid array) cpu socket with zero insertion force facility, where in pga 370 pentium socket you need to hardily press cpu till then it mount properly in cpu socket, but lga 775 and other pin less cpu socket you don't need to press hardly cpu just put microprocessor in hand carefully established in lga cpu socket now pull down cpu socket level/lever properly till it proper connect

at bottom switch, install heat sink connect heat sink with supply unit and wait open bios view microprocessor information mhz/ghz etc. If everything correct it mean microprocessor installed correctly.

Cpu fan – cpu fan make cool cpu temperature while cpu in working mode, cpu fan installed on microprocessor it maintain cpu temperature voltage level and stop cpu from overheating, if cpu temperature over from normal temperature microprocessor will be burn and stop working, cpu fan continuously supply air at bottom installed cpu component, single computer installed one or more cpu fan or other fan graphic card fan, cabinet rear fan, smps fan, all these are design to keep out hot air from device and increase device performance, cpu fan contain aluminum heat sink along cpu

fan with power unit connector, remember for better microprocessor life and performance cpu heat sink fan running in properly condition, while it stop working it burn component of microprocessor and move computer in halt mode.

Simm 1 slot – simm abbreviated as (single in line memory module) slot contain sd ram installed in it, these type of memory slot used in sd ram previously used in computer, these simm slot quantity depend on computer motherboard manufacturer it may be 2 slot or 4 slot, simm type of memory slot used in 1980 to 2000 era, installation of simm memory to be very easier buy ram and push its according to given instruction, while ram properly installed it pin contact to simm slot given on motherboard pin, and ram started proper functioning it store retrieve or contain electronic information till than user computer moves in switched off mode.

Dimm1 slot – dim slot used to fitted or install new generation memory called ddr ram, dimm slot enhance speed of memory device created great compatibility and storing capability than simm slot ram, dimm stand dual inline memory module these types of ram used in today's environment personal and commercial computer, dimm slot performing ram in dual operation form both side while computer and other component exchange information with it.

Fdd connector – fdd connector abbreviated as (floppy disk drive) connector, installed by motherboard manufacturer company, fdd connector connect fdd cable with floppy drive device, floppy drive device read write copy paste 3.5" floppy object content, now days floppy would be outdated storage media, it replace with smart card or pen drive but 20 year ago floppy is a reliable portable secondary storage media that allow portability between multiple computer, fdd cable similar to ide cable used in hard disk or cd rom, dvd rom, it carry/moving data and information between installed floppy disk drive and mother board floppy connector.

Atx 1 connector – atx 1 connector allow computer hardware engineer to connect power supply called smps to the computer motherboard, these type of atx connector contain at least 24 pin of power connector used in pentium 2 to pentium 3 generation computer, it allow to connecting smps 24 pin power connector and supply electricity to further component of computer motherboard hardware device, now days these type of atx connector completely replaced with modern atx power connector.

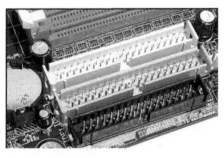

Ide cable mother board connector – ide slot established on computer motherboard these type of ide slot used on computer motherboard form pentium generation of computer, it depends on your computer motherboard manufacture it may in size of one or two or may be more, these slot directly allow computer user to connect ide hard disk connecting form computer motherboard, before installing ide hdd drive you must know about its function and structure ide slot have a middle notch than indicate to ide cable installer to how to install ide cable properly without any error, these ide slot carry or move computer generated instruction between computer hardware or hard disk drive.

Cmos clear – cmos clearing method allow computer hardware engineer to move back computer motherboard in factory setting, it discard all manually changes made by user, cmos clear better for system performance, hardware error, hardware compatibility issue, and related problem, cmos battery store information manually recorded by computer user, while we clear it, it free all function in factory mode even it better for any personal computer troubleshooting while some normal or serious error/issue generated.

How to clear cmos

- ➲ **Bios menu.**
- ➲ **Cmos battery.**
- ➲ **Jumper setting.**

Bios menu – start computer press del, f10, f2, for entering in bios menu, now select load setup default, or optimized setup default, you get different option in different bios manufacturer company like amibios, phoenix, award bios, etc. Now you all manually changes added by you all are discarded and system restore previous/original mother board status, here we compare motherboard bios with computer nervous system, it mean each computer hardware motherboard function will be control and manage through system bios settings easier while user need to manually modify it, but be strict while changing settings of bios, don't modify those settings and control that one you not familiar, because it cause serious error in system performance during working order.

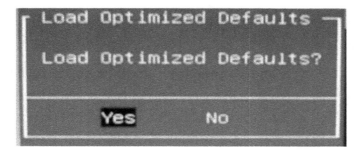

Cmos battery – cmos battery are small design cell that prevent all manually store bios information in it, cmos store battery electric power consume by cmos while you remove cmos battery/cell it release store bios setting and information store in it, move back bios in factory setting mode, now start bios again and reconfigure required setting necessary for proper system booting, while you unplug cmos battery it restart all cmos function in default mode, apply carefully if you have less it skill because it stop manually configure services and settings and turn back system in factory settings/mode.

Jumper setting – jumper setting store cmos information preserve in bios, default jumper set on 1 and 2 while you hold them 2 or three jumper pin it release/destroy all cmos store information in it, jumper located on motherboard, open cabinet case view carefully cmos jumper and clear it from place it in pin 2 and 3, again restart machine and place it at default location set it in 1 and 2 pin location, jumper also move you in motherboard original state/factory settings.

Sata port – sata abbreviated as (serial advance technology attachment) new generation motherboard port replacement of pata (parallel advance technology attachment), pata port used in pentium 3 or pentium 4 motherboard, but now days sata port common for connection cd rom, dvd rom, hard disk, and other sata capable secondary storage media device, sata port carry information between connected optical device, hard disk and mother board component, ide port comes in 40 pin or 80 pin pata connector they also carry information between ide hard disk same as sata port do sata port come in 7 pin port, plug sata cable in sata hard drive and other end cable plug in motherboard placed sata connector, sata reduce amount of cable, space, amount, and faster data moving between mother board and computer component.

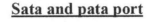

| **Sata port** | **Sata and pata port** | **P - ata port** |

Panel/connector – mother board panel connector are device control place on mother board, while mother board properly screw up in cabinet, later connect all motherboard connector with smps, sata, optical drive and important panel connector look outside front view of computer cabinet many switch and led appear at flat cabinet panel, plug all cabinet panel in to mother board panel connector connect start, restart, hdd led, cd/dvd rom led, power led, speaker, button properly connect with mother board panel component.

Explain briefly front panel connector

Power sw – power sw connector connect cabinet front cable with flat panel, push outside mounted start button for turn computer in display mode.

Reset sw – reset sw button restart personal computer if any error occurs system halt or generate any other type of error, reset place new o/s copy in ram and discard all problem in new o/s copy load during restarting process

Hdd led – hdd led connect with hdd performance during hdd processing data and information, while hdd deal with any process and activity it blinks continue in red color and indicate system in process mode, hdd led blink or stable when hard drive read write or process any information

Power led – power led (light emitting diodes) used in cabinet to display power if turn on/turn off or standby mode, press esc to move back from stand mode to normal mode

Speaker – speaker panel connector connects internal cabinet connector with cabinet, speaker beep sound while it moves in turn on mode, speaker design in small size only for any troubleshooting error it may be ram beep system another category of beep.

Usb connector – usb abbreviated as (universal serial bus) standard port replacement of old lpt and com port, usb port tiny in size connect many modern peripheral device with usb port, transfer faster data transmission then other port, connect mouse, pointing device, keyboard, card reader, printer, usb hdd, pen drive, smart card, audio/video player, handy cam, digital camera, scanner, projector and other remaining usb supported device easily connect with usb port, connect up to a single usb 127 device, configure them manually, all usb port are design as plug  & play some device no need to install software and some refer to install manually software for better working performance, single mother board contain one or more usb connector in from and rear usb port connection plug cable and device and use it.

Audio

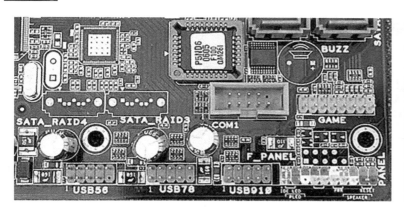 

Pci slot – pci slot are important slot in motherboard it used while need to install additional vga card, sound card, printer card, modem, network adapter/nic, graphic card, tv tuner card, and many more other remaining card easily to fitted/install in pci slot, pci abbreviate as (peripheral component interconnect), pci slot extend mother board capability if you want to install new technology or card pci slot permit to you install them easier on pci slot.

Agp slot – agp abbreviated as (accelerator graphic port) short called agp, agp slot fitted agp slot that accelerate/enhance speed of graphic video card and 3d animation game playing software, by default some motherboard contain video graphic card inbuilt and some need to be install manually on agp slot, buy video card now open system case and easily push agp card in agp slot, now days company don't make agp slot because newer version of motherboard contain high amount of graphic video card enable facility.

 **System fan** – system fan connector established on motherboard it connect cpu cooling fan from motherboard, if properly installed cpu fan now plug fan connector into motherboard system fan, it put out heat from microprocessor and maintain system cooling level, generally mother board provide two system fan connector one reserve for microprocessor and second one is for draw out heat from computer case called rear fan connector, it is essential to install computer cooling fan they control cabinet environment and maintain system cooling level status.

Atx – atx 4pin motherboard connector provide electricity motherboard component, it generates +12 volts for microprocessor voltage, 4 pin atx connector specially design to provide additional power direct into the cpu, two common pair of wires used by atx power cable connecter 2 black and 2 yellow wire for motherboard socket.

Rear panel connector

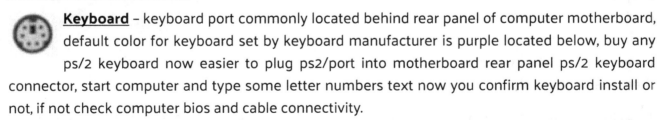 **Keyboard** – keyboard port commonly located behind rear panel of computer motherboard, default color for keyboard set by keyboard manufacturer is purple located below, buy any ps/2 keyboard now easier to plug ps2/port into motherboard rear panel ps/2 keyboard connector, start computer and type some letter numbers text now you confirm keyboard install or not, if not check computer bios and cable connectivity.

Mouse – mouse is a common pointing device which enable you to select windows control dialog and manage windows operation, default green color set for mouse connect any ps/2 mouse directly plug in ps/2 mouse port in rear panel of motherboard, start computer check mouse movement if proper it mean mouse installation is in proper order.

 **Vga** – vga (visual graphic arrays/visual graphic adapter)common port using to connecting computer output device media like monitor, projector, television, 15 pin vga connector plug between lcd monitor and cabinet vga port, it carry moves analog signal and convert it into digital signal form.

Dvi port – dvi extend version of old vga display cable, dvi cable increase lcd monitor resolution, device performance, dvi abbreviated as (digital video interface) dvi port connect digital video device like lcd computer monitor, dvi port produce high quality digital interface  video output signal for better graphic video quality, dvi port convert analog signal into digital format, now days modern computer contain vga, dvi and hdmi video port for better computer resolution with high quality frequency just similar like television.

 **Hdmi port** – hdmi abbreviated as (high definition multimedia interface)new port available and produce on newer generation computer motherboard, for connecting laptop, video game, dvd player, tablet and other hdmi capable device directly connecting with lcd television or computer monitor, hdmi port create strong resolution need for hd(high definition)video, you can play or run high quality video movie song and game if you have hdmi port facility on available motherboard, newer generation intel, giga byte and other company motherboard contain dvi, hdmi port enable facility, just buy and use it.

Esata port – esata port abbreviated as (external serial advance technology attachment) external sata port placed in laptop or desktop computer for connecting external sata storage device directly from laptop or desktop computer, generally connect external hard drive and share faster data  information between esata device and computer hardware, these port located outside computer rear or laptop back side in left right or back side located attach related device share required information and data among it.

Usb port – usb port externally placed at rear panel of computer motherboard, connecting usb external device directly from usb port, you may connect at least 127 devices with single usb port, connect usb printer, mouse, keyboard, joystick, scanner, digital camera, web camera, handy cam, cellphone, smart card and many other external devices for sharing externally and internal system data and information with these port.

Ethernet/lan port – ethernet port special design to providing connectivity between computer devices, connect two or more computer as client server nature with rj 45 connector, new generation all computer have built in ethernet port but previous time manually need to install lan/ethernet card on pci slot for lan connectivity, connect computer network device and share data information and network software hardware resources, ethernet port design by xerox communication for connecting computer in same building and region.

Audio connector – audio connector connects audio speaker microphone jack to the rear panel audio port connector, plug audio pin in given audio socket.

Printer – connect printer with lpt printer or usb port directly install printer software driver for proper printer configuration installation with computer system.

Booting process – booting process involve some series of booting process check manually every instruction and steps when computer start every time in windows, rom every time check all bios store instruction and step of booting process from start to end when everything properly checking and proper it will copy operating system fresh copy from rom to ram device.

Pc busses – pc busses are computer highway or route path connected to various hardware component share, move and travel hardware component electronic information in computer through these pc busses devices, pc busses hardware path or wire of computer motherboard that reliable to copy, carry, travel data from source to destination location.

Input output i/o busses – input and output computer busses used to communicate input and output computer data information carry through connected input or output attached hardware component like microprocessor and other component, these busses travel or carry system created signal or data from its source location target location.

About memory – memory is type of storage container medium of reserve computer data and information in temporary or permanent nature, every personal computer has two type of memory it includes primary and secondary memory both kind of memory install on computer motherboard for reserve/fix operation some it play role of storing data and manipulating information in primary(volatile) and secondary (non – volatile) order both memory dedicated for specific task and purpose for its user need.

Types of computer memory

- ➲ **Primary memory (volatile memory).**
- ➲ **Secondary memory (non-volatile memory).**

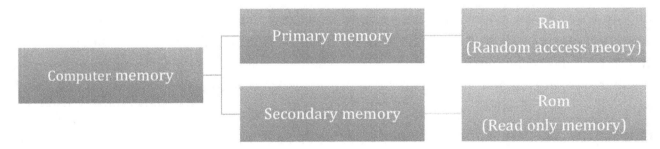

Description of primary memory

- ➲ **Ram memory.**
- ➲ **Rom memory.**

- ⊃ Prom memory.
- ⊃ Eprom memory.
- ⊃ Eeprom memory.
- ⊃ Virtual memory.
- ⊃ Auxiliary memory.
- ⊃ Bubble memory.
- ⊃ Cache memory.
- ⊃ Resister memory.

Ram – ram abbreviated as random access memory primary store information till than power switch is in turn on mode, while power switch off ram lost all information and data store in it, ram install on computer mother board on dimm1, dimm2 ram slot, ram process faster information and data in computer than rom memory, ram store information and data only in condition while pc switch on mode, so we called it volatile memory, if power failure lost all content stored in ram, ram contain small register, chip for storing

information and process content, ram available in many size, we start from bottom from pentium 1 to pentium 4 now, days intel i3, i5, i7 processor supported 2/4/8 giga byte of ram, ram available in various size, 4mb, 8mb, 16mb, 32mb, 64mb, 128mb, 512mb, 1gb, 2gb, 4gb, 8gb and more size available specially for server computer.

Types of ram

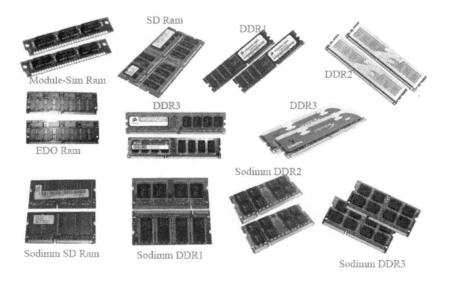

Dynamic ram – dynamic ram is type of computer memory may be install in desktop laptop and other electronic gadgets, a quality of dynamic ram it refreshed every few second during working system order, dynamic ram store information as capacitors and transistors.

Static ram – static ram another type of computer memory part of ram, static ram produce result faster and higher performance, but its nature of store information is volatile it release store information in few second, sometime static ram known as cache memory working with personal computer microprocessor very expensive but faster result performance device that contain static ram.

Rom – rom abbreviated as read only memory which nature store and process information permanently, while computer motherboard manufacture/program in company rom instruction placed on mother board, rom written information can't erase while power switch off mode, rom contain computer bootable instruction every time run while pc switched on mode, ram established in motherboard as integrated circuit or chip form, rom information can't be altered modify edit by normal user, but computer programmer edit it with specific relevant experience or knowledge these process called updating system bios cmos settings but it risky it cause of permanent damage system bios setting permanent so be carefully while doing related activities and operation.

Prom – prom meaning programmable read only memory category of primary/volatile memory perform only while power switched on mode, meaning full use of prom write and install computer program application software into rom, after adding prom application it can't be alter or modify, specially prom design by computer manufacturer for write program information.

Eprom – eprom meaning erasable programmable read only memory, commercial use of eprom in computer eprom erase all information written by prom or information placed in rom, eprom spread/focus ultraviolet rays for erase instruction and information written by rom and prom, while user format any computer secondary device store information and data contain in it, these kind of memory work internally we can't see them but know about its working structure.

Eeprom – eeprom meaning electrically erasable programmable read only memory, eeprom extend version of eprom, eeprom specially used for erasing information electrically placed in computer memory or secondary storage device these memory very similar other one memory but similar we can't see its but know about its working order and structure.

Virtual memory – virtual memory created in personal computer fixed hard disk, while your buy pc contain minimum/fixed amount of installed ram and when process many more data, application software, web browsing, editing, installed ram would be full in size and

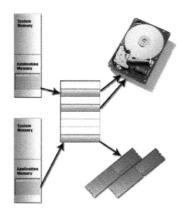

no space available for additional storage data, now you create manually virtual memory on hard drive partition and placed additional data and information in virtual memory ram read additional information form virtual memory and process with main memory/cpu, virtual memory better choice for those pc have less amount of main memory created virtual used as ram save money and deal with huge amount of data, remember while virtual memory created it used hdd space so hard drive space size reduce automatically used amount of virtual memory.

Auxiliary memory – auxiliary memory is not part of computer internal storage devices, special purpose of auxiliary memory for storage data and information in faster storage method without involvement of cpu memory, nature of storage different from primary memory, many secondary storage come in auxiliary memory, most external secondary storage device play role of secondary memory.

Bubble memory – bubble is type of computer memory nature of bubble memory store information and data non-volatile, concept of bubble memory storage information use thin film of magnetic material for hold small magnetized area recognize bubble store one bit of data.

Cache memory – cache memory type of primary memory store information till power/electricity on, cache memory design for computer microprocessor, microprocessor read information more quickly than random access memory and any other primary memory, cache memory installs nearest computer cpu, cache memory design in case l1 or cache l2, cache provide high memory storage area than other primary or secondary memory.

Resister – register is hardware memory type register memory store data and information directly in register so they don't need to exchange information with primary memory, register capable to store data as well as instruction.

Secondary memory

- ⮩ Punch card.
- ⮩ Hard disk.
- ⮩ Floppy disk.
- ⮩ Zip disk.

- ⮑ **Magnetic tape.**
- ⮑ **Magnetic disk.**
- ⮑ **Optical disk.**
- ⮑ **Compact disk.**
- ⮑ **Digital video disk.**
- ⮑ **Pen drive.**
- ⮑ **Memory card.**
- ⮑ **Audio/video cd.**

Punch card – punch card is historical computer data processing and storing device used in early/traditional computer, it known as hollerith card, punch card based on paper several/many hole sequentially placed on paper these punch manually created by human or computer processed, computer data company industrial or organizational data store in small punch hole than it can be processed any time according to need, these small punch hole store as well as retrieve store contain data and information while its user need.

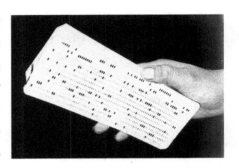

Hard disk – hard disk recognize as permanent secondary storage device fixed in every new brand purchase computer, hard disk store file, folder, image, graphic, text, audio, video, animation, document, report even all type data and information in shape of electronic process data and information, hard disk is a default storage medium of any computer device, popular had disk prefer by scsi, segate, or western digital hard disk available in market pata, and sata port, now days hard disk manufacturer create production of sata hard disk easier fixed in new computer, hard disk available in size 256mb, 512mb, 1gb, 2gb, 4gb, 8gb, 16gb, 20gb, 30gb, 40gb, 60gb, 80gb, 160gb, 250gb, 500gb, 750gb, 1tb or 4tb i start hard disk from pentium 1 to today's date, sata and pata cable used as data bus they carry information between computer mother board and other component and hard disk ide cable ide connector or sata connector connection with main board, hard disk completely screw up surround by metal box, hard disk internally fixed on platter/plates a spindle that tightly screw up different platters individual read/write head read or write information in hard drive from track and sector, rpm(revolution per minute) read write and display information frequently no air dust water reaching in to hard disk during it performing or process computer data and information, each computer use hard disk for storing retrieving and manipulating electronic data and information.

Floppy disk – floppy disk use in year earlier 1990 and after 1990, that time floppy recognize versatile reliable storage medium, it allow computer user to copy and move data information from copied location to share between many computer user, floppy appear as rectangular plastic disk, storage data and information 1.44 mb and dual density

floppy store 2.88 megabyte, floppy available in size 8" inch 5.25" inch 3.5" inch, now days floppy completely outdated storage media it replace with micro/mini sd card, pen drive, flash card, or memory register/chip, these storage devices store more data and information then floppy device include it more reliable, more space data and information container, plug and play and heavy duty then floppy device, but the legacy of floppy device established in 1990 to year 2000.

Type of floppy disk

- ➲ **8-inch floppy disk.**
- ➲ **5.25-inch floppy disk.**
- ➲ **3.5-inch floppy disk.**

8-inch floppy disk – 8 inch first floppy disks of world design by ibm (international business management), it available for storing data and information in read write format, the common problem with 8-inch floppy disk with size of storage carrying and portability so it would be unfamiliar in short time.

5.25-inch floppy disk – disk used in early time while less secondary storage available in year 1990, these floppy disks come in huge size and less storage amount of computer data and information, the actual problem of using these devices of carrying information even volatility or portability issue with it, but after some time company generate new floppy disk in size 3.5 inch, the actual storage size of 5.25 floppy disk are 1.2 megabytes or 360 kb.

3.5 inch floppy disk – floppy disk smaller in size easier to carry with pocket greater amount of data storage than 5.25 floppy disk and more reliability provide, it come in dual density both side storage of data and information, it store 1.44 megabyte and some grater version store 2.88 megabyte or more data and information, floppy disks available in many colors shape design even many company manufactures it for their clients, but after development of other greater volume of device floppy device would be outdated storage media, we sad that floppy is completely replace with modern secondary device name pen drive/flash drive etc.

Zip disk – zip disk is recognition as secondary storage media extend version of floppy disk where floppy 3.5" store data 1.44 megabyte dual density 2.88 megabyte but zip disk storage size of data in 100 mb, 250 megabyte and more 750 megabyte, zip disk use to take backup of data and information move this data and information between one to more computer because zip disk portable secondary storage media, zip disk became more popular for it size, storage, durability, and portability even reliability, now day's zip disk don't used at zip disk place computer user used usb pen drive, smart card, memory card etc.

Zip disk created and developed by Iomega, in today's environment zip disk is old back up media people used pen drive memory card for data and information moving between one or more client server machine.

Magnetic tape – magnetic tape is popular secondary storage media for recording music information, record movie, telephone voice and computer data related information, these devices available in audio video cassettes in various size and shape, the common magnetic tape using for data collection storing and backup storage device, plastic tape coated with ferromagnetic material, these tape look like reels, it stores analogues or digital data.

Optical disk – optical disk are commercial secondary storage media that contain/store higher volume of data and information than floppy or zip disks, the common optical disks are cd, dvd, and blue-ray, cd stands compact disk plastic disks store data and information 700 megabyte some version 800 megabyte or 1 gigabyte of storage size, dvd stands digital video/versatile disk store data and information up 2 gigabyte, 4 gigabyte, 8 gigabyte, 16 gigabyte and more but blue ray storage media store data and information up to 50 gigabyte and more size in computer.

Compact disk – compact disk are popular secondary storage media used for store game, computer software, multimedia, audio, video object, moving secondary storage object between multiple computer with compact disk facility, commercial of compact disk create/burn multimedia object and play with supported device, cd rom (compact disk read only memory) hardware device that read compact disk with ultraviolet rays, compact disk available in two format first that write once and read many and cd-r rewritable that use again and again for storing information and data, common compact disk available with 650 megabyte or 700 megabyte storage space, compact disk created with plastic circular disk on coated polycarbonate, common diameter of compact disk are 4.75 (12 cm) diameter, compact disk store more information than floppy disk, zip disk, regular storage size of compact disk 700 megabyte some 1gigabyte in higher version play 80minute of audio store in compact disk, compact disk introduce sony and philips company.

Digital video disk – dvd extend (digital video disk/digital versatile disk) another secondary storage media store more information than floppy disk, zip disk, compact disk, common storage size available in market is 4.7 gigabyte and more size available is 8 gigabytes or 16 gigabytes, and some more available size, for reading dvd need dvd hard drive device, store game, software, multimedia object, film, movie etc. Play with supported software, data information access rate of dvd between 600 kbps to 1.3 mbps you need hardware device/component that enable to play dvd.

Pen drive – pen drive versatile usb storage media allow portability moving of database and information between one or many computer pen drive use to take backup computer data from source location to moving destination location, pen drive new invention and replacement of floppy disk, zip disk, all pen drive are plug and play device just use it and unplug it you don't need to install additional hardware for using pen drive in computer, you can store file, folder, image, graphic, text, content, audio, video, multimedia, animated object, and many more that just can be copy and paste, pen drive available in size 1gb, 2gb, 4gb, 8gb and 32gb, and 64 gb, maximum size 512gb, many company design pen drive in various size, with pen drive you can transfer data, backup data, send and receive data easier, pen drive used as removable storage media just according to use plug and play it.

Memory card – memory card small in size use in digital communication store photo, audio, video, files, folder, image used as flash card plug in usb port, now days memory card/smart card used in cellphone, laptop, digital camera, audio player, video player, video game, handy camera and many more used, memory card available in mini sd, micro sd, compact flash, xd picture card size plug in memory card slot available in laptop or externally card reader

device which read copy and paste computer database among memory card and computer hard drive partition, memory card store information as non- volatile nature while plug you card in device store content display and read by user.

Simms memory – simm stand single in – line memory module, sim circuit are memory module that hold computer memory, each simm circuit memory module contain one or more ram chips, these simm module established on computer motherboard, simm memory module available in 32-bit data type model, simm now replaced with dimm memory module, simm memory module contain sd ram contain small amount of storage and slow processed used in year 1980.

Dimms memory – dimm stands dual in – line memory module replacement of simm memory module, dimm circuit placed in pentium 4 or later motherboard common dimm slot hold dram (dynamic random access memory) memory type, working pattern of dim, memory is more reliable faster and time consuming than simm ram it support 32 - bit operating system.

What is cpu – cpu is device which is strongly responsible for all windows/ unix/linux/mac os computer operation input and process by user, cpu abbreviated as (central processing unit) brain of computer/decision maker in computer all logical, statically, ordinary, algebraic, numeric, textual, multimedia, data and information task perform by cpu, cpu control system activities alu (arithmetic logic unit) cu (control unit) operation, register/memory used for storing and retrieving information, desktop computer motherboard install at least one cpu/microprocessor some motherboard install two or more processor/cpu for multi-processing (used in server), microprocessor execute between computer hardware and software processed information by user.

Component of cpu

- ➲ Alu.
- ➲ Cu.
- ➲ Memory/register.

Alu – alu stands arithmetic logic unit part of cpu(central processing unit) brain of computer, main responsibilities perform by alu is arithmetic and logical operation like doing math include (addition, subtraction, multiplication, division), logical operation include(true, false, not), statically, algebraically, numerical, textual, multimedia, boolean expression include and, or, not, nand, nor, xor, xnor gate operation and all other remaining decision produced by alu, alu is real part of microprocessor that generate or produce meaningful decision.

Cu – cu stands control unit a controlling instruction generated by computer microprocessor, it control computer operation and related activities, cu ensure all computer hardware software function working in proper order, even receive instruction from cpu and apply on computer operation.

Memory/register – register placed with computer microprocessor called cpu, register high speed memory processing device, all data and information by microprocessor firstly stored and processed in cpu register device, even it deliver processed data result to external device media, number of small register built in during microprocessor manufacture in company.

Pin less processor – pin less processor new generation microprocessor that are replacement of old pentium one, two and three microprocessor, where pin processor hardily placed on motherboard placed microprocessor socket, but in pin less microprocessor easily placed on new generation computer motherboard printed circuit board, first all remove pcb cap now hold firmly pin less processor in pcb socket properly with zero insertion force adjust according to given instruction or view notch placed on microprocessor or pcb circuit, now easier move rotation clip till than processor properly install, wait install microprocessor heat sink and start computer for further installation, the common pin less processor fitted in lga 775 or later microprocessor printed circuit board.

Type of cpu

- ➲ Single core microprocessor.
- ➲ Dual core microprocessor.
- ➲ Quad core microprocessor.

Single core microprocessor – single core microprocessor used in year 1960 to 1990, they operand single process and data at one time, while any process already in process mode we wait till finish it, we can't process two operand simultaneously at a time, single core cpu slow in process wait for result even can't support multitasking, multiprocessing facility, but dual core microprocessor advance than one core cpu, modern cpu provide more processing layer of data and information at single time.

Example of single core cpu

Dual core microprocessor – dual core cpu function in two layer two different process path for input and output cpu processing, it very similar to two cpu in single microprocessor input two or more task simultaneously, it mean process many task and job with single installed dual core microprocessor at time because dual core cpu used two different path for input and output programmer instruction, it is very fast to single/one core cpu because in one core single path play role of input or output cpu data and information, modern motherboard manufacturer manufactures dual core cpu socket for new generation motherboard.

Example of dual core cpu

Quad core microprocessor – quad core cpu extend version of dual core microprocessor, where dual core microprocessor divide process in two part where quad core microprocessor process data in dual layer with multitasking multiprocessing task and job process facility, quad core microprocessor has inbuilt memory and instruction to deal with large volume of a task simultaneously processed by programmer.

Example of quad core cpu

Microprocessor/cpu generation

- ➲ Pentium microprocessor/cpu.
- ➲ Celeron microprocessor/cpu.
- ➲ Xeon microprocessor/cpu.
- ➲ Intel i3 microprocessor/cpu.
- ➲ Intel i5 microprocessor/cpu.
- ➲ Intel i7 microprocessor/cpu.

Pentium microprocessor – pentium is popular category of microprocessor, pentium introduce by intel company in year 1993, 32 bit microprocessor pentium 4 processor is a extend version of earlier pentium 1 and pentium 2,3 cpu, intel company produce widely pentium microprocessor for desktop, laptop and note book computer after year 1993, it became so popular for it tremendous performance like multi-tasking, multi-processing, and multi-  threading and more, processing capabilities with dealing all kind of computer process data and information depend on user need.

 **Celeron microprocessor** – celeron microprocessor introduced by intel company in year 1998, it is completely inspired by intel pentium microprocessor, but it run at slow speed approximately 200, 300, and 500, 900 mhz processing speed, the reason of designing celeron microprocessor for design computer for those people or client who can't afford pentium architecture based personal computer microprocessor, celeron based computer cheaper than other computer pentium or other brand available microprocessor based computer.

Xeon microprocessor – xeon microprocessor belong to intel family, the reason of designing xeon processor for high speed with accuracy and reliability for client and server platform computer, inbuilt cache memory is grater of xeon based microprocessor than previous intel processor release, big advantage of xeon microprocessor is these microprocessor highly heavy duty and task performer depending on user tasking.

Athlon microprocessor – athlon microprocessor introduced by amd (advance micro device) company who capable to design intel capable microprocessor, amd introduced 200 mhz in year 1999 speed 650 mhz for 32 - bit supported operating system, amd athlon microprocessor hold additional cache memory dealing with multi-tasking and multi programming server operation in networking mode, amd microprocessor clock speed is more than it generation compared microprocessor list, even amd processor capable to dealing with 32 – bit and 64 – bit operation.

Intel core i3 cpu – intel core i3 cpu belong to dual core family 64 bit and x86 based microprocessor design for laptop, desktop, and ultra-book, even for mobile users, core i3 processor launched by company in year 2010, advantage of core i3 microprocessor is these microprocessor get larger cache memory many core for processing multitasking, multiprocessing, multithreading, or many layer deal with multi-processing, it support better surfing, browsing networking, client, server, multimedia, graphic, games, movie, with easier or smoothly it mean you don't need to install additional hardware along it.

Intel core i5 cpu – intel core i5 microprocessor belong to intel dual core family new microprocessor technology better than core i3 processor but lesser than core i7 microprocessor, it support hyper threading technology with enhanced intel speed step along turbo boost include integrated graphic processor for dealing graphical processing application, higher cache memory multi-layer/core for dealing with multi-tasking and multi-processing task, core i5 better for game, multimedia, graphic, networking, and server operation support high quality video and gaming operation.

Intel core i7 cpu – intel core i7 microprocessor belong to intel quad core processor family, it is top of line series microprocessor design by intel corporation, intel core i7 is better than intel core i5 and core i3 microprocessor, core i7 cpu contain hyper threading, enhanced intel speed along turbo boost features, that make intel core i7 processor different other lineup company microprocessor, intel core i7 microprocessor dealing higher graphical application hd multimedia support, networking support, even manage windows multitasking, multiprocessing, client server order capable, high definition visual graphic animated 4th generation protected microprocessor, but it is more costly than core i5 and core i3 microprocessor.

Hard disk

Type of hard disk – hard disk computer most essential secondary hardware component which is reliable for storing computer application created and processes data electronic information store at local hard drive partition space, traditional computer use ide hard disk for storing data and information ide cable carry electronic information between computer and ide storage device, but after invention sata hard disk more reliable and rotate on more rpm speed then ide hard disk cable, default these kind of hard disk used on various computer hardware name ide(integrated drives electronic), sata(serial advance technology attachment) and scsi(small computers system interface), any kind of hard disk use on computer play a role of storing data and information as secondary purpose for storing movie, sound, audio, video, graphic, program, projects, and other installed application software created electronic information storing hard disk in track, sector called spindle shape.

Hard disk architecture

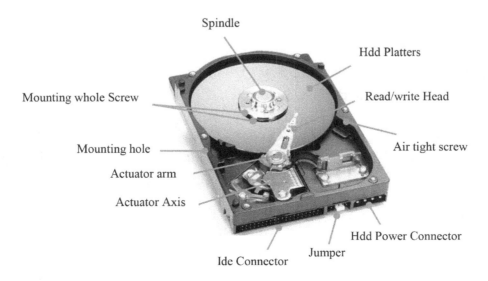

Cd rom – cd rom abbreviated as (compact disc read only memory) cd rom hardware device use to read and install software, game, computer document, content, and other database information, cd rom device connect with mother board ide cable, store more data than floppy and zip disk now day's replace dvd with cd because dvd store more data and information than cd, popular size of cd drive 650 megabyte may be 700mb or 1 gigabyte.

Dvd rom – dvd extend version of cd where compact disk store small amount of data and information but dvd(digital versatile/video disk) store greater amount of data and information than cd, dvd design with same size of compact disk, commercial use of dvd drive to read dvd produce/burn new dvd install software, game, play music, video, animation, and other multimedia object etc. Dvd rom device

connected in computer with sata and pata/ide cable, dvd use huge amount of data so it popular than cd, floppy, pen drive etc. Dvd available in two categories normal dvd write one and read many time till than track sector damage, read/write dvd used many time burn and erase dvd data and information according to need, remember your installed dvd rom capable to burn data and information, dvd available in 2gb, 4gb, 8gb, 16gb and more size available, dvd commercially refer for video, audio, data and information as a storage media.

Zip drive – zip drive represent floppy drive but more reliable and greater amount of storage than floppy data and information, zip drive popular in year between 1995 to 2000 and portable storage media, zip drive may fixed/internal or external with zip connector and ide cable connect zip drive with other mother board component, zip disk used in zip drive for recording data and information size 100 megabyte and 250 megabyte, zip disk rewritable it mean you can read write erase zip disk many more time, push zip disk hardily inside zip drive open my computer and record desire information and content in it according to need.

Type of zip drive

Input device – input device refer to entering data into computer, there are many input design for computer entering information, some time we think if no input device attach with computer then no possible to insert, edit, cut, copy, paste, control dialog, window, application, enter information will be impossible, so here input device play important role while entering and recording or storing data at computer storage media for its user need.

Keyboard – keyboard is a popular input device similar to type writer unlike in type writer write everything on paper text but can't change or revert text, edit or modify written information, but in computer immediately change erase unneeded text, every computer must have one keyboard for create document, letter, perform numerical calculation, keyboard connected from computer may be com port, ps/2 port, usb port, or bluetooth wireless port, keyboard allow you to manage editing customization in written text with supportable application software, keyboard used as input device for entering numeric, alphabet, text, password, symbol and other similar operation remember no possible to create textual based information and text without possible using keyboard device.

Mouse – mouse use as input pointing device, it allow you to control windows application dialog, select control, input process, drag and drop windows, follow windows wizard, select and apply any dialog control, choose between many tabs, on off control and many more than your basic requirement, mouse connected with now days ps/2 or usb port it may be wireless port also, no matter what kind of mouse/pointing device you attach or installed on current machine but fix task and role of each and every installed mouse device while dealing computer application and its control.

Web camera – web camera capture live streaming video and picture, video camera used as input device in computer, while making online chatting, video chatting, in online meeting, or video conference, web camera preview your video and picture other side sitting client same as you watch him/her video sitting other side in network, talk live discuss any topic agenda or solve any query online in small global village with video conferencing device, now days many web site offer online video chat program even you can join any online social community web site, you can be a member of face book, twitter, link din or other online web site, web cam connected with computer, laptop, notebook from usb port even built in laptop, notebook, or ultra-book, now days web cam capture live picture, record streaming video, and transfer video etc. Web camera record voice video attach microphone device during online conversation.

Digital camera – digital camera take live picture used by photographer for taking picture of picnic, birthday, marriage, any background, function occasion, while somebody enjoy their life they record their important moment of picnic tour used digital camera to take picture with video recording facility record video live picture, in field of computer digital camera used for input picture recorded video and edit with video editing software easily, connect digital camera with pc via usb port or card reader for reading digital camera flash card, share picture among friends relative and colleagues, print edited picture make new picture edit video and many effect and many more you can do with recorded video or picture.

Scanner – scanner used as input device for scanning image, picnic photo, wedding image, photos, newspaper article, movie posture, background, letter, any document text, content and other text graphic based information, edit and modify content of scan document information with relevant application software, scanner convert text graphic in computer (digital format), you can send e-mail upload scan content world wide web through connected internet broadband network services, even using scanner as scan somebody identity, authentication, with supported technology.

Type of scanner

Touch screen – touch screen used as a input device which enable you to touch menu, control, option, choice from your hand finger or pen, choose directly any command option and process it immediately, touch sensitive interface, now day's tablet, smart phone, cellphone, touch laptop, notebook, photo copier machine, medical touch gadgets and devices follow touch screen technology, use human hand finger or touch pen device for touch device sensitive control for operating and controlling its operation.

Light pen – light pen is a input device which enable you to write text, select menu, option control dialog, windows operation without keyboard or mouse, light pen similar to any other pointing device, it use pointer to point out any object and content at touch screen device, light pen connected with computer through ps/2 or usb port catch light pen in hand finger now write any text select screen windows and operation directly, light pen display similar ordinary pen but use light sensitive method for any crt operation.

Micr – micr abbreviated as (magnetic ink character recognition) input device used for read special pattern of character, symbol, number, while micr read any document micr device used by bank to check special character printed on cheque, even it check cheque authenticity, it read document ink and translate it into magnetic information, micr used special ink for read information from checks, document, and other similar document.

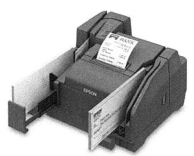

Omr – omr abbreviated as (optical mark reader) used to check objective type question answer book, now days most of exam online student fill answer with black pencil or black pen omr device read these fill round circle, square shadow by omr scanner it read as well as check answer sheet, omr device check thousands of answer sheet in short time more than hand work, because answer key already fill in omr machine while some omr sheet inserted for scan in omr sheet its system check automatically true/false fill circles values and information according to its user need.

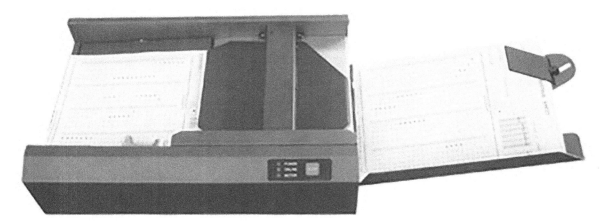

Video capture device

Bar code reader – bar code reader is special kind of scanning (scanner) input device, hand held device which focus on product printed bar, bar code read or capture bar code information contain on newly purchase product or commodity, bar code scanner convert bar code into number or letter format and describe digital specification information about current bar code reader scanning device and its information while user need.

Card reader – card reader is internal/external input which read flash card, memory card of cellphone, smart phone, digital camera, handy camera and other similar digital media device, card reader may be fix in pc or externally used with connected usb port, push mini and micros smart card in card reader slot read, cut, copy, paste information between card reader smart card or laptop, desktop computer hard drive, external card reader prefer you variety of card slot used in digital media device.

Microphone – microphone used as input device it read human voice and convert it into electric form output in speaker, microphone connected with computer usb port even wireless hand-held device hold by anchor in any program, microphone read or digitize voice put on external output media, microphone use in computer headphone with microphone or individual microphone, television program anchor used microphone, telephone, recording tape, cellphone recording device many more application available of recording function, used microphone normally in computer while online video chatting, online collaborative computing during video, text conversation, or chatting mode, listen sender voice and send your voice at recipients address through microphone device easier.

Touchpad – touchpad is primarily input device already fixed in laptop or notebook computer, some smart phone these refer as primary touch sensitive input sensor which communicate with human touch and interaction, move human touch interface while control windows features function control windows dialog boxes application menu and other function, generally many touchpad manufacture create touch pad with right click left click even horizontal vertical scroll function include along it, in modern touch device touchpad use as pointing device which is replace mouse device even working similar pointing device for selecting text, control dialog and window, or enter command..

Data glove – data gloves are common input device that working like mouse or touchpad, common data glove contain sensors sense move or operated by human hand finger while human interact with data glove it create movement in specific software of computer desktop windows, now control any virtual image, scan image, robotic motion in specific software apply specific control and menu operation with easier data glove device.

Joystick – joystick is popular pointing input device similar to mouse which is commonly used for playing normal and three dimensional video game, connect joystick device with ps/2 or usb port now start any game and pull joystick level/lever from all direction, joystick control movement of playing game hold joystick level/lever in hand now move it in all side according to play game movement, joystick base contain joystick lever rotate lever orientation and move from all direction, you can move in back forward up down direction, joystick technology used in aviation industry for controlling air plane operation include computing technology for control computer device operation and control.

Graphic tablet – graphic tablet is special input device which enable you to create direct any visual, sketch, design, diagram, and other image with the help of touch pen input device, graphic tablet consist electronic tablet and cursor/pen, artist can draw desire graphic of using pen moment along print view and modify existing electronic design graphic and design, computer photo maker, artist, animation photo maker or drawing design artist use these category of graphic tablet device for making finest and fantastic graphic images on customer need.

Output device – output device belongs to category of displaying result of input device produce text and information, each output device design/build for specific purpose in computer technology some output device produce result, some output device play input as well as output devices during using and controlling these categories of devices.

Monitor – monitor is popular old output device in personal computer technology, now days monitor replace with lcd(liquid crystal display), led(light emitting diode), plasma technology, monitor contain crt(cathode ray tube) create picture pixel(picture element), while electricity light focus in crt two horizontal and vertical deflection plates move electric rays on electron, electron create chemistry with its hardware component finally produce high resolution output input by user text or information three color code use during creating any kind of visual, text and background create on the base of **rgb**(red, green, black).

Lcd – lcd abbreviated as (liquid crystal display) new invention in computer technology which is completely replace old crt monitor technology, lcd are small in size less electric power consume, less weight, faster performance, consume minimum space for displaying on flat table or desk even it hang on wall easier at home, office, building, and other places, today lcd and led craze in computer market use these technique for upgrade your machine.

Led – led abbreviated as (light emitting diode) technology used in modern television sets and led monitor, led resolution and performance are better than lcd, led contrast, color accuracy, view angle, power, size and price lower than lcd, now days led became market need for buyer because these technology in grow in this time and most hardware monitor manufacturer design led monitor screen as output device.

Plasma – plasma television output device using in entertainment to view live television serial, movie, news, sports, and other live broadcast information in computer, plasma tv preview flat panel screen display television sets, now days plasma popular in market more 32" inches sizes, quality of viewing picture and videos of plasma television sets better than other television sets, using these media for entertain purpose only at home or office.

Printer – printer is popular output device which commercial recommended to everyone who print document, letter, graphic, and other textual material, printer may be connected with computer lpt or usb port, while purchasing new personal computer you have choice of three kind printer for home and personal use buy ink jet printer but you also have choice of buy new inkjet and laser printer but above discuss these kind of printer come in commercial category or installed at large level for producing high quality of graphic, text, and printed material, each printer print softcopy data into a hard copy information.

Plotter – plotter is popular output media device which is used to produce highly graphical picture, graphic, advertisement, and brochure, wall add, flex board add, and any graphic picture that produce in large size or scale with best high resolution and major size, printer are not capable to produce maximum size of picture and graphic so plotter use, plotter connected with personal computer designer draw edit advertisement and graphic while send for print, small plotter device pen draw continues image on

paper size select by user, in simple plotter is a high quality, high resolution printer use to produce print maximum size of print content, commercial use of plotter to design cad (computer added design) object large scale company advertisement and commercial hoardings banner hold on large scale on any wall, building, or other location, use plotter device for printing huge size of graphic on paper or plastic banner paper.

Projector – projector are output device which highly used for company, industry, organization for present/preview meeting presentation video, picture, text, animation, multimedia object, content on large screen with maximum cover of client/viewer list in meeting company hall or any occasion, connect projector device with computer cpu or television puss television or cpu cable in  projector focus projector beam on flat large wall/white cloth surface, it depend on your projector how much space cover by used projector resolution size, you can see the size of picture and graphic produce by projector display in maximum level connect additional speaker and large area cover by your projector device during preview or play some multimedia and textual object information in meeting or conference.

 **Speaker** – speaker are commonly output device which output playing audio video sound from computer to speaker, speaker connected with sound port from computer motherboard rear part audio jack, mother board installed sound chip decide sound and preview it with attach sound speaker device in voice or sound format, it depend what kind of speaker you installed with your personal computer, primary role of each speaker is producing sound of playing any multimedia object like audio, video, animation, sound, and other kind of system voice easier to listen with speaker.

Television – television is popular entertainment output device which completely entertain you watch movie, serial, news, audio, video, animated object, now you can connect your personal computer with television with given television vga, dvi, or hdmi port produce direct display and better resolution of given monitor screen display, television produce high definition video picture quality available on new generation hdmi television sets, lcd monitor size restricted but television size available in more larger  size than lcd monitor so you get better and large screen resolution screen, television became necessary equipment for entertainment at home, office, and other places without television sets no possible to entertainment somebody or everybody even it use as output device while its connect with pc.

Pc assembly and operation.

Assembly and disassembly of pc and its various parts.

Collect essential computer hardware component.

- ➲ **Computer cabinet.**
- ➲ **Smps unit (power supply).**

- ➲ Microprocessor (cpu).
- ➲ Optical drive/dvd rom.
- ➲ Memory/ram.
- ➲ Sata cables.
- ➲ Mother board.
- ➲ Processor (cpu) fan.
- ➲ Rear fan.
- ➲ Hard disk.
- ➲ Screw.
- ➲ Screw driver.
- ➲ Keyboard.
- ➲ Mouse.
- ➲ Lcd.
- ➲ Printer.

Assembly pc various part – assembling pc refer to generate/build computer on the basis of raw computer hardware component device, assembling include install all computer essential component at proper place in given position at different component location in computer cabinet, install microprocessor, smps, ram, graphic car, bios, heatsink, front and rear fan, similar other component comes in category of assembly pc part.

Open computer cabinet case – buy computer cabinet and install all computer mother board and other device properly mount screw in exact hole location screw them correctly till fitting properly on cabinet screw bottom location, remember if you have skill to assemble computer then you know how to do it properly but you don't know about then try it till then somebody guide you about computer assembling steps.

Step involve during cabinet installation

- ➲ Buy any company computer cabinet/case.
- ➲ Open left, right, front cover for installation computer motherboard, hard disk, optical drives, and other media device.
- ➲ View all screw position placed in computer cabinet case.
- ➲ Now ready to install all computer peripheral device into computer case properly.

Smps installation – smps main supply in computer install smps in computer cabinet case, properly screw up it from all side till than it completely fitted, now plug different smps power supply connector in different motherboard component, plug 24 pin atx connector into atx connector, install 4 pin cpu power connector, install additional 4 pin hdd, optical device power connector same add all other smps connecter at proper place.

Step involve during power supply (smps) installation

⮕ Open cabinet case cover.

⮕ Place exact location of power supply at proper hole align hole position with smps hole position.

⮕ Screw it up properly till fitting.

⮕ Install all power supply connector with mother board connector.

⮕ Plug smps power cable into main power supply (home/office).

⮕ Start computer and see display, if everything ok, it mean installation proper.

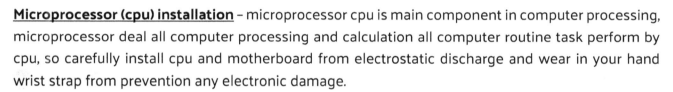

Microprocessor (cpu) installation – microprocessor cpu is main component in computer processing, microprocessor deal all computer processing and calculation all computer routine task perform by cpu, so carefully install cpu and motherboard from electrostatic discharge and wear in your hand wrist strap from prevention any electronic damage.

Installation procedure of microprocessor

⮕ Buy new generation intel/amd microprocessor.

⮕ Remove microprocessor cover.

⮕ View microprocessor location on motherboard in cpu socket.

⮕ Now days company create zif(zero insertion force) cpu socket.

⮕ Place cpu into zif cpu socket properly with alignment notch.

⮕ Now down cpu load lever retention tab properly, and fix it.

⮕ Now apply small amount of thermal compound on microprocessor properly spread it all side of microprocessor, it keep cool cpu or maintain microprocessor temperature heat level during long/heavy duty working.

Heat sink installation – after microprocessor cpu installation it's time to installation heat sink fan, take heat sink fan properly screw up, install heat sink fan power connector on computer motherboard connector, view properly all its connection point and location then start computer for check or confirm installation of cpu or heatsink on microprocessor.

Heat sink/fan installation procedure

- ➲ Open heat sink fan cover.
- ➲ Properly place it at microprocessor location.
- ➲ Fix it microprocessor location from all side.
- ➲ Connect heat sink/fan connector to the mother board heat sink connector.
- ➲ Check while power is on if working correct, it mean installation succeed.

Memory/ram installation – random access memory installation essential because ram store data primarily while computer is switched on mode, ram play important role in computer performance and working order, ram store data and information temporary it mean while power is off it release all information store in it.

Step involve during ram installation

- ➲ Buy ddr 3 or modern version ram module and uncover it.
- ➲ Place properly it notches according dimm ram module slot.
- ➲ Now press ram module hardily into dim slot till it automatically lock.
- ➲ Check ram module properly install in motherboard ram dim slot.

Mother board installation – motherboard is most common or important component in computer case which handle all computer processing, logic connectivity and hardware software activities, motherboard divide in two part north bridge and south bridge both side individual motherboard component work together and perform single output, depending on user input request, you always remember each and every component work simultaneously during exchange desire information and content while communicating or interchanging some information with motherboard south and north bridge.

Installation procedure of computer motherboard

- ➲ Buy latest generation computer motherboard category motherboard.
- ➲ Open cabinet case and properly mount screw hole.

- Matches all side cabinet hole with motherboard hole.
- Place plastic or paper cover at bottom motherboard installation from any power grounding.
- Place properly motherboard into computer cabinet align all cabinet and motherboard hole in proper position.
- Screw up all motherboard screw from screw driver till properly tight, and move or drag board to check screw fittings.

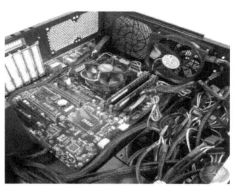

Hard disk installation – hard disk is popular secondary storage media in computer it stores file, folder, image, graphic, text, audio, video, multimedia object, program, project and any secondary computer visualize object that electronically treated in any software application, hard disk store all information as a permanent method, it store till than we manually delete or remove these information from its storage location.

Hard disk installation procedure

- Buy sata/scsi/western digital any one other company hard disk.
- Install hard disk into computer cabinet properly, see blank slot position at cabinet case and install in hdd.
- Now place all screw correctly position of install hard disk, properly screw tight hard disk if not proper it destroy or damage hard disk as well as motherboard component.

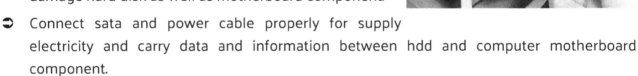

- Connect sata and power cable properly for supply electricity and carry data and information between hdd and computer motherboard component.

Optical drive/dvd rom installation – optical drive include floppy drive cd dvd roam and combo drive installation, you can install one or more optical drive according to your buy cabinet size, it may be tower and mini tower in tower cabinet you get many additional slot to install additional optical drive and hdd, now day's company stop production of making floppy and zip drive they are replaced with pen drive.

Step involve during optical drive installation

- Buy dvd rom zip drive floppy drive uncover it.
- Place optical device into computer cabinet inside given slot.

- Properly place optical device into cabinet slot and align all side screw according to cabinet hole.
- Now tight screw from screw driver till than all are completely fitted.
- Start computer test optical device if work correct it mean proper installation otherwise repeat all process.

Sata cables installation – sata cables are smaller in size carry more data and information faster than other older ide cable, now days many company manufacturers create production of sata cable for optical device hdd device and other storage media, buy sata cable connect additional hard disk, optical device, zip disk and other kind of sata port attaching device using for storing and sharing secondary storage devices information.

Installation of sata cables

- If everything properly screw up in computer case now times to install computer cables.
- Take one sata cable plug it one side into hdd drive, and similar other side plug into motherboard sata port slot.
- And check after computer installation if everything ok than installation proper.
- Start computer check hard disk, optical drive, open hdd files folder, open optical drive content etc.

Rear fan installation – rear fan control computer temperature level while computer working long duration, motherboard component automatically heated and spread/release heat in computer case, so it can be harmful or burn from overheating of your computer motherboard component, so install cabinet rear fan they may one or two or more in quantity, they drew out heat from computer cabinet component or maintain cooling level, if they are not working properly it may damage/burn computer cabinet important hardware component.

Installation procedure of cabinet rear fan

- Buy cabinet rear fan according to given rear fan empty fan block.
- Now properly screw position of cabinet rear fan and cabinet mounting hole.
- Screw up them proper position till than tighten.

Screw installation – screw bound/catch properly completely computer component include motherboard, optical drive, hdd drive, smps, computer additional card slot, etc. Each screw design for specific purpose it mean you see all component placed different screw, while you buy computer cabinet company provide free bag that collection of different screw, pick them exact level that needed to fit in computer case.

Screw driver set – screw driver is collection of super set tool of different screw drive tool, pick any one of them even see screw top and assume which screw drive fitted on it, now properly tighten given screw from its orientation location.

Computer cable installation

Connect 24 pin atx connector – install 24 pin atx power connector, in atx 24 power connector placed on mother board some mother board at contain 20 pin connecter but now days most of motherboard designer design motherboard with 24 pin atx connector, push hardily 24 pin atx power connector in mother board located 24 pin atx socket adjust power connector lever and finalize it, start computer check motherboard if everything ok it mean installation proper of 24 pin atx connector.

Molex power connector – 4 pin molex power connector connect optical and external hdd media, plug in 4 pin molex hardily in hdd dvd rom given power socket, start machine and check performance device if everything ok it mean installation proper otherwise reconfigure it.

Connect data cables stata/pata – data cable move and carrying data and information between computer motherboard and other device, pata (parallel advance technology attachment) used in pentium 3 type computer it plug in master and slave ide slot place on motherboard, pata comes in two type 40 pin and 80 pin used them according to better availability, sata (serial advance technology attachment) use in now days computer sata small thick and havier data transmit between connected computer devices.

Connect usb cables – some motherboard designer company two or more usb connector placed on computer motherboard, by default two or more usb 3.0 version located at rear panel of motherboard some placed on motherboard and at least two usb located at front panel of computer cabinet case, if you want additional usb in active machine plug usb cable card or install two or more cable usb jack with usb slot appear on main board.

Connect audio cable – now days all design motherboard inbuilt audio device chipset facility, but in starting computer development state need to manually install sound card on each motherboard, sound card produce sound, plug in all audio cable at proper audio cable point.

Connect 4 pin cpu connector – 4 pin 12 - volt power connector specially design to supply power to the microprocessor, plug in 4 pin power connector, in 4pin cpu power socket located at motherboard, cpu consume all electricity generated by 4 pin cpu power connector.

Install rear panel cables

Keyboard installation – keyboard is popular input device for using input alphanumeric and text in any computer electronic application software, attach keyboard to the rear panel of computer motherboard default color set for keyboard is purple plug in 6 pin keyboard connector and start computer check and type any key, if everything ok it mean installation proper of keyboard in computer system.

Mouse installation – mouse is a very essential input pointing device which enable computer user to operate computer instruction control windows dialog and windows, default color set for mouse ps/2 port is green install 6 pin mouse cable in rear side mouse connector located start computer move mouse movement and finalize installation process of mouse installation.

Lcd installation – lcd monitor installation include to install two different port one is power code that plug in main electricity, second one is vga cable that are plug between lcd vga connector and motherboard rear connector, both port install correctly and start computer see display resolution of computer screen and finalize step of lcd installation.

Printer installation – printer is popular output device that are manually attach with modern computer, if you want to be install printer with active computer buy printer open printer install printer lpt/usb cable in lpt or usb rear panel port install printer software provides by printer manufacturer company, follow instruction properly and wait till installation succeed print test page confirm installation of printer process.

Scanner installation – scanner is another essential device that are used to scan document, graphic, content, picture, image, and other paper electronic document material, plug scanner cable into rear cabinet panel install scanner version driver check with scanning any electronic material and finalize process of scanner installation.

Dissembled pc various part – dissemble pc various part option involve process of detach all computer hardware parts manually one by one, but must have skill to detach computer hardware properly otherwise it will serious cause of system proper booting function, i will explain in detail how pc component detach in step by step.

Steps of personal computer dissemble pc parts

➲ First of all, disconnect all computer power plug from main power supply.

➲ Detach cabinet connected lcd/led monitor wires name power cable and vga cable properly.

➲ View cabinet move on rear panel of cabinet unplug manually mouse, keyboard, vga port, audio jack, hdmi port, games, printer, usb port, ethernet port, video and other all kind port.

➲ Open cabinet case view front on motherboard unscrew all motherboard mounting hole screw from all side.

➲ Unplug smps main 24 pin power connector, similar disconnect 12-volt 4 pin power connector form motherboard.

➲ Now drag motherboard from computer cabinet, uninstalled all installed usb port, hdmi card, ethernet, or other card cables, unplug power panel connector, installed ram or removes cmos battery, sata and pata cables or connector.

➲ Finally, all connector disconnects from computer motherboard, now times to uninstall computer heatsink fan unscrew it properly, now you see bottom microprocessor chip move retention clip angle at 90 degree angle to drag out microprocessor from its location, place properly microprocessor properly at its location.

➲ You see all component of your computer properly unplug or disconnected from computer component.

Startup process (booting) – booting process involve series of step that load operating system from secondary memory to primary memory, while we hit start button bios start computer function check all internal external attach hardware device and component search boot sector where computer bootable instruction stored, boot sector boot or load bootable instruction and start operating system, post (power on self-test) program check all computer peripheral, if everything correct copying boot instruction into ram, otherwise produce console error if nay device fail to load, it process repeated many time when we start and restart computer in routine process.

What are bios – bios abbreviated as basic input output system first program loaded in computer by computer motherboard manufacturer, bios contain all bootable instruction program that are necessary to normal booting and proper computing function, bios control all computer component and peripheral like keyboard, mouse, printer, scanner, usb, irq, ethernet, ram, serial and parallel com ps/2 port, computer security features component enable disable option and many other function required for normal booting a computer system, bios control and managed computer hardware software windows operation, bios store in read only memory (permanent memory) and every time while computer start it placed operating system bootable instruction from ram to rom, remember bios is a first program that area pre-installed while computer motherboard design, after configuration proper bios menu now install windows operating system for boot graphically operating system environment, you can update older bios version from newer one after detail getting knowledge of bios up gradation process, if you have less skill don't try this it make permanently damage your computer hardware so be careful before apply these step.

Bios setup – bios setup mean entering into bios screen there are many option to access bios menu screen some computer allow press del while computer switched on some laptop allow press f2, f10, tab key, now you see bios screen windows, bios screen display multiple bios screen that are necessary to proper function computer component, remember if you are beginner don't change bios function and menu otherwise it interrupt booting process and other bios services even it because of bios damage.

Multimedia – multimedia is essential component of business industry it include television, movie industries, online video conference web visual animated multimedia object resources, it became media of human entertainment source anybody watch/listen directly indirectly multimedia resources through personal use electronic gadgets.

What is multimedia – multimedia combines much visual non – visual object stuff, multimedia is a combination of sound, audio, video, text, graphic, animation, movie, visual material common application of multimedia are computer video/movie/animation cinema hall movie television projector lcd display visual hoardings multimedia animated product website are common example of multimedia, multimedia became important part in human life illiterate understand anything visual image audio video impact human brain directly even fulfill requirement of business industry.

Text – text include letter, introduction, matter, heading and other information represent during multimedia object display with supported electronic gadgets, text play a role of understanding audience meaning related multimedia object.

Graphics/images – graphic include visual theme picture image background foreground map sketch and other graphic media included/recording during multimedia object generated graphic add visual attractive interface you created multimedia object.

Animation – animation include graphic cartoon image visual animated content as a shape of multimedia now days many web site display online catalogue of animated image include sound audio video picture that demonstrate to their client about product.

Audio – audio include voice recording mp3, mp4, wav, wmr and other audio extension recorded and play with multimedia object, audio describe nay multimedia object easier.

Video – video contain all multimedia material include text graphic image animation audio video etc. Video recorded for commercial education or non-commercial product.

Multimedia application in education

Entertainment – entertainment need everyone to relax him/her self, using entertainment in shape of computer playing moving, using software apps, games, using multimedia movie contents, virtual world application, using windows xbox game, use windows media player and other application view movies, view multimedia website, web content and many more entertainment content easier to get and access through internet application.

Marketing – use computer in marketing to promote marketing business, demonstrate product worldwide through using internet technology, explore product 360-degree angle, show online product specification, product photos, views, and other graphical status, post with using product description online, include many user advantage of using computer and internet technology worldwide through internet application when user need.

Computer software – computer software computer developer created source code or event of series task or command create or design some specific purpose, software develop by computer software developer, software developer develop category of software according to their customer need, generally developer created system software, application software web software, database software, application management software, security software and other one category in software list, computer software play important role between installed hardware installed operating system provide user working space or area to easier deal with desire application for fulfill some application related commercial task and information.

System software – system software specially design for system called computer, these category of software handle computer operation, task, manage system services, control user behavior, secure and manage system data, provide infrastructure operating to working long duration or time in safer mode, sometime system software using like a system tools to manage and control other system activities, some common system software is windows, dll files, group policies, registry, services and more other tools and control.

Application software – application software design for windows user or consumer, these application provide graphical interface each computer user to work and close system related task and activities, system software communicate with installed operating system and installed operating system integrate services with computer hardware device and component, user have various category of application software in market if you need to application for office then use microsoft office or libre office suites, if you want to create code use c, c++, java, c#, vb.net, python, shell and more, similar you created database use microsoft access, or libre office base, similar like many category of application license and open source application you have choice to install on your computer to work easier in installed operating system.

Compiler – compiler is also system utility program which translate c programing code in high language code into low language, compiler read all program source and translate equivalent source code to object code and produce all error at the bottom of program application exception error windows, remove all error one by one and make program error free in simple compiler translate source language code into target language code.

Interrupter – interrupter is also translator interrupter translate source programming language into target programming language one by one, interrupter read one line statement and convert it into equivalent target language, these process repeat till then all line interrupted from top to bottom, interrupter play a role of mediator between two different language.

Names of some high-level languages

C language – c programming is a general purpose programming language originally design and developed by dennis ritchie in 1972, at bell laboratories in california c programming derived from b language created by ken thompson in 1970, in c programming we deal with arrays, function, union, typedef, structure, pointer, file handling, loops, and other many hidden concept, create with c programming project, application, software, operating system kernel coding, boot loader, games, and many more, now days c programming is popular between engineer developer student scientists even other computer user.

Syntax of c program

```
#include <stdio.h>
Int main()
{
Printf("\n welcome to c programing !");
Return 0;
}
```

C++ - c++ programming language which is inspire from c programming, c++ borrowing concept feature syntax similar in c programming mainly c++ describe oops (object oriented programming system) concept, c++ developed by bjarne stroustrup in 1980, c++ is a general purpose programming language which is combine features of low level language and high level language, c++ design and created at bell lab, important features of c++ it to introduce classes, c++ run of different platform may be windows linux unix mac or other, c++ provides features of classes function arrays file handling inheritance polymorphism etc.

Syntax of c++ programming

```
#include <iostream>
Using namespace std;
Int main ()
{
Cout << "welcome to c++ programing!";
Return 0;
}
```

C#.net – c # known as see sharp advanced version or combination of c c++ programming concept, c # is multi paradigm programming language, c # completely developed and redesign by microsoft dot net team developer, in c # create console based application program even graphical windows ide form based common or advanced control, c# popular in year 2000 when microsoft combine multiple individual programming in single, net project it combines features of c, c++ or visual basic programming language.

Visual basic – visual basic programming concept introduce by microsoft company in 1991, vb is third generation event driven programming language, visual basic programming generate on the basis of basic programming language, vb adopt all concept features of basic programming vb introduce first programming on gui (graphical user interface programming) concept, drag and drop method which mean user just drag and drop some vb control and create code for it, visual basic created by john makeny vd allow raid (rapid application development import database from microsoft access sql oracle and other programming method support backhand behind now days visual basic derived from new name called vb.net a project started by microsoft company since 2000 visual basic programming easier then c programming because it provide list of tool active x control pop up oledb control.

Basic windows of visual basic program

Visual basic.net – visual basic .net upgrade version new release by microsoft company vb.net keep all function features structure derived from visual basic programming, it based on concept object oriented programming method which implement net frame work, net frame work allow to globalize share project code application among multiple client two main release of visual basic .net microsoft visual studio or microsoft visual basic express edition both version allow you to create robust client server enterprises company standalone level application development support.

Different version release of vb.net

- ➲ Visual basic studio 2000.
- ➲ Visual basic studio 2002.
- ➲ Visual studio 2003.
- ➲ Visual studio 2005.
- ➲ Visual studio 2008.
- ➲ Visual studio 2010.
- ➲ Visual studio 2012.
- ➲ Visual studio 2013.
- ➲ Visual studio 2015.

Cobol – cobol is outdated oldest programming used in midterm 1960 for business, government, agencies, private organization, company, school, universities, etc. Cobol abbreviated as (common business oriented language) early 1960 cobol popular in industry business administrative finance other business activities we can say that now days we use for finance software like tally, net stock, and other for business and finance that time cobol use for these purpose and task.

```
$ set sourceformat "free l"
Identification division.
Program-id. Shortestprogram.
Procedure division.
Displayprompt.
Display "welcome to cobol programming".
Stop run.
```

Version of cobol programming

- ➲ Cobol-68
- ➲ Cobol-74
- ➲ Cobol-85
- ➲ Cobol 2002

Java – java is object oriented programming language which is completely derived features function structure of c and c++ programming, java programming concept developed by james gosling at sun microsystem, java derived from oak programming used in 1990 for microwave and small chip coding, java programming use method syntax follow in c and c++ programming, java code compiled into byte code to source code and execute in any jvm(java virtual machine), java specially design for microwave vcr firmware chip circuit coding, but now days new release of java used in software development web development and other use.

Java program syntax

```
Public class hellojava
{
Public static void main (string [] args) {
System.out.println ("\n welcome to java");
}
}
```

Basic windows of java Version of java programming

- ➲ Jdk 1.0
- ➲ Jdk 1.1
- ➲ J2se 1.2
- ➲ J2se 1.3

➲ J2se 1.4

➲ J2se 5.0

➲ Java se 6

➲ Java se 7

Pascal – pascal high level computer programming language develop by blaise pascal, using pascal programming in 1970 to create systematic structured computer generated program, user of pascale follow strict program creation steps, create program following various similar programming pattern and syntax in other popular programming language in this era, pascal user properly literate proper programming syntax and logic during any source created.

Prolog – prolog stand as programming logic, a general purpose logical programming language, prolog used to find artificial intelligence, computational linguistic solution, predict future logic, prolog design by alain colmerauer in marseille, france, in the before year 1970.

Free domain software – free domain software are intentionally loaded by their developer designer on public domain server free post web site for everyone, who access free of charge use/download, you can access all features of software in some condition, if you want full access of freeware software features than buy license, in this category of free open sources software developer by unix and linux even for windows user developed application utilities software are free of cost in gpl(general public license) called foss(free open source software) system, developed millions of application for customer/client/developer/designer download and installed them no need to pay anything to anyone.

3. Operating system

Why need operating system – the question remain for all computer user they may be beginner, or advanced include a computer developer or administrator, can possible to work with computer without installing operating system, so the answer is no possible to work and communicate without installing copy of operating system, important function of operating system is that operating system provide user interface for working with many windows system and user application, while user buy computer system company must installed a fresh copy of operating system, after installing operating system, user able to install his/her desire application software into a installed operating system, remember it depend on your system hardware specification what specification minimum meet during installation of operating system process, depending your system hardware may be 32 - bit or 64 - bit application support installed required application and take advantage of computer system for making personal and professional task easier during system interaction.

Function of operating system – important function of any operating system installed on a working machine is that operating system is master/collection of many small packages necessary to proper boot/run and execute system task, remember any user may be ordinary or system administrator no able to communicate with system hardware devices, during system communication, but installed operating system provide user interface for working with computer system, while user interact or communicate with computer system he not able to direct work with microprocessor, input/output, system busses, and other hardware component, installed operating system translate binary/machine language into human readable/understandable code or instruction, now operating system interact with system, busses, system hardware, logic gates, binary, decimal, octal, and hexadecimal number system, and provide interface for ordinary and advanced user to work with computer technology.

Operating system and system software – operating system we already discuss what is operating system and how it function, but now we difference between operating system and system software so you know about both are a category of computer software but both function and role of working is different, where operating system play role of master software it run many individual system or application software, but system software design or work with particular software, like you need to properly run any input or output device you must need to install a related system software or necessary hardware, like we need to proper function of web camera then first we plug – in web camera with attach computer hardware or installed related system software for proper function of web camera with installed operating system through system hardware, but you always know major difference is operating system just provide environment/infrastructure for running and supporting many application in working system hardware.

Operating system and application software – we already discuss about role of operating system in field of information technology why operating system required and necessary for any fresh buy computer, remember operating system is huge collection of small or large system, utilities, and user application, after installation of proper operating system, computer administrator user able to installed application software the question remain unsolved, why application software so answer is application software specially design to meet requirement of a particular system or user, application fulfill desire requirement of a particular field subject need, like you need to create document, print, edit, or modify document then you just need to installed word application for managing documents, similar installed a various kind of application software for photoshop for design photos and graphic, similar coral draw for creating professional advertisement and design for publication.

Operating system and hardware – operating system and hardware both necessary component of computer remember hardware is physical component of computer system that play role to build/ design computer devices, or hardware is collection or type all attach input/output, processing, storage, devices that play important function of control system operating, system hardware and operating system both necessary for each and other first hardware build computer system and operating system integrate and communicate between system hardware software and user while user perform desire function and task with computer system.

Windows popular operating system

Sl. no	Operating system name	Version available	Company
1	Windows 10 technical preview	32 – bit or 64 – bit	Microsoft company
2	Windows 8.1	32 – bit or 64 – bit	Microsoft company

Sl. no	Operating system name	Version available	Company
3	Windows 8	32 – bit or 64 – bit	Microsoft company
4	Windows 7	32 – bit or 64 – bit	Microsoft company
5	Windows vista	32 – bit or 64 – bit	Microsoft company
6	Windows xp	32 – bit or 64 – bit	Microsoft company

Choice of available operating system – choice of available operating system for windows user allow microsoft windows user to installed desire operating system from available choice of operating system, remember microsoft company every time launch new kind or client and server operating system with new environment support and additional modern features, but now days many computer hardware manufactures design new hardware support modern operating system and devices, like if user buy a new laptop, or desktop then restricted choice of installed modern windows 8 or windows 10 operating system, even if you installed modern operating system then it much more support than old operating system, and modern operating system provide greater speed, performance accuracy, system communication with user and devices better then old operating system so always installed modern operating system on new buy computer system, in list of choice available operating system is microsoft window 10, unix based operating system, linux based ubuntu, or apple operating system, android o/s and other one.

Why world most user prefer windows – these question remain unsolved and controversy between computer user beginner and advance user why world most user prefer windows based operating system, instead user can access android, linux, unix, or apple mac operating system, so the answer is microsoft is a leading company in field of information technology or these company design easier user interface operating system, company main focus to give technology its client easy as learn for fun concept, even company target all kind of computer user may be beginner, advanced, or developer, company intention provide computer technology in all hand with easier environment and robust features, the reason of choosing windows operating system is it available everywhere, low price, support client and server, all required application collection in it, easy to install update, getting online support, huge market of windows share, company reputation in field of information technology, global access, meet all type client requirement, and most about windows world 90% computer hold/installed windows based operating system across worldwide, last but not least huge share of windows market globe wise.

About microsoft – windows project started by microsoft company after year 1990, in year 1995 microsoft successfully launch windows 3.1 or microsoft windows 95 operating system, it became soon popular between computer user, because it provide tremendous graphical environment features include small application package media player sound recorder, small utilities software windows control panel and more necessary application package, in that time mac unix and linux became popular between developer and computer engineer.

An overview of different versions of windows

Windows 98 – windows 98 o/s popular in year 1998 this release by microsoft organization cover almost of it market across the world, windows 98 combine many built features and hardware control for windows operation, windows 98 have great features and hardware tools for all client and other thing, it is a stable plug and play o/s support and cover run install almost platform.

Windows 2000 – windows 2000 operating system belong to server category even it design in four different platform, windows 2000 server upgrade version of windows nt operating system, specialty of windows 2000 server it design on client and server framework for connecting internet and intranet share printer access files and folder, microsoft provide of windows 2000 server in server, advance server, data center, windows 2000 operating support new hardware interface, plug and play device support, design or build networking between connected client, share hardware resources, printer, scanner, storage device, network information etc.

Windows xp – windows xp release after windows 98, me windows 2000 windows xp operating system first time windows xp windows xp graphical multi user multi-tasking multi-threading os designed for client user windows xp based on winnows 98 windows xp popular and stable version for long time without produce any error debug best support of windows xp it is totally designed on concept of previous windows release best part of its that microsoft company release windows xp different version name windows xp service pack 1, service pack 2, service pack 3 last release.

Windows 2003 – windows server 2003 operating system successfully upgrade version of windows 2000 server operating system, company built windows server in 32 bit include 64-bit operating system, even company launch these in four different version categories, it making update in group policy management include active directory.

Windows vista – windows vista release after windows xp windows vista highly graphical and strong restricted group policy provide operating system, software which is totally designed on concept of stop piracy copy or misuse of source code by illegal user windows vista don't break software restriction and group policy settings, generally it allow only genuine software and hardware support tools windows vista control dialog windows button title and other features completely differ from previous release by microsoft company, windows vista add new generation tools and control for new environment with easily access and reduce software piracy and misuse of legal resource even strong windows client and server restriction.

Windows 7 – windows 7 operating system launch after windows vista successfully working in market, windows 7 operating system advance or upgrade version of windows vista os, windows 7 launched in october 2009 but windows 7 provide and smoother user interface with upgrade software hardware booting kernel instruction then windows vista os, company add new web browser, windows media player, personalization, better security environment, new control panel, networking support, device attachment liberty and many newer concepts add these are included in any version of previous windows operating system.

Windows 8 – windows 8 release by microsoft organization after windows 7, windows 8 foundation designed based or construct on windows 7, windows 8 include most of similar features configuration windows foundation but new idea or new concept identity of microsoft company for always create new thing and control for microsoft os user windows 8 add many new features control and environment company create new.

Windows 10 – windows 10 os new operating system developed and launch by microsoft company, windows 10 upgrade version of windows 8 operating system, it contains all features available in windows 8 but it gets back start menu (new start menu) that contain apps include programs for user, include sleek design new generation robust features for modern hardware and software, windows more reliable, stable, fast, easier, modern, multiuser, multi-tasking, and other features contain operating system.

Basic windows elements

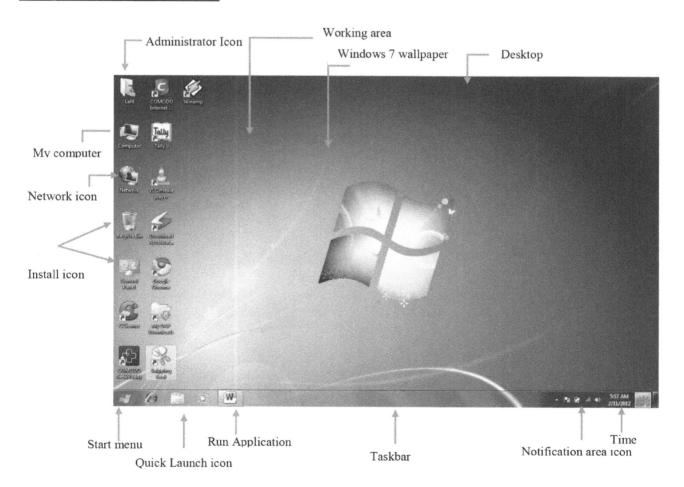

Windows 7 icon

Active user icon

Comodo Antivirus

My computer icon

Tally 9 icon

Network   icon

Vlc Media Player icon

Recycle bin   icon

Dap   icon

Control Panel   icon

Google chrome
Browser   icon

Ccleaner   icon

My Dap Download
icon

GeekBuddy   icon

Snipping Tool   icon

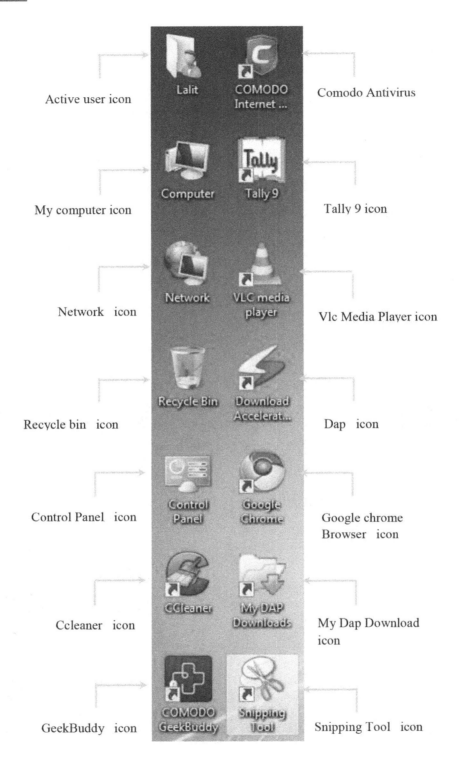

Windows 10 project – windows 10 or windows technical preview project started by microsoft company developer/group of student, for creating something new in field of compute information technology, the whole used and access microsoft various kind of operating system flavor company decided to create new concept with new idea even offer microsoft customer new type of operating journey with sleek design, robust features, strong platform for client and server platform.

Windows 10 operating system – windows 10 operating system is operating system, but i telling you about what is operating system, in term of information technology operating system integrate or share information between system hardware and software resources, even operating system is collection of system program, utilities, basic application, library, even we called operating system a master system software play role between computer and its user, remember no possible to work with computer system without installing operating system copy, windows 10 operating system foundation design on new technology, it add new concept of start menu, better graphic and design, modern application with better startup speed, and many more new features that introduce by author in this book.

Flavors of windows 10

Sl. No	Flavor name	Company
1	Windows 10 technical preview client	Microsoft company
2	Windows 10 server	Microsoft company

Hardware installation specification for windows 10

- ➲ Dual core processor at least greater (3 gigahertz (ghz) is recommended).
- ➲ At least 1 gigabyte ram (2gb recommended).
- ➲ At least 20 gigabyte space on hard disk (recommended 80gb or more).
- ➲ Bootable cd-rom or dvd - rom, usb bootable pen drive.

How starts setup

- ➲ Start computer press del, f2, f10, f12 for entering in bios menu.
- ➲ Select first boot device cd/dvd rom, if boot first device usb select first boot device usb.
- ➲ Insert cd/dvd in cd/dvd rom usb in usb drive.
- ➲ Press any key to cd/dvd .... Continue click enter and follow instruction.

Installation of windows 10 operating system

Step involve during windows 10 operating system installation

Press any key to continue – first set bios bootable device it may be dvd or usb drive or lan ethernet network connection, in short time wait you see message display in console windows press any key to continue press any keyboard key, but prefer enter key, now windows 10 installation begin it blink a character of number dots continue now you able to press any key for starting window 10 new installation on laptop, desktop, notebook or other kind of computer hardware device.

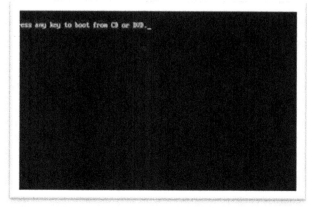

Starting windows – starting windows 10 installation windows it indicates windows 10 installation begin, juts wait and watch till than next screen dialog windows appear, it flashes windows 10 new start menu logo in slow moment view it, it shrinks from small to larger size and rise continue, at bottom a circle process bar continuing moving in round direction at windows logo bottom, it moving continue with round of dots till the next windows 10 next screen appear.

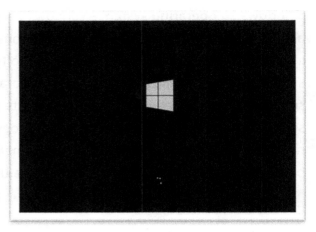

Location – select your default windows 10 installation language english (united states) by default, customize time and currency format according to your region, select keyboard and input method, automatically detected keyboard belong to active computer hardware device, click next to continue getting screen of windows 10 installation, remember in this dialog user decide a basic format of install language continent region, include using keyboard hardware method use on active computer hardware devices.

Install now – install now option starting beginning installation of windows 10 operating system procedure, click and wait till next windows 10 installation dialog appear in screen, even in this dialog allow user to repair existing windows operating system installation even start new fresh windows 10 installation begin on click next to continue loaded windows 10 operating system according to the user need.

Product key – insert windows 10 product key for activate purchase/buy downloaded download windows 10 operating system version, remember without insert windows 10 product you can't access next dialog in setup procedure, enter 25 alphanumeric key of current windows 10 product in large empty text box, it allow user to make active your windows 10 operating system version online/ offline even you get new update features and function from windows 10 website, you get windows

10 license key behind dvd label even beta version get from microsoft web site, after properly insert alphanumeric key of windows operating system click continue for installation continue.

License term – license term indicate strict policy design by microsoft company for their windows 10 user, eula(end user license agreement) you follow all terms and condition created by microsoft company before using their product, click check box on the i accept the license terms, generally eula bound every windows user to learn and better understand company product issuing and using related policy set for every windows 10 user, click next to continue running windows 10 operating system installation.

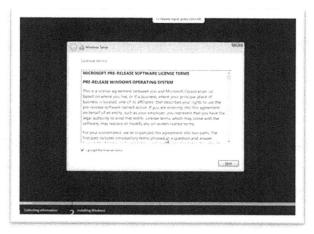

Installation type – if existing version install of windows 7 or windows 8 and you want to be upgrade windows 7 include windows 8 install earlier version with upgraded new windows 10 version click on upgrade it will upgrade completely your existing version keep file and directory structure as well as default, if you choose custom install windows 10 version it remove all files and directory from root drive, fresh installation and new file and directory structure created, click next to continue in setup step, this windows allow you to getting two individual choice for fresh include upgrade existing new or old windows 10 operating system after selection click on next to continue begin installation.

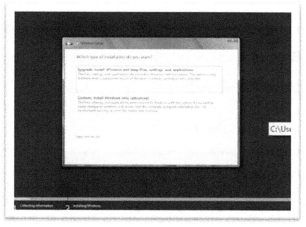

Partition information – all/overall hard disk space available in partition windows, include view another existing along new created windows 10 partition size, now select hard drive partition and click on drive option advance new option appear, click and equally divide current hard drive in two part or desire hdd partition size, create at least three and more partition in partition windows if you want to create more windows 10 partition install windows 10, even press right click on my computer icon after installation of windows 10 on desktop choose manage option select disk management and create number of remaining partition according to need, click next to continue installation procedure.

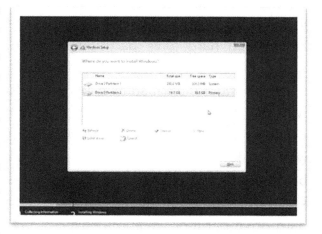

Created partition – created partition appear in next windows, if you create one or more windows 10 partition, now view any one select any partition where reside windows 10 installation files and folder.

Partition windows option

Refresh – refresh all created windows hard drive partition table if any error occur, click refresh after create windows hard drive partition.

Delete – delete existing partition table partition even newly created partition also and new create size of partition.

Format – format option erase all entire information store existing and newly created partition and make new track sector cluster at hard drive partition always format installation c drive format, because c drive reserve for window root directory, here a and b drive reserve in previous for floppy/ zip drive, so created partition started from c, d and continue.

New – create new number of partition, of existing hard drive, select hard drive space click on new enter partition size now click to new partition generate apply same process for remaining new partition creation.

Load driver – load driver of hard drive partition and other information related driver information.

Extend – extend options extend size newly created partition size from extend menu.

Installation partition – select partition form existing partition table created in windows 10 hard drive partition table, by default it create 350 megabyte partition for swap memory area, in windows 7 swap memory size is 100 megabyte, but in windows 10 it keep or leave 350 megabyte partition select above installation partition for windows 10 installation file, finally making desire changes in a partition table include it option customize according to user need, click on next to continue in setup procedure of windows 10 operating system.

Installation begin – windows 10 file and directory copy at selected hard drive partition by default it will be windows c drive location, start copying file and system folder configuration installing windows 10 features in windows 10 version, installing update add new update windows 10 new releases from microsoft windows 10 web site, for these broadband internet connection must be required or connected and should be faster, finishing setup windows 10 file and information correctly move at hard drive partition location, now just wait and watch

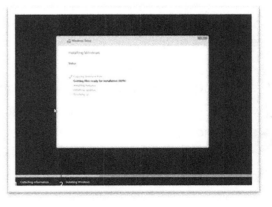

approximate 30–35 minute for installation of windows 10 operating system, it depend on your computer hardware specification.

Restart windows – restart windows appear after windows 10 installation dialog finishing number of installation process name copying windows 10 files, getting files ready for installation, installing features, installing update, finally configure windows 10 setup or finish it and restart windows 10 setup dialog appear these dialog arrange setup file and configure installation operating system between hardware software services in windows operating system, wait for second even click on restart windows now command button to manually restart windows 10 operating system setup.

Getting's device ready – after windows 10 installation restart next screen appear name getting's device ready these screen configure operating system services between computer hardware and software, even it configures properly computer plug and play services include attach all hardware component for properly boot every time windows 10 operating system in normal mode, wait till these dialog automatically configure its services while installation in running mode.

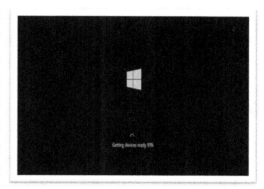

Personalization – in personalization windows select background color of using metro style apps, series of color offer by personalization windows you may free to select desire color behind metro style apps preview, drag slider from start to end select the desire one personalization color and leave it, type personal computer name, computer name used in networking while used lan or wan it show system identity online, pc name should be different from user name other collision occur, click next to continue dialog.

Setting – choose use express setting or customize, if you are connected through internet than choose use express setting and continue otherwise select customize option it enable you to live sign up in microsoft windows 10 online account sign with microsoft company user e-mail account and password services, enter microsoft live e-mail detail and sign in to microsoft company online account, if you choose express setting than enter offline user name and password for log in account windows 10 install operating system for accessing and controlling its function and features when user need.

Use express settings – use windows 10 express installation setup mode option, provides facility to windows installer to installed windows 10 with automatically windows updates recommended, keep help protect windows from files and internet defect website, use upgrade microsoft software features, configure automatically windows apps according to your system location and settings, and many more other features you automatically updates and modify automatic in use express windows 10 installation settings.

Customize – customize option enable microsoft user to manually configure and customize installed windows services, application, control application, network, system, online/offline control, include system additional features manually configure and customize by dialog by dialog or windows configuration, set final settings that you like to work or install with installed windows 10 operating system.

Share into with microsoft and other services – share info with microsoft and other services windows enable windows 10 user to, configure default share behavior of windows 10 apps name microsoft bing, internet explorer, and other windows 10 supporting apps while configure these services it provides freedom user to turn on or off share info with microsoft or other services in windows 10 operating system, click next to continue screen appear.

Sign into live microsoft account – enter microsoft online e-mail account/address information for opening and accessing microsoft live account features, remember if you are using microsoft live user e-mail account then you protect your system, getting live update, configure installed new apps from microsoft company provide apps store like apple mac or android play store, for these you must be online user even you get many more advantage offer new launches provided by microsoft company but remember online account id and password enter one time and its configure properly you no need to enter configure online microsoft account information more and more time you always login as a microsoft online or live user in windows 10 account.

Settings – configure settings of attach install or connect windows 10 pc devices and network public accessing related content in windows 10, while you click on these dialog for configure its services you must remember the network connection must be connected or in online mode before using these services, select your choice between yes and no according to your need.

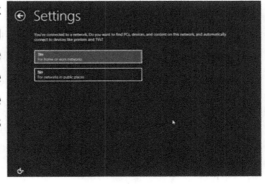

Update your pc and apps – update your pc and apps setting dialog enable windows 10 user to configure turn on or turn off windows 10 update related apps and pc settings, if you configure these dialog properly then you getting automatically window new apps, device driver, system hardware software function when user click on update pc and app settings, modify help and protect your pc and display privacy settings, related option making turn on or turn off.

Check online for solutions – configure check for solution dialog option in windows 10 installation, in these setting a or configure a gap between computer hardware and software devices, get online solution for microsoft product and services you get by default two option of choice for making turn on or turn off settings related improving check solution related to microsoft product services.

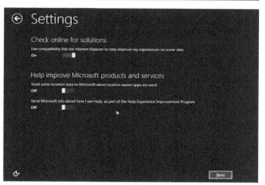

Sign in to microsoft account – sign into microsoft online account, if you already created a microsoft online account then just enter microsoft user e-mail id include id password for log in online microsoft user account for getting accessing new advantage features of newly installed version copy of windows 10 operating system, even you don't have online microsoft user account then you have freedom to create online microsoft live user account for log in as a live user.

Create microsoft account – create a microsoft live user account on fill available microsoft account form, in this windows enter user first name, last name, e-mail address, create password, re-enter password, enter password must be alphanumeric or more than 8 character similar add country/region information from drop down combo selection finally click on next dialog to configure or verify live user account for every time entering in windows 10 user account.

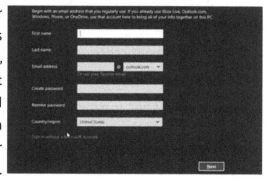

Sign into your pc – create a single user account enter user name type password follow password restriction policy, password should be strict complex combination of alphanumeric symbol collection, and never share password with unknown, type password hint if you forget password hit indicate idea about lost password, click next to log in created windows 10 user account and access newly install windows 10 features from microsoft collection.

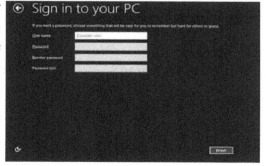

Installing apps – after installing most features of window 10 operating system, you getting a screen name installing apps windows, these windows continue to installing windows 10 modern apps in computer background, must remember in that time you don't get windows 10 desktop screen windows till then finally setup properly of windows 10 modern apps, at the time of installing apps many color full background flick or changing all kind of color appear and finally it configure all installing apps related information and windows 10 desktop screen for user access.

First look of windows 10 – as you see before during windows previous version installation, default screen you will get default windows 10 desktop screen and its elements name recycle bin, welcome to tech preview and other icon will be displayed at windows desktop even this pc, network, document, or, control panel icon show from personalization change desktop icon settings, click check box icon to making check turn on or turn off for previewing these items at windows desktop screen, even see default

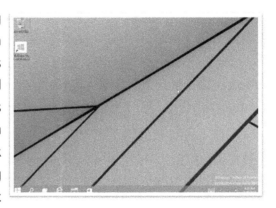

legacy of windows desk top include new features new windows 10 start menu quick launch taskbar and notification area settings available for user modification, click on any on for making desire changes even if below desktop windows appear it mean your windows 10 operating system copy successful install at user machine and installation succeed.........

Installation of other software packages such as microsoft office 2016
Where to buy

- ➲ Buy microsoft office 2016.
- ➲ Buy online license microsoft office 2016.
- ➲ Download 365 microsoft office 2016 trial from microsoft official web site.

Minimum requirement for office 2016 installation

Sl. no	Component	Requirement	Recommended
1	**Microprocessor**	1 gigahertz (ghz) or faster x86- or x64-bit processor	3.0 ghz intel amd processor
2	**Memory (ram)**	1 gigabyte (gb) ram (32-bit); 2 gigabytes (gb) ram (64-bit)	2 gb or more for faster performance

Sl. no	Component	Requirement	Recommended
3	**Hard disk**	3.0 gigabytes (gb) available	500 gb or more available
4	**Operating system**	Windows 7 (32-bit or 64-bit) Windows 8 (32-bit or 64-bit) Windows 8.1 (32-bit or 64-bit) Windows server 2008 r2 (64-bit) Windows server 2012 (64-bit)	Any new version release by microsoft company like windows future release windows 9
5	**Browser**	Internet explorer 8, 9, 10, or 11; mozilla firefox 10.x or a later version; apple safari 5; or google chrome 17.x.	New version of ie 10 firefox 25.0 safari 5.0 and above newly version
6	**.net version**	3.5, 4.0, or 4.5	

How to set up

- ➲ Open microsoft office 2013 source folder.
- ➲ Double click on setup or right click on setup click on run as administrator.
- ➲ Follow number of setup dialog during microsoft office 2013 setup.

Click on below given microsoft office 2013 setup icon

Collection information – microsoft office 2013 installation began wait till microsoft office 2013 get essential hardware software information about required office installation.

License term – read carefully microsoft office 2013 office installation setup procedure agreement, move down vertical scrollbar continuously till end of line, finally click on i accept the terms of this agreement check box on, generally this agreement telling you about using microsoft product policy you follow microsoft eula (end user license agreement), click continue to step in installation of microsoft office 2013 software.

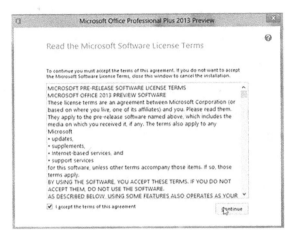

Choose the installation you want – microsoft office 2013 setup dialog provide you two default option for office installation, first one is install second one is customize if you choose install now option during microsoft office 2013 setup you install microsoft office with 2013 minimum installation configuration, and if you choose customize option now let's choose microsoft with desire microsoft office component if you want add some additional component or even install microsoft office 2013 with desire install features click select and enable disable office 2013 customize installation function.

Installation option – installation option allows you to customize default microsoft installation type, many default office 2013 function already selected and if you want to add or remove other microsite group menu then click on category select or deselect make it according to need.

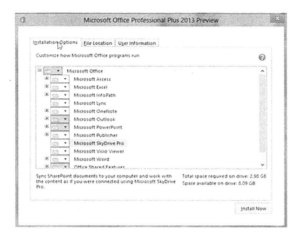

File location – change default microsoft office 2013 installation location default location is c:\program files \microsoft office, if you want changing location of install microsoft office 2013 default location, click on browse command button select desire location of microsoft storage location, then click on install now if all desire changes made.

User information – add installation user information, like user full name, initials, organization name and other essential information in given text box, if all information fill click on install now option to permanent microsoft office reside in your computer.

Install now – finally all tab configures properly like installation option, file location, user information now click on install now option to start remaining installation procedure.

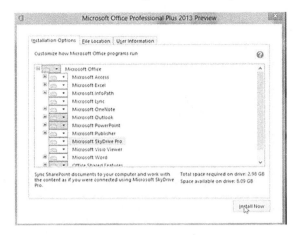

Installation progress bar – installation start from 0 to 100 it indicates your microsoft office 2013 installation begin and wait till progress bar automatically finish from start point to end point, remember during progress bar microsoft office 2013 set storage location of office files and folder.

Complete installation – while microsoft office 2013 setup complete it show you dialog which moves you on microsoft office 2013 installation website now you check newly microsoft upgrade features install new update function features on existing microsoft office 2013instllation.

Windows 10 additional features

Start screen – windows 10 start screen very familiar to windows 8 or windows 8.1 start screen in windows, all the by default installed windows apps and pin to start screen application listed as a metro style apps for touch and mouse control, at windows 10 start screen you see thumbnail all default loaded apps include online update, installed software shortcut, windows name, windows control like, shutdown, restart, switch user, sleep, include search features that allow you to search apps program and content in local computer, windows 10 installed on desktop, laptop, notebook computer, if you have a touch device then it easily allow you to manage metro style app with sliding effect, at bottom of start screen you get a horizontal scrollbar that easer you to moving from left to right direction in metro style apps start screen, windows 10 contain some windows 8 apps and some new apps added, by default at start screen you see, mail, calendar, video, music, one drive, photos, people, skype, weather, news, reading list, camera, windows store, food & drinks, sports, maps, health & fitness, alarm, calculator, reader, sound recorder, apps at start screen in windows 10 include lots of new features in newly launched microsoft windows 10 operating system.

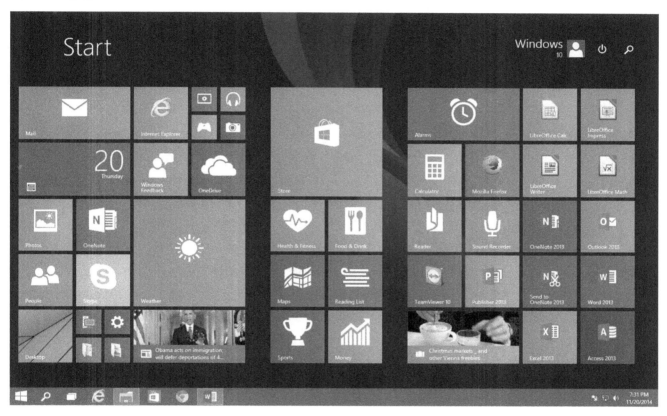

Start menu – you see them previously in windows vista, windows 7, but in windows 8 and windows 8.1 microsoft developer remove start menu and place start menu location start screen, start screen contain metro style apps and program in windows, but its back windows 10 new start menu look and feels, that feels you again start menu concept in windows operating system, let's describe you start menu function of new windows 10 start menu, it contain some windows 8.1 apps and menu, in windows 10 start menu you

arrange windows apps in wide, small, large, even change default apps position from their current location to new location, add installed apps at taskbar menu bar according to need, by default new start menu appear visually more attractive previous one even it display separately windows apps, program, control, administrative control, document, pc settings, with new inbuilt search function to search in start menu even hole computer.

Windows 10 charm features

Search – search option in windows 10 option enable you to searching desire object in windows 10 with search tools just move windows mouse cursor at right bottom corner or notification area appear at windows taskbar in windows 10 operating system, when you click on search option it display you empty text box for write information about search term it will show you many search location select by it give you many search location and these are settings, everywhere, files, web image, web video, select any one of them and start process of searching elements in window 10 operating system.

Share – share option in windows 10 operating system option allow you to sharing current e-mail object with microsoft outlook express, these option work while you click on any windows object and selecting process of share current object with microsoft outlook software, remember before applying these operations you should be must configure outlook 2013 account setting, then add other recipients remaining detail final share it.

Start – start option enable you to moving you in windows metro style app selection, while you click on start or press windows key on windows 10 operating keyboard, in windows 10 metro style app include access all installed automatic or manually windows 10 application software, system utilities, admin tool and many more, finally in metro style apps it also provides search tools that we discuss previously in windows 10.

Devices – device option in start selection windows enable you to selecting and choosing device play media object include printing printed object files information from desktop printed location in windows 10, finally project current windows desktop screen with single pc, duplicate, extend, or second screen only mode select desire one to put current display with given category choice in windows 10.

Settings – setting option in windows 10 start selection strip allowing you to configure or access windows desktop, control panel, personalization, pc info, getting windows help, include view configure or customize windows 10 wi-fi setting, sound volume, windows brightness, notification, power and keyboard setting configure or customize according to need in windows 10 operating system, remember it allow some additional advance change pc setting option that giving liberty to customize setting depending your need.

Windows 10 start menu

About windows 10 start menu – we already discuss windows 10 new start menu above, it's back again in new windows 10 technical preview operating system, in windows 8 start menu completely removed but lots of feedback receive microsoft company from its user, microsoft company decide to replace start screen location with start menu, but it slight different from windows 7 start menu, you get here windows installed apps, application, and program for user access, even right side you get metro style apps as thumbnail view to get online update related display aps in windows 10.

Windows 10 - Default start screen

Windows 10 metro style apps

Windows 10 start screen – windows 10 start screen different from previous windows operating system release, start command permit windows user to getting all windows related task and function including windows desktop, e-mail, calendar, photos, games, windows store, reading

list, sky drive, weather, camera, music, skype, maps, travel, and remaining windows element easier to access from windows 10 start screen, these type of start screen enable windows user to getting all information task and action get from single location, here you meet with your clients, check e-mail, create appointment with calendar, view stock prices, install windows 10 apps store apps, view world map, get latest news, browser www resources with internet explorer, update yourself with windows update help+ tips even many more similar to get in previous windows classic style start menu, including in windows 10 start screen allow option to control lock screen windows screen, sign out account, change account picture, even sign in, sign out, including switch user between windows available user account, control windows power option setting like, shutdown, restart, sleep, with searching every in windows 10.

Windows 10 installed application/system/and all software

Windows 10 apps – windows 10 apps features of windows allowing windows user to getting all windows default and manually installed windows application software by default listed in app metro style view, it show all installed windows app as a stack one by one every windows apps, all the apps display while you click on start windows key, it immediate moves you in start screen now here you click on down arrow keys to view installed windows apps view icon display at left  bottom corner of windows 10 start screen, you just click on them even move it with finger to slide up it to view installed windows apps, every time whenever you are installing any windows 10 software app online including off line all these apps listed as category in windows 10 apps view, you can view all these windows 10 apps view in different category view, it allowing you to view or arrange all windows 10 apps in by name, by date installed, by most used, or by category view, by default these apps arranging as by category view in windows 10.

Windows 10 setting control

Desktop – desktop option in windows 10 setting, it moves you at windows active desktop location where you can have accessed this pc, document, recycle bin, network, control panel and many other remaining windows 10 element in windows operating system, just click on desktop and access its content according to need.

Control panel – control panel is all windows gui based operating system command center where user/administrator can control or manage even provide privileges to each user interaction with windows operating system, while you click on control panel you getting all windows important control listed here you can pick anyone from given category and customize or configure related setting in control panel.

Personalization – personalization decorate or make attractive even adding some additional attributes in windows boring desktop style, click on personalization and pick desire windows 10 theme, even configure lots of personalization setting like desktop background, desktop color, desktop sound, screen saver, change windows desktop icon, display, task bar and navigation or finally ease of access center setting, now pick any one of them and start to explorer or configure according to your requirement.

Pc info – pc info option enable you to know everything about your pc information about all installed information like installed windows operating system detail include system processor, installed memory, system type, pen or touch device info, computer domain workgroup setting information, and finally windows activation information getting easier from pc information, even control windows admin control like device manager, remote setting, system protection, advance system setting, action center, or final windows update setting pick someone and configure related setting according to need.

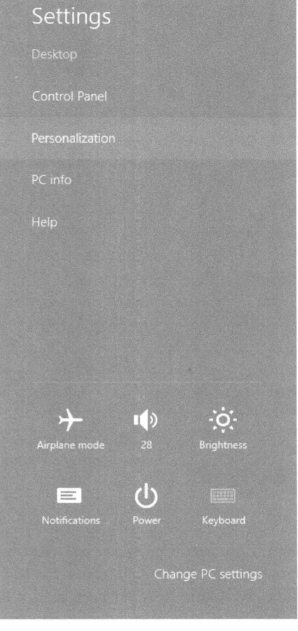

Help – help option immediately moves user to know more about windows 10 use features and control help with basic guide.

Additional windows 10 setting

Airplane mode – airplane mode appear while you're using system desktop or laptop even ultra-book wi-fi wireless services is available in turn off mode, you just click on wi-fi button in turn on mode to display as wi-fi to airplane mode, generally airplane mode indicate all wireless radio frequency services are disable by user manually while they are not available in using mode, when wi-fi button turn off than the wi-fi button indicate in red light mode, when you click on wi-fi button it display all network setting for exist internet broadband connection, even it show number of connection created manually or automatically in network.

Volume level – volume level control enable you to manage playing multimedia audio or video application software volume level between 0 to 100, here 0 indicate minimum volume level and 100 indicate maximum volume level, even volume level set below 0 it turn volume in mute, now adjust playing multimedia object volume level according to need, even entertain yourself in moment or relax while you free or not using your machine.

 Brightness – brightness option enable you setting laptop, desktop, ultra-book, brightness level between minimum to maximum, here minimum is 0 and maximum is 100 brightness level set the brightness level according to need, remember more or maximum computer brightness level glow you desktop screen, but it impact your eye resolution, even consume more computer battery power or electricity include during long working session it negative impact on user eye, so keep using windows desktop brightness level wherever you best fit your need between to minimum to maximum.

 Notification – notification option display you notification about windows operating system, windows produce many notification during user working session, notification option allow you to hiding notification related element for a few moment or a complete 1 or more hour according to your need, how much notification time you set it, till that time windows notification will became disable from using mode, how it enable or available for use than single click on notification icon to making it enable or disable from user access in windows 10 operating system.

 Power – power option allowing user to control windows computer shutdown, restart, or sleep, hibernate, even it may be hibernate or switch user option if these option enable from gpo, while you move your laptop cursor position in right bottom corner that you getting change pc setting and here you getting control name power, these option allow you to power your machine mean computer immediately all closed application and moves in turn off mode, second one is restart option these option close all windows open application and services and restart machine with new windows 10 operating system copy, finally sleep option allow to move active machine in sleep mode for a short moment while you leave machine for a reason or any business cause, then you again move your system in normal mode boot order, now you control power option that best meet your requirement.

 Keyboard – keyboard option enable you to display setting of using default keyboard language even if another keyboard language added or included these added keyboard language display here, if you adding two or more keyboard language than it allowing to make selection/choice of using single language from given category according to need, remember keyboard is essential popular hard ware media that allow you to interaction with computer allow us to create write text enter text and control windows operating.

Change pc setting – change pc setting is a collection of various windows 10 pc setting, it allowing you to configure desire setting related to your installed windows 10 operating system, just click on change pc setting now pick any one setting from given choice and configure or customize it according to need in windows.

Windows 10 control panel

About control panel – windows 10 control panel is not differ from previous windows control panel release, similar that control panel contain all installed windows application, software, services, hardware, network, administrative control, that can be modify, editable, customizable even configurable only the system approved user now here approved user mean a windows administrator user who getting full privileges to allocate and manage all windows resources according to need, even control panel is a collection of windows administrative setting, your installed computer operating system all function and features configure or customize through only windows control panel option, click control panel and view many administrative setting related your computer device, from control panel you decide how computer function, control windows operation, how windows behave, how share, how control, and many more other setting required to need configure by windows user that are configurable through windows 10 control panel.

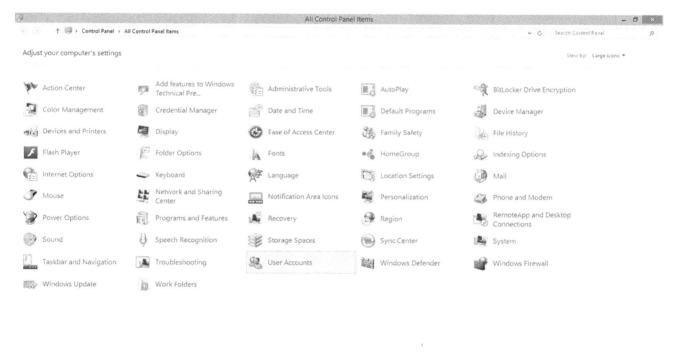

Windows 10 – Control Panel default appearance

Windows 10 personalization

About windows 10 personalization – personalization decorate or make attractive even adding some additional attributes in windows boring desktop style, it emphasis user to making some cool and commercial look like desktop appearance, click on personalization and pick desire windows 10 theme, each windows default installed or manually download theme contain sound, wallpaper, background, animated video, picture and more theme contain like mouse cursor taskbar and windows style changer, even configure lots of personalization setting like desktop background, desktop color, desktop sound, screen saver, change windows desktop icon, display, task bar and navigation or finally ease of access center setting, now pick any one of them and start to explorer or configure according to your requirement.

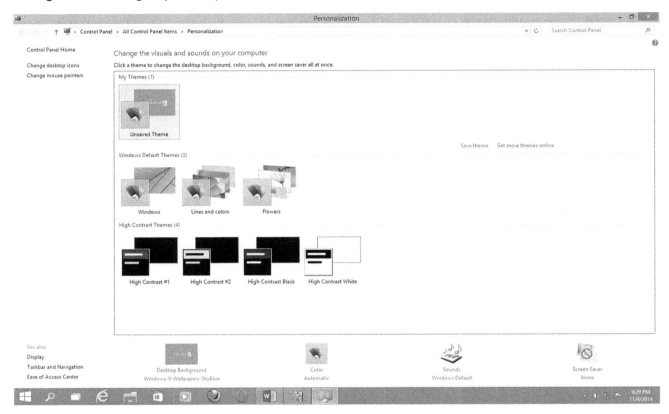

Windows 10 – Personalization default appearance

Change desktop icon – change desktop icon setting enable user to change desktop icon in windows installed 10 operating system, when fresh copy of windows 10 installation of operating system, then window 10 default desktop only recycle bin icon display other remaining icon display manually at windows desktop, click on change desktop icon in windows 10 personalization, you can display icon name is computer, control panel, network, user's files icon, show from change desktop icon menu, change icon option allow you to change default icon view of your desktop with change icon command, or restore default command button setting restore of change icon default icon in original state mode.

Desktop icon elements

Computer – computer check box elements responsible to show my computer icon replace my computer icon with new name this pc in windows 10 operating system, by default it uncheck while you fresh install copy of windows 10 operating system you need to manually turn on it on click check box option in windows 10 operating system.

User's files – user's files option enable you to show user' contain folder icon placed at windows desktop location, you see these user's folder with first user account creation process in windows operating system during installed window operating system.

Network – show network icon at windows 10 desktop location, by default it invisible while firstly windows 10 operating system installed by user, you manually turn on it on click check mark on same as you make these check mark turn off, if you don't want to show network icon at windows desktop screen.

Recycle bin – recycle bin folder contain windows deleted removed unnecessary files, folder, image, audio, video, web content and other electronic resources, contain by windows recycle bin by default recycle icon automatically display at windows 10 operating system installation, if you need to make turn off these setting then you made check mark option to turn off in windows.

Control panel – control panel option always added in any windows operating system, windows control panel store windows hardwar, software, firmware setting, you may enable to configure enable disable them according to need, by default control panel icon disable when fresh windows installation, you may make check mark turn on to display control panel, or make check turn off to making disable control panel option.

Change icon – change icon button enable you to change default icon of select windows 10 icon in windows, first of select any one icon of windows now click on change icon option to replace current icon with available new icon choice finally click to change it, you see at your windows desktop selected icon will be change in windows.

Restore default – restore default option remove user made manually changes default icon behavior display at windows desktop screen, while you need to restore windows in default mode then you try to restore these setting on click restore default it discard all manually impact added on current dialog.

Allow themes to change desktop icons – allow themes to change desktop icons option enable you to allowing theses change desktop icon when these changes in windows manually or automatically by system, if you check mark turn off these option then it works otherwise it remain default for use in windows 10.

Change mouse pointers – change your default windows 10 desktop mouse moving pointer setting from mouse properties default windows aero (system scheme) display mouse pointer change with inbuilt mouse pointer scheme then ok new mouse properties will display without any restart process.

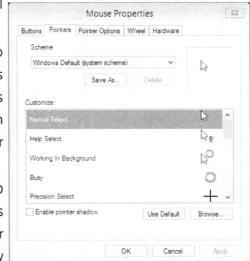

Taskbar and start menu properties

Elements of pointer tab

Scheme – scheme drop down combo box enable you to select choice between many windows available mouse pointing operation like select, help select, busy, text select, handwriting, vertical horizontal resize, move, link select, and many other pointing device operation task symbol, you can change them on click drop down scheme available microsoft company provide various category of scheme, even you click each scheme object icon and browse or replace with new one, or discard these changes with use default option.

Enable pointer shadow – enable pointer shadow check box option choice allowing you to display shadow behind mouse pointer while user working mouse or pointing device in any windows based application or software by user, by default these option remain uncheck but you make them turn on or turn off according to need during operation.

Use default – use default option rollback all changes made in using any pointer scheme, it re-back default pointer scheme effect in windows, during user dealing with many windows operating or task.

Browse – browse button allowing freedom to manually customize each pointing device operating symbol from selecting default or replace with give browse choice in windows, set whatever type icon with existing icon in windows 10 operating system.

Display – change reduce or extend size of windows 10 screen size on click display option, select smaller, medium, large resolution of windows text display screen, adjust windows resolution customize windows brightness display setting connect display attach projector device and many setting related windows screen and display.

Taskbar and start menu properties – customize default properties setting of taskbar and start menu setting change taskbar appearance, start menu display enable disable taskbar toolbar in available list.

Elements of task bar tab

Lock the taskbar – lock the taskbar option allowing windows 10 user to lock windows task bar at bottom of windows desktop screen, if check box on it mean task bar turn to lock if check mark is turn off it mean lock task bar turn off mode during use.

Auto hide the taskbar – auto hide the task bar option enable windows 10 user to making invisible or hide during working in windows 10 apps, it appears while you click at position of windows 10 taskbar location, while check mark is on it mean task bar auto hide while check mark is off it mean taskbar auto hide turn off features in windows 10.

Use small taskbar buttons – use small taskbar button option in windows 10 desktop enable windows taskbar contain all item visible in small taskbar display view, when check mark turn it mean taskbar item display in small view, but when check mark option turn off it mean taskbar button display in large screen view.

Taskbar location on screen – configure or set a windows default task bar  location by default in all windows operating system windows placed at bottom of screen every windows operating system taskbar, but in taskbar properties you getting choice change to display default taskbar location in windows, you map placed default taskbar screen location at left, right, top, bottom, by default it placed at bottom now you decide wherever you want to placed new location of your windows 10 taskbar.

Taskbar buttons – taskbar buttons option show open windows apps, 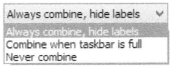 software, application, label in different view, you may select between always combine, hide label, combine when taskbar full, or never combine, select one of them for open windows app during windows 10 taskbar location, by default it loaded with always combine, hide label order in windows operating system.

Notification area – notification area contain item notify by windows, by default many windows installed application automatically placed shortcut icon at windows notification area in windows, but you decide each and every notification apps behavior from customization of notification area setting in windows, you may click on any icon now change its default behavior from given category of show icon and notification, hide icon and notification, only show notification, now you may select one of them for display notification icon behavior preview order, according to your selection your define notification item display in notification area in windows operating system.

Ease of access center – customize windows accessibility control start magnifier, start on screen keyboard, start narrator, set up high contrast, explore windows elements control from ease of access center control.

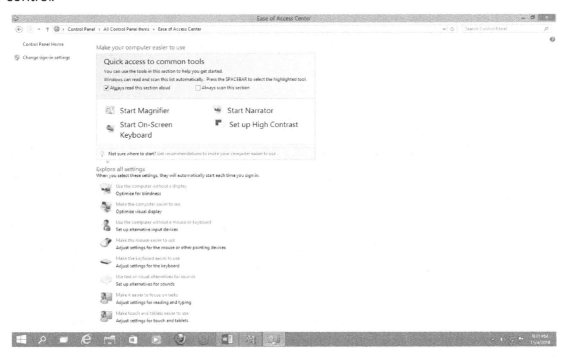

Windows 10: ease of access center

Pc info

About windows 10 pc info – pc info option enable you to know everything about your pc information about all installed information like installed windows operating system detail include system processor, installed memory, system type, pen or touch device info, computer domain workgroup setting information, and finally windows activation information getting easier from pc information, even control windows admin control like device manager, remote setting, system protection, advance system setting, action center, or final windows update setting pick someone and configure related setting according to need.

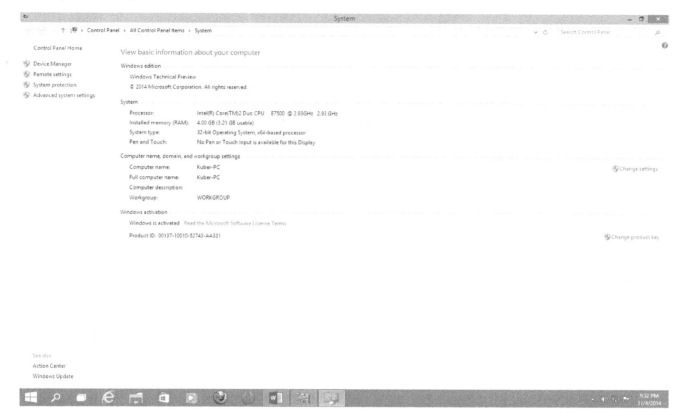

Device manager – device manager is important control function in computer, where we know about actual installed hardware component devices information in computer, by default it display your computer disk drives, display adapter, cd dvd drive, human interface device, keyboard, monitor, network adapter, microprocessor, sound, video, and game controller, system devices information use service etc. List display even any newly installed hardware automatically added in list of device manager category, you can update desire device manager hardware component, software install/ uninstall, update hardware, software removes, hardware or hardware driver view properties, and scan for devices changes.

Remote settings – remote setting dialog enable you to configure windows remote desktop related configuration and services, remote desktop is an important function of windows that enable you to working virtually all over geographic location of the world but remember you need administrative privilege and setting before do remote desktop setting, remote setting dialog allow you to configure remote desktop related all setting in single windows, remote assistance access you network remote computer from any geographic location you must leave these dialog box as check box on mode, configure advance setting that allow you to maximum limitation of remote connection with active machine even you can configure remote desktop radio button choice from give below choice.

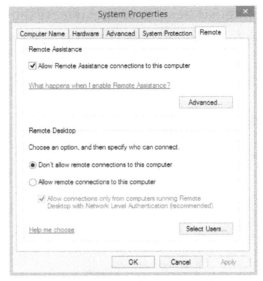

System Protection properties

Don't allow connection to this computer – don't allow connection to this computer radio button enable than you can't access remote desktop on active machine, while any remote desktop user trying to access active computer as remotely than remote access discarded by system default, because active machine configure with don't allow remote desktop on active machine.

Allow remote connection to this computer – allow remote computer for this computer settings enable windows 10 user to allow other connected computer with remotely with active computer, remember these possible while these check box must be enable, configure advance settings, set remote computer behavior for allow or don't allow other computer with this computer include select manual user of remote computer.

System protection – system protection system features enable you to move system in previous mode we say that it mean your current system position move back in the time when actually computer operating system and windows application loaded on active computer, if these features enable in system protection than you can remove or discard unwanted unnecessary changes effect on active machine, it restore computer in previous restore point mode, configure system protection setting configure or create system restore point.

Windows 10: System

System restores – system restore command button enable you to start windows system restore wizard to move back system in actual restore point, in restore point you see actual system restore date and time even view scan for affected programs, finally, you start system restore point and move back system in actual system restores point.

Configure – configure system restore point setting you can check how system restore point work is it keep previous version of files or turn off system protection, customize system disk usage space, you can delete previous system restore point information.

Create – create a system restore point for restoring system if any problem occurs, than turn on system restore point for active system drive, finally type the name of system restore point and activate it.

Advance system setting – advance setting option enable you to configure system advance setting according to need, advance setting option gives you choices of system advance setting like performance, user profiles, and startup and recovery or system environment variable system configuration.

Elements of system setting

Performance – performance command button enable you to customize system windows visual effect these setting enable you to improve system appearance and performance, configure system processor scheduling adjust the best system performance, configure system virtual memory size increase decrease system virtual memory default amount, you can manually or custom changes amount of using hard drive partition as virtual memory on current system even configure data execution prevention setting according to need.

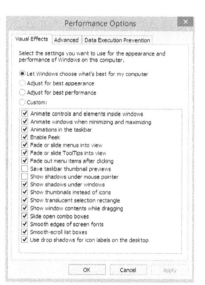

User profiles – user profiles are collection of windows login instruction include windows startup to windows logoff setting user roaming profiles store in user profiles setting, you can change existing windows profiles type local profile to roaming profiles, even delete existing windows profiles each created windows profiles contain/keep important instruction related to windows logon.

User profile properties

Startup and recovery – view system startup default installed operating system detail, number of time display operating system in seconds, computer startup moment increase decrease system startup second time according to need, even view system failure error notification, it write all event in system log file, or automatically restart, write debugging information in kernel memory dump, etc.

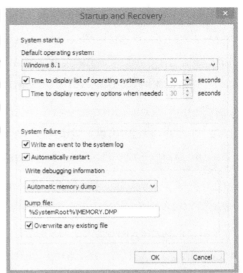

Startup and Recovery properties

Windows 10 search setting

Search features important features of windows 10 operating system, remember these search different from previous windows search technique and method, in this search dialog type name or start keyword of search term and information after wait it produce list of related search query, these search features searching at all area of a computer like it search in windows software, drive location, system application, system software, finally these option listed all search related similar query at below important features of these search tool is it search or find all search category in whole computer while user try to search.

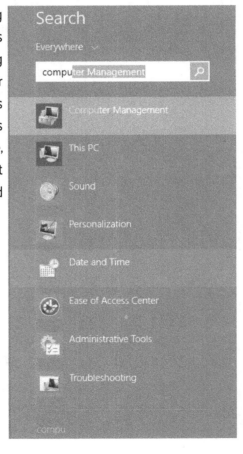

Windows 10 personalize setting

Background – used windows 8 windows 10 decorative background used for display as windows desktop screen, by default windows 10 installed with default theme or default background you able to change default background with available personalize choice of background all these listed background, default collection of background provided by microsoft company team, you just click and select apply desire background from personalize collection after applying desire system desktop background you will be able to change its default background include accent color from personalize settings, after adding new desktop background again apply another one desktop background.

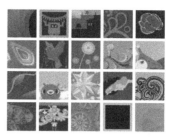

Background color – apply background color for working windows 10 desktop screen, first of all select a desire background for active windows desktop now click on collection of background gallery here you get normal, standard, or more dark, light color ready for apply in working desktop wallpaper background color, click select and replace background color till then user need, even you may replace existing one with new background color.

Accent color – change or apply accent color at working windows 10 desktop screen, remember these option effective area of windows 10 desktop accent area, similar above you also get here choice of dark, light, and medium color choice for apply as accent color at windows desktop background while user need.

Windows 10 tiles setting/tiles

Show administrative tools – these option show windows 10 administrative tools in tiles windows, administrative tool huge collection of administrative task control that allow or provide control windows administrator for control and manage windows 10 operation and services, by default these option turn on but according to need you may turn on or turn off administrative tools with tiles preview in windows 10 start screen/start menu window.

Clear personalize info from my tiles – clear personalize information from my tiles windows these option removing user personalize information from tiles area in windows 10 operating system, by default these option remain untouched while user click on clear option it will clear user personalize info from tiles window.

This pc – this pc is a windows 10 new style my computer explorer, windows that display you information about installed local hard drive multiple partition, installed optical device, removable device, network information, web cam installed application software, it allowing to easier moving between multiple computer hard drive partition, optical drive, view explorer edit or delete this pc electronic content and information, even you can easier view or move content of this pc desktop, document, download, music, pictures, video and another important object according to need, just click and view desire object in it, the major different between windows 10 and previous release microsoft my computer/now this pc it contain menu style as tab format you can easier to pick and done desire task from given option choice in this pc object.

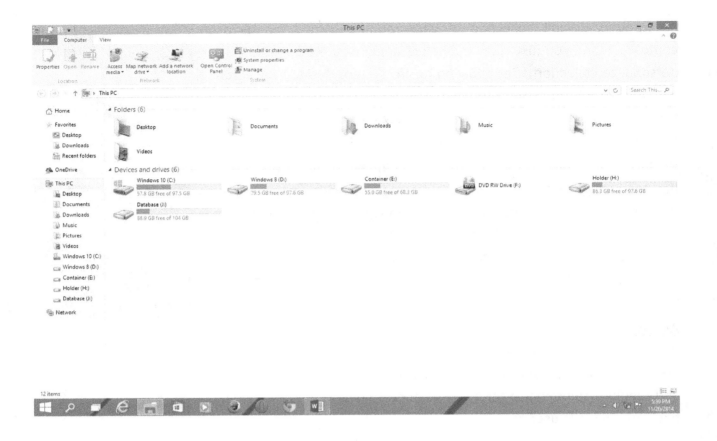

Element of windows 10 this pc

Menu tab – this pc in windows 10 contain by default the common purpose of menu performing this pc operating and these are file, computer, and view remember by default display three common use menu but if you selecting any individual object and content in this pc hard drive partition than according to selecting and use object some additional tab display automatically while you accessing related object in windows 10.

Desktop – desktop is computer important workplace or area where all computer routine task perform even it display you installed application icon, this pc icon, network, recycle, control panel icon, and other installed object, it enable you to quickly move and access windows 10 desktop elements according to need.

Document – document folder in this pc contain by default location of microsoft application software storage content, it can store documents, presentation, spreadsheet, database, text file, html sources, computer program, even other default or manual set location of my documents object in documents, now you can pick your desire electronic document object from document location, it allowing to opening it modify cut, copy, paste, or delete, current documents object according to need, by default it display some common used folder of custom office template, fax object, notes, or scanned documents etc.

Download – download folder is default storage location in this pc where computer network download object store in download folder, by default download folder contain compressed files like, win zip, pkzip, tar files, download electronic document, download music, software programs, downloaded video object store individually in separate folder according to selected folder category in download folder location.

Music – music folder contain default or manually storage music audio files that play with windows 10 music player it inbuilt with windows 10 operating system, it allowing you to playing music application, now you can store your latest hollywood, bollywood, cultural, or traditional folder of song store or save in music folder and listen while you tired or in relax mode for getting some pleasant environment.

Pictures – pictures folder contain installed web camera videos, picture or other camera pictures you can manual store and playing or view them depending on need, picture folder may able to contain your holiday, picnic, festival, marriage, cultural, images even it allowing to some editing tools to customize them depending on need.

Video – video folder stores this pc videos it allowing to store videos file, movie videos, animated video, 3d video even you can store your functional, marriage, picnic, festival video in videos folder, even play with suitable video player software application inbuilt installed in windows 10 microsoft operating system.

Hard drive – hard drive is an essential computer hardware in computer, always windows operating system start computer hard drive partition from drive c letter and so on depending how much partition you created in windows 10 operating system, first hard drive partition drive c contain windows 10 bootable drive it contain operating system or windows installed application software setting in it, than other remaining hard drive partition contain additional windows document, videos, files, folder, picture, multimedia, animated, web resources and any other electronic object, hard disk size may be in gigabyte or terabyte.

Optical drive – optical drive called cd/dvd rom drives that capable to read or write information in shape compact disk or digital video/versatile disk, but now days compact disk or versatile disk became outdated it completely replaced with flash card, pen drive, insert cd or dvd or read or write plastic disk information with installed optical drives, it enable you to installed software, play or installed game, view or play video movie, mp3 songs, play animated clips, read or write electronic document object etc.

Removable drive – removable drive information display in this pc in windows 10, you can easier to plug and play removable media like, pen drive, flash card, memory card, zip disk, electronic chip, floppy drive or many other thing easily to share play read or write with removable devices in windows 10 operating system.

Network detail – network detail display you installed network information joined workgroup/ domain network, work group member and other related detail in windows 10 operating system, you can view or configure windows 10 network related information from network folder in windows 10 operating system.

Windows 10 – windows 10 release by microsoft organization after windows 7 and windows 8 foundation designed based or construct on windows 7, windows 10 include most of similar features configuration settings windows foundation, but new idea or new concept identity of microsoft company for always create new thing and control for microsoft o/s user windows 10 add many new features control and environment company create new.

Windows 10 desktop screen

 Desktop - desktop area or surface on every computer where we found some common control for handling windows operation, like execute any program shortcut menu drag and click desire control and whatever you want to be perform on windows desktop, all installed application shortcut my computer icon, my network place, recycle bin, internet explorer, and other program shortcut which can easily to play and run by every windows user most of short cut similar and common in previous operating system.

This pc – windows my computer icon display and long journey from windows previous release, microsoft company continue add my computer icon on every windows release included windows client and server, my computer icon keep many control like hard disk, hard drive partition, floppy disk, zip disk, cd/dvd writer information, installed web camera, and system info, control panel, favorites, and network information.

Network icon - my network icon display network and sharing, and network control, network control preview list of all connected client, server, share printer, hard drive partition, dvd rom, scanner, or other sharable tools and resources which one ready edit for local permission move and copy data resources and information between any connected ping reply client similar with server also do with clients configure server setting client setting change lan (nic) card setting ip address manage all adapter wired and wireless connection setup new connection connect with network and changes advance setting for resource information sharing.

 Recycle bin – recycle bin icon located below network icon like empty basket, recycle bin play role of dust bin in computer like home or municipal corporation wastage container similar all file data folder text deleted material automatically move in recycle bin basket it provide two types of remove deleted data and resources.

Recycle bin option

Empty recycle bin – this option removes permanently all recycle deleted item permanently from hard drive partition you can't get recover back primarily sad this but if use strong backup program of any company then remove most of type file will recover back in recovery mode its depended which backup program you use.

Restore this item – this option work on single selection by user operator mean you can send back your deleted data that previous location without any loss sometime after remove data an information but next you need it again then restore this item at its original deleted location now use and edit with restore item.

Restore all item – restore all deleted selected item all item move at their original deletes location with single click all restore item use again as simple common data, if you delete any item with shift + delete key its remove data permanently its location and data can't move in recycle bin.

Control panel – icon display at the desktop of each and every flavor of windows operating system, may be windows client or server control hold all windows setting tool and menu, where we can configure customize and enable or disable windows main function and operation, all or most of windows 7 control function will be edit and control with control panel option some are hardware, software, printer, date & time, windows firewall color management and other properties in control panel.

Administrator/user info/active account – icon display at the top left corner of windows 10 desktop screen this icon keep multiple setting related to windows 10 common control operation like contact, desktop, downloads, favorites, links, my documents, my music, my picture, my videos, saved games, searches etc.

Describe briefly them

Contacts - keep business commercial, non-commercial, private relationship contact, in contact list for quick connectivity like name, address, contact, phone, fax, photo, home, business, address, web page, web site address, store birthday, anniversary, notes, about any contact and digital id of related contact phone title fax office pager number etc. May be in a simple contact with add new contact group e-mail edit delete import export new group and contact.

Windows contact window

Windows of contact

John mathew headen

New contact – option enable you to adding everything information required during create new user, friend, commercial or non- commercial contact, you may add user name, e-mail, title, nick name, home, work contact, address, phone, fax, pager, address, detail, family, birthday, anniversary detail, adding a noted about current contact, even view digital contact created new contact in windows 10.

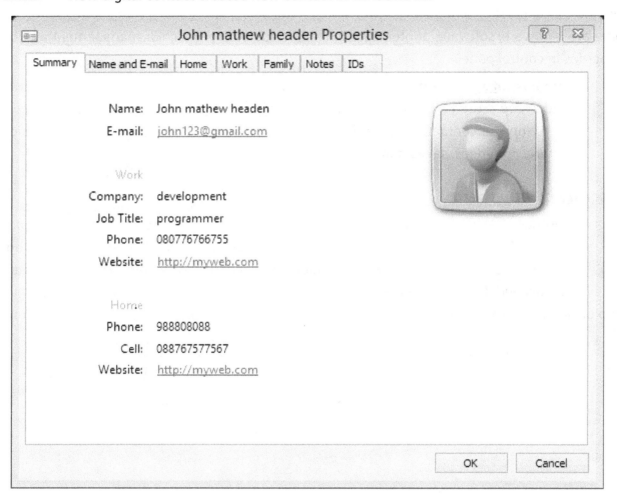

Elements of new contact

Open – open option enable you to open a select contact, new contact group even new folder created item with supported installed windows apps in windows.

Share with – share with option allowing windows user to share selected windows contact, new contact group, include created new folder in contact apps, you configure how these item electronically share among windows user even which user access or not access these item according to need.

E – mail – e-mail option enable windows user to send selected contact at define e-mail address, according to user need.

Edit – edit option allow user to edit or customize input user contact detail even replace old information with new information, click on edit option you see contact previous add information now edit them.

Delete – delete option allow user to delete selected windows new created contact according to user need, so remember these option apply only when you really don't need any created contact in windows.

Print – print option enable user to print a user contact created information in windows, turn on printer and apply print command to print user summery or contact related important contact.

 New contact group – new contact group option enable you to creating new contact of group, once you created a new contact group after that you add existing user created contact one by one as a group in new contact group, even you created new contact group from here, add contact name e-mail address, similar add other contact detail like address, postal, state, country, web site, add notes, phone fax, detail about current contact.

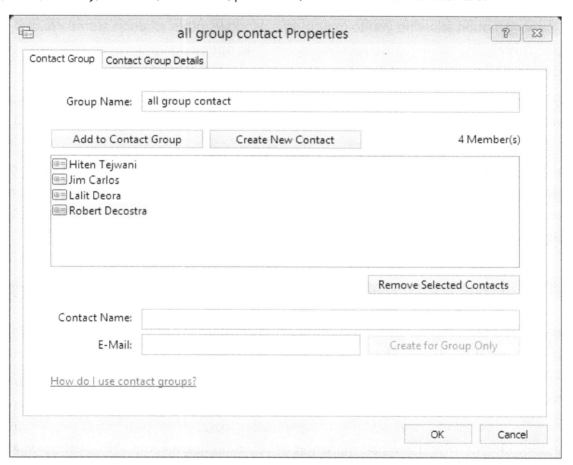

Elements of new contact group

Open – open option enable you to open select contact, new contact group even new folder created item with supported installed windows apps in windows.

Share with – share with option allowing windows user to share selected windows contact, new contact group, include created new folder in contact apps, you configure how these item electronically share among windows user even which user access or not access these item according to need.

E – mail – e-mail option enable windows user to send selected new contact group at define e-mail address according to user need.

Edit – edit option allow user to edit or customize input user new contact group detail even replace old information with new information, click on edit option you see new contact group previous add information now edit them.

Delete – delete option allow user to delete selected windows new created contact group according to user need, so remember these option apply only when you really don't need any created contact in windows.

Print – print option enable user to print a user new contact group created information in windows, turn on printer and apply print command to print user summery or contact related important contact.

Import – import option allowing you to importing a windows other location stored created contact or group of contact import at contact location in windows operating system, you may import contact in csv, ldif, vcard, or microsoft installed outlook express contact format.

Export – export option enable windows user to export a selected windows user based created contact in common format like csv or vcard file format, in exporting you send contact based created contact at other location in windows.

New folder – new folder use as container that contain computer electronic item as a container, every new folder keep/store files, folder, image, graphic, multimedia object, contact, and many more other electronic item according to need, after created new folder you may whole different item in it even you may delete or customize its item according to need.

 Desktop – move in windows desktop icon to getting view desktop installed located program icon with quick execution shortcut view and run desire shortcut whenever need whenever we or computer software maintainer install additional software or program me installed software some shortcut icon in program me folder in start menu some short will place in notification area quick launch area and even windows main desktop of computer.

Downloads – view the list of all download item in active machine computer most of default download software game program me matter documents image and other download if not additional downloader installed in your machine like download accelerator or idm(internet download manager) or you tube downloader also then download item display in default in this folder.

Favorites – view list of favorites item listed in favorites item group like favorites bar microsoft website msn website windows live and other self favorites and bookmarks or linked pages list for quick navigation and reach on bookmarks or favorite links without follow long or manual procedure simply favorites folder keep information of favorite web pages.

Favorites Bar
Microsoft Websites
MSN Websites
Websites for United States
Windows Live

Links – manage different links installed on active machine links related to desktop download and recent file in computer with quick move in above link with easily move and run required item in linked folder etc.

Documents – documents is default container documents image, file, folder, letter, fax e-mail, sheet, budget, presentation, rtf word pad, notepad, microsoft paint, excel, word, power point, file default, storage file, related and other default file automatically when save store in this my documents folder without change location most of programmed and application save associated extension and file move for save and storage in my documents icon folder.

Music – music folder design to store favorite song classical hollywood and new bollywood song store in my music folder and listen play when entertain yourself in free time for relaxation music item copy and paste as group or copy them individual folder separation launch each item by choice.

Picture – view your windows default storage image in format of jpg gif bmp tif etc. Even you can store and copy wallpaper image background of movie rock sports entertainment nature god and other type of wallpaper also store in this folder and view with photo viewer and image editing program.

Videos – my videos are another type of icon folder consist store different type of entertainment movie sports hollywood bollywood movie even camera mobile clip also you can view and play them in free time.

Folder tree – display all windows 10 element drive desktop download documents, picture, music, videos, my computer, local hard drive partition, c drive d drive e drive f drive and so on all created partition installed pen drive floppy disk zip disk web camera links dvd cd rom.

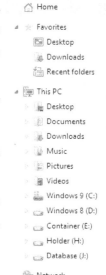

Desktop – display windows desktop item loaded program and other icon view in desktop browsing.

Downloads – view the list of all downloads music song video documents program and other download.

Documents – display my documents folder of default location of windows installed program source by default most program store in my documents folder.

Music – display stored listen music from hard drive location.

Picture – view preview windows default loaded and self-copy download image in this folder.

Videos – view play video song video movie in video folder.

Computer – view list of windows hard drive partition floppy drive zip disk web camera and other my computer elements.

Network – display list of shareable server list of local area network client, all network client view at only one place name my computer, open client share drive copy paste delete data and information in shareable network.

Windows 10 desktop right click item/menu

View – display windows 10 desktop item in different provided view on desktop generally view provide different choice of windows icon view order.

Large icon – display windows 10 icon in large or maximum order size, while you turn these option view as large icon view, it make maximum enlarge size of windows desktop placed or created icon regularly accessed or use by windows user, remember you use large icon view only when you have a maximum size of computer lcd/led screen resolution present or attach with your personal or commercial computer, large icon increase immediate size or pixel resolution of computer used default icon accessed by windows user in windows.

Medium icon – display windows 10 desktop icon in medium view it is default system windows 10 o/s define view we see most of windows 10 icon in medium icon view, medium icon view keep many more application shortcut placed at windows desktop screen, you may use medium icon view only when you need to display many more windows based created icon on computer desktop scree, how it work, right click on computer desktop now select view option at top – in sub menu select medium icon view display for windows 10 operating system.

Small icon – change view of medium icon view to small icon view according to need if one or more icon reside on your desktop then set them in small icon view for displaying all icon at same time in desktop, remember user always access a small view icon when many more apps install in windows operating system, small icon view show in large screen of computer desktop for arranging or previewing number of computer desktop icon at same place in windows 10 operating system.

Auto arrange icon – auto arrange all desktop icon in in sequence not ascending or descending order it arrange desktop in random icon view, when you see gape between computer icon even individually placed computer apps icon at different places then you apply auto arrange icon view to arrange them stack in windows desktop screen.

Align icon to grid – align all icon in alignment of desktop gridline order, these option allowing windows user to align all windows 10 display desktop elements at align according to its grid display in windows 10.

Show desktop icon – by default system show some popular windows icon my computer administrator network recycle bin with system installed desktop icon if you don't want to be see them on desktop then make checkmark disable in right click view menu all icon placed in desktop will be hide on screen of windows.

Show desktop gadgets – appear and disappear windows 10 gadgets icon on windows screen by default it sometime show or sometime hide in windows 10 installation you can set permanent on windows 10 desktop icon display.

Sort by – sort windows 10 desktop icon windows folder file database in different provide order according to need display preview set icon in by.

Name – set all desktop icon in ascending or descending alphabetical order, these option arrange all desktop item as a name wise at windows 10 desktop screen, by default windows desktop display icon in name view order.

Size – set desktop icon by their hold data size from low size to high size, even these option arrange all windows 10 desktop icon item according to size as a stack order at windows 10 desktop screen.

Item type – set desktop item by item type order similar name time type order, you may arrange all desktop stored item as item wise order at windows 10 desktop screen.

Date modify - display desktop icon by their date modify ordered date simple icon preview last modify date order, it mean today date folder or item display at top or first of computer screen in windows.

Refresh - refresh desktop icon after long work process to reactivate desktop performance it restarts and refresh active running windows service reduce hang and halt time with better performance it plays role like additional fuel in machine performance.

Paste - paste copy item on desktop or other hard disk folder location it just places copy content at new location which decided by us or tell to machine.

Paste shortcut – paste short cut in windows desktop and other location where you set move them with paste command.

New – new right click option give choice you to create direct application document shortcut at desire location, create application link of microsoft word, microsoft power point, microsoft access, folder, shortcut, zipped document bitmap, briefcase shortcut.

New sub item

Folder – create new folder with unique desire name generally folder like container which hold different thing like documents video audio file itself folder and other data base which can group together like sub item single folder store program me game software or other important material.

Shortcut – create new short cut of any program me icon and install application browse the location of shortcut then click next type the name of shortcut and click finish button for final place shortcut on desktop.

Microsoft access database – create new shortcut link to quick open microsoft access database windows for create new database form query table label or report with macro create double click on desktop icon.

Bitmap image – create new for bitmap image to quick open microsoft paint image graphic application for creating new image drawings or sketch according to user need in windows operating system.

Contacts – create new contact group contact shortcut with all detail name address home business e-mail fax postal zip code e-mail web site etc.

Microsoft word documents – manage microsoft word links to quick edit microsoft word document fax e-mail brochure table smart art graphic etc.

Journal documents – create a journal documents short cut on desktop windows create edit customize active journal.

Microsoft power point presentation – create microsoft power point links quick edit and manage power point presentation on desktop define with shortcut with project plan overview etc.

Microsoft publisher documents – create microsoft publisher shortcut with design edit website brochure pamphlet menu envelope greeting card etc.

Text documents – simple place short cut of notepad text documents with small text file editing less than 64 kb limitation without high formatting.

Microsoft excel worksheet – put shortcut of microsoft excel worksheet work book empty now write data and information within active microsoft worksheet create new sheet agenda budget plan sales purchase transaction report in row column.

 Compressed (zipped) folder – create new compress zip folder with name now put drag or copy zip and non-zip item and folder for compression or without compression some file and folder store in low space and size with folder compression many utilities are available for compression like win zip, pkzip, gzip zip etc.

Screen resolution – change windows 10 screen resolution according to your graphic driver or motherboard vga graphic chipset best resolution 1024 * 768 if you use 14" inch or more lcd led then you set best meet resolution form 800 * 600, 1200* 600 1280 * 720 1200 * 800 or more depend on lcd scale and resolution.

Screen resolution windows

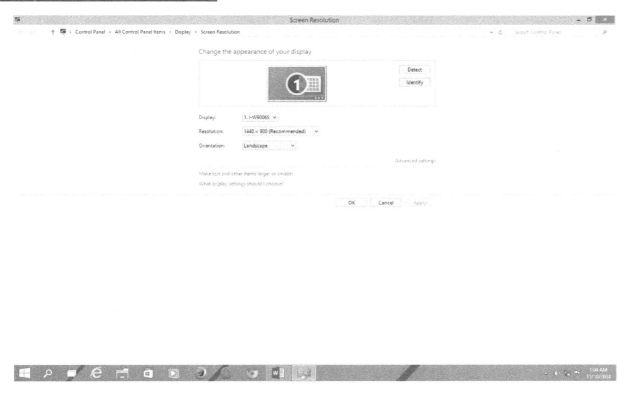

Gadgets – we already explain windows 10 gadgets a collection of basic windows common usable tools which decorate windows 10 desktop even display time slide show weather puzzle clock and calendar etc.

Personalize windows

Customize windows desktop appearance include desktop icon, mouse pointer, account picture, apply new theme in background of your windows 10 desktop environment, theme is collection of style font background style and color pattern that change overall look of your desktop presentation, click on any desire theme from theme gallery and apply it in extra change desktop background, windows color option gives you choice of different color for your windows 10 background select any color adjust color from color mixer change windows sound for different windows event click and change sound test sound browse new sound for current event apply screensaver background of your windows desktop while you are not working in windows, apply desire screen saver from drop down combo box choice click on setting change customize screensaver elements see also display setting, taskbar and start menu, ease of access center setting.

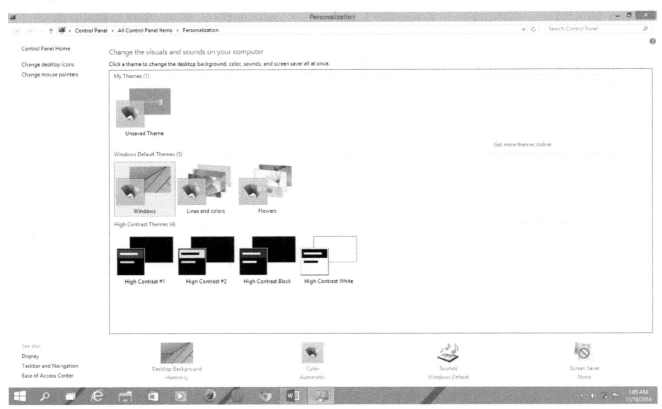

Desktop icon settings

<u>Change desktop icon</u> – change desktop icon setting enable user to change desktop icon in windows installed 10 operating system, when fresh copy of windows 10 installation of operating system, then window 10 default desktop only recycle bin icon display other remaining icon display manually at windows desktop, click on change desktop icon in windows 10 personalization, you can display icon name is computer, control panel, network, user's files icon, show from change desktop icon menu, change icon option allow you to change default icon view of your desktop with change icon command, or restore default command button setting restore of change icon default icon in original state mode.

Desktop icon elements

Computer – computer check box elements responsible to show my computer icon replace my computer icon with new name this pc in windows 10 operating system, by default it uncheck while you fresh install copy of windows 10 operating system you need to manually turn on it on click check box option in windows 10 operating system.

User's files – user's files option enable you to show user' contain folder icon placed at windows desktop location, you see these user's folder with first user account creation process in windows operating system during installed window operating system.

Network – show network icon at windows 10 desktop location, by default it invisible while firstly windows 10 operating system installed by user, you manually turn on it on click check mark on same as you make these check mark turn off, if you don't want to show network icon at windows desktop screen.

Recycle bin – recycle bin folder contain windows deleted removed unnecessary files, folder, image, audio, video, web content and other electronic resources, contain by windows recycle bin by default recycle icon automatically display at windows 10 operating system installation, if you need to make turn off these setting then you made check mark option to turn off in windows.

Control panel – control panel option always added in any windows operating system, windows control panel store windows hardwar, software, firmware setting, you may enable to configure enable disable them according to need, by default control panel icon disable when fresh windows installation, you may make check mark turn on to display control panel, or make check turn off to making disable control panel option.

Change icon – change icon button enable you to change default icon of select windows 10 icon in windows, first of select any one icon of windows now click on change icon option to replace current icon with available new icon choice finally click to change it, you see at your windows desktop selected icon will be change in windows.

Restore default – restore default option remove user made manually changes default icon behavior display at windows desktop screen, while you need to restore windows in default mode then you try to restore these setting on click restore default it discard all manually impact added on current dialog.

Allow themes to change desktop icons – allow themes to change desktop icons option enable you to allowing theses change desktop icon when these changes in windows manually or automatically by system, if you check mark turn off these option then it works otherwise it remain default for use in windows 10.

Change mouse pointers – change your default windows 10 desktop mouse moving pointer setting from mouse properties default windows aero (system scheme) display mouse pointer change with inbuilt mouse pointer scheme then ok new mouse properties will display without any restart process.

Elements of pointer tab

Scheme – scheme drop down combo box enable you to select choice between many windows available mouse pointing operation like select, help select, busy, text select, handwriting, vertical horizontal resize, move, link select, and many other pointing device operation task symbol, you can change them on click drop down scheme available microsoft company provide various category of scheme, even you click each scheme object icon and browse or replace with new one, or discard these changes with use default option.

Enable pointer shadow – enable pointer shadow check box option choice allowing you to display shadow behind mouse pointer while user working mouse or pointing device in any windows based application or software by user, by default these option remain uncheck but you make them turn on or turn off according to need during operation.

Use default – use default option rollback all changes made in using any pointer scheme, it re - back default pointer scheme effect in windows, during user dealing with many windows operating or task.

Browse – browse button allowing freedom to manually customize each pointing device operating symbol from selecting default or replace with give browse choice in windows, set whatever type icon with existing icon in windows 10 operating system.

Display – change reduce or extend size of windows 10 screen size on click display option, select smaller, medium, large resolution of windows text display screen, adjust windows resolution customize windows brightness display setting connect display attach projector device and many settings related windows screen and display.

Windows 10: display default appearance

Taskbar and start menu properties – customize default properties setting of taskbar and start menu setting change taskbar appearance, start menu display enable disable taskbar toolbar in available list.

Elements of task bar tab

Lock the taskbar – lock the taskbar option allowing windows 10 user to lock windows task bar at bottom of windows desktop screen, if check box on it mean task bar turn to lock if check mark is turn off it mean lock task bar turn off mode during use.

Auto hide the taskbar – auto hide the task bar option enable windows 10 user to making invisible or hide during working in windows 10 apps, it appears while you click at position of windows 10 taskbar location, while check mark is on it mean task bar auto hide while check mark is off it mean taskbar auto hide turn off features in windows 10.

Use small taskbar buttons – use small taskbar button option in windows 10 desktop enable windows taskbar contain all item visible in a small taskbar display view, when check mark turn it mean taskbar item display in small view, but when check mark option turn off it mean taskbar button display in large screen view.

Taskbar location on screen – configure or set windows default task bar location by default in all windows operating system windows placed at bottom of screen every windows operating system taskbar, but in taskbar properties you getting choice change to display default taskbar location in windows, you map  placed default taskbar screen location at left, right, top, bottom, by default it placed at bottom now you decide wherever you want to placed new location of your windows 10 taskbar.

Taskbar buttons – taskbar buttons option show open windows apps, software, application, label in different view, you may select between always combine, hide label, combine when taskbar full, or never combine, select one of them for open windows app 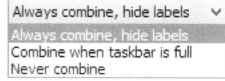 during windows 10 taskbar location, by default it loaded with always combine, hide label order in windows operating system.

Notification area – notification area contain item notify by windows, by default many windows installed application automatically placed shortcut icon at windows notification area in windows, but you decide each and every notification apps behavior from customization of notification area setting in windows, you may click on any icon now change its default behavior from given category of show icon and notification, hide icon and notification, only show notification, now you may select one of them for display notification icon behavior preview order, according to your selection your define notification item display in notification area in windows operating system.

Ease of access center – customize windows accessibility control start magnifier, start on screen keyboard, start narrator, set up high contrast, explore windows elements control from ease of access center control.

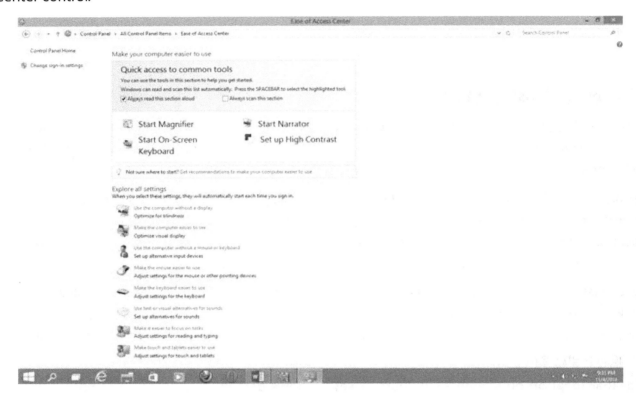

Task bar properties

Task bar right click properties menu

Toolbar - make visible or invisible common toolbar appear in list of toolbar like address links table pc input and drag or select any folder location for new desktop preview at windows 7 taskbar list toolbar hold different type of toolbar these are explain individually below.

Type of toolbar

Address – address bar view in list of taskbar right click address bar direct open any internet url website address without open any particular web browser by default it open type web address with preloaded internet explorer by microsoft web browser type any url then press enter button remember internet connection must exist and on.

Icon of address bar

Links – bar show common microsoft and other guide links for user to quick explore navigate microsoft other features if you make add some links in list of category they will display automatically in list of links but it holds some predefined links by company.

Icon of links bar

Tablet pc input – tablet pc input features add windows tablet pc or tablet supported windows 10 operating system device, direct input keyboard command and function from touch keyboard in windows operating system, now if you have touch device then you may enter all character command from touch input keyboard device it make easier of entering text direct without from touch input device in windows 10.

Tablet pc writing pad window

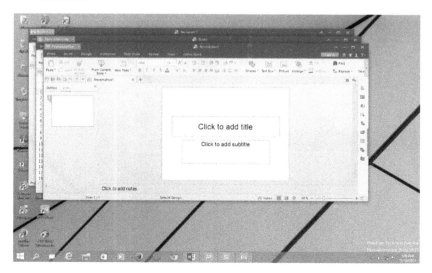

Desktop new toolbar – create new desktop toolbar form windows 10 operating system, select folder location for new desktop toolbar in windows 10 o/s.

Desktop toolbar icon

Cascade windows – cascade windows option preview multiple windows open as cascade view one by one view display of open application window, open two or more application windows, now click on cascade windows option to view available windows in cascade order, click on group of cascade windows which one you need to work.

Display of cascade windows

Show windows staked – show open two or more application software windows in staked order, open windows display same size one above one preview, now select staked window, windows activated and make desire changes in it.

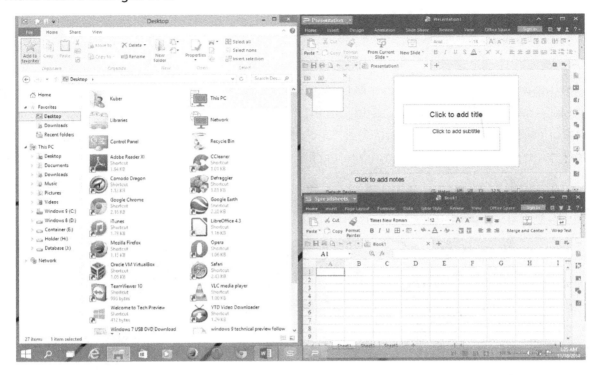

Show windows side by side – show open document, application windows simultaneously at same time vertical view, work in both windows at same in click individual window, both windows show same size but remember single windows display at time.

Display of windows side by side

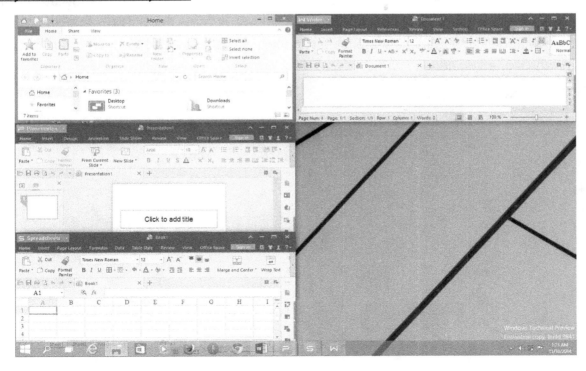

Show the desktop – show desktop option display content placed on desktop, desktop display all necessary icon created on windows desktop, easily open related application on double click application software icon.

Properties of this pc hard drive partition

General tab – general tab appears first tab in windows 10 selected drive properties like type of local disk, file system, total used and free space, total capacity of using hard drive partition size, apply disk cleanup command to remove unnecessary types of files and date store space on selected hard drive partition, or make turn on or turn off available check box features on selected hard drive partition.

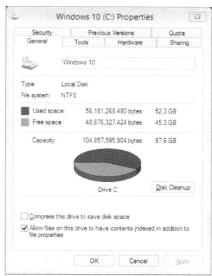

Elements of c drives properties

Type – view detail information about using or selected hard drive partition type information like it may be local disk, network disk, or other storage type category in windows 10 operating system in simple identify disk type here.

Files system – file system title represent type of used file system format on selected hard drive partition like, it belong to old file system called fat32(file allocation table) or modern o/s support new file system type called ntfs(network file system) that more reliable in client server or directory structure then previous one.

Used space – used space title represent consume space from total space available on selected hard drive partition in gigabytes or terabytes format, if you have 50 gigabytes partition or consume 10 gigabytes then it shows 40 gigabytes free space on selected hard drive partition, used hard drive partition space show with blue color in graphical circle view of display hard drive used space.

Free space – free space option represents total free space after remaining consume/used space on local hard drive partition in windows 10 operating system, the free hard drive space represents with pink color in display graphical view of hard drive partition show picture in general tab.

Capacity – capacity title represent total holding/storage capacity of current used hard drive partition, even show how much space allocated to the selected local hdd partition size, show total capacity in number of bytes include gb(gigabytes) or tb(terabytes) format.

Disk cleanup – disk cleanup identify selected disk space contain unnecessary unwanted files that contain hdd drive space the files may be download programs files, temporary internet files, recycle bin item, temporary files, clear temp folder, select given dialog check box turn that files to ready delete and click on cleanup system files to remove them permanently from active system hdd size, it similar to your home or working desk that you always clear or clean before begin new work, these option increase system speed, free system space, or provide greater efficiency on selected hard drive partition you may use these option every day or in week three or more time to get better system performance to improve working experience on working windows 10 os.

Compress this drives to save disk space – compress this drives to save disk space option compress selected hard drive partition to store more data and files on selected hard drive partition size, but remember during disk drive compression it compressed all store windows files folder data information and other electronic content some time it loose data naturally during access mode.

Allow files on this drives to have contents indexed in addition to file properties – allow files on this drives to have contents indexed in addition to file properties option enable you to allowing files for current drives contents indexed in addition to file properties in windows 10 operating system.

Tools tab – tools tab contain some important tools for checking maintain and play role to continue performance of current used system hard drive partition, you may able to checking selected hdd partition size store files and folder error checking, and optimize and defragment drive, option arrange hdd partition size files and folder arrange in a particular sequence these process increase system speed increase hard drive life time and fast open or accessed electronic content files and data on working system drives according to need in windows 10 operating system.

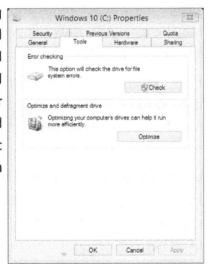

Elements of tools tab/error checking

Check – check option analyze selected hdd partition size store files and electronic store data for checking system errors and related issue, when you access these option in windows you wait till these dialog starting and manager process related finding error and debug in system files or data structure, it play important role to manage system

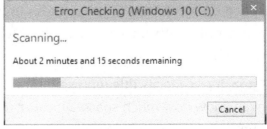

files system, in windows 10 while many user access system data from their own client server system it made reliable file system during working in windows.

Optimize and defragment drives

Optimize – optimize tools windows based hard drive performance improve tools, that arrange all computer bits remove free space arrange data and information as sequence order, it optimize or defragment your local hard drive one by one selected by you every time you using optimize features of windows, it increase your system speed, data accessing speed, retrieval process of computer data and information, even analysis system partition drive produce system health report include available disk space, free space even damage area of disk on local hard drive.

Hardware tab – hardware tab displays hardware information about using optical media device hardware information like all disk drives view name of installed storage and optical device name, device properties, device manufacture detail, location of used device, include device current status in windows 10 operating system, and get other related information to the using properties of current device in windows operating system.

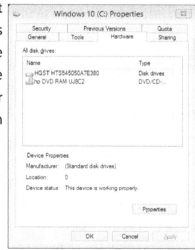

Elements of hardware tab

All disk drives – all device option enable you to show information about installed windows secondary storage device include used optical device information in windows 10 operating system.

Device properties

Manufactures – view detail about installed used hardware device include optical device information, manufacture is device manufacture who design working device in windows operating system.

Location – view location of current using hardware device properties of hdd or optical device used in current operating system.

Device status – check current using device status information like mode of using current device is enable or disable in windows operating system.

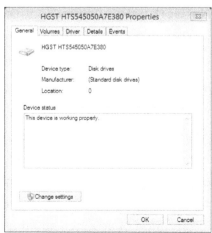

Properties – properties windows display detail properties of selected optical device detail, view secondary device type, manufacturer, location, device status, and change settings, view device volume information, installed secondary device information, device driver details, or view all generated events related information in advance properties of secondary device.

General tab – general tab display you detail information like device name, device type, device manufacture, location, device status, change settings, and other general information view in general tab according to need.

Volumes tab – view using hdd device disk information like disk volumes, status, partition style, capacity, unallocated space, reserved space, volume capacity and other volumes information of selected hdd partition in windows 10 operating system.

Driver tab – driver tab displays driver name of hdd selected partition, driver detail like, driver provider, driver date, driver version, update driver, rollback install driver, disable and finally uninstall current driver of secondary storage device partition in this pc windows.

Details tab – view selected secondary hdd device partition in formation like device property, include disk drive usage value in windows 10 operating system.

Events tab – event tab contain all event generated or created by selected hard drive partition in windows 10 operating system, view listed events dates, time, description, event information and view all events created on selected hdd partition in windows.

Sharing tab – sharing tab display information about using current hdd partition size sharing detail like shared drive name, advance sharing option, password protection during sharing or communicating with shared component in windows 10 operating system, sharing option helping windows group network user to exchange files, folder, data, and, information, easier to access between connected multiple windows operating system user, you may share hardware component and other windows resources in sharing tab so you configure sharing system and its control how to use and allocate among multiple windows user.

Elements of sharing tab

Network files and folder sharing – view information about sharing network files and folder sharing related settings and query in sharing tab according to need, even configure another setting according to need.

Network path – network path enable you to showing a shared network path detail or shared device information related information in windows.

Share button – shared button show shared detail of selected hdd partition information, after you making to click on shared device to turn on it mean your device ready to shared component and resources.

Advance sharing – advance sharing option enable you to select share this folder, share hdd partition share name, add share name, and remove share name, configure limit the number of simultaneous user to, comments, configure permission of shared device properties, and edit caching information of advance sharing control in windows operating system.

Elements of sharing advance tab

Settings

Share name – share name title represent you the share name of current hard drive information like using current hdd share detail etc.

Add – add option enable you to adding shared name in current in windows 10 operating system.

Remove – remove option enable you to remove share device name in windows 10 operating system.

Limit the number of simultaneous users to – configure limit the number of simultaneous users to share name information in windows 10 operating system.

Comment – view comments information about usage shared device hdd information in windows operating system, add own comments of selected shared hdd component in windows.

Permission button – permission tab displays information about to display permission or group or user name, add user name, remove user, view list of permission for everyone, view everyone individual permission and other detail in share permission tab.

Elements of permission button

Group or user name – group or user name option display you share permission provided to the number of user and client created in windows operating system, view each user individual permission and control for everyone that are created on local machine in windows 10 operating system.

Add – add name of existing user in windows operating system, similar adding number of user individual permission, type name of each user configure object type, object location, or check name of existing user that created in windows 10 o/s.

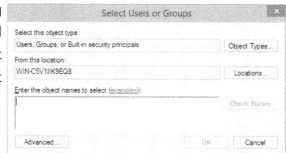

Remove – remove option enable you to removing number of user or group that one already provided to exclusive permission in windows 10 os.

Permission for everyone

Full control – full control option allowing to full control on windows hard drive usage, computer resources, network control, admin control, system backup and restore usage allowed by full control access user list in windows 10 operating system.

Change – change control allowing selected windows user to allowing to changes in windows 10 operating system related installed or allocated resources in windows operating system.

Read – providing everyone user of windows 10 created user for reading shared windows hdd partition information in windows 10 operating system.

Caching button – caching button option enable windows 10 users to which files and programs available offline when network are disconnect, it provide three different radio button choice are only the files and program that users specify are available offline, no files or program from the shared folders are available offline, all files programs that users open from the shared folders are automatically available offline in windows, select one of radio button according to your need in windows operating system.

Password protection – password protection option enable you to access password while you accessing system resources password for getting system shared folders, and information in windows.

Security tab – security tab display security information of users group of users, view list of user detail, change each user security permission, modify allow or deny permission for authenticated users, even customize advance user security related settings and configuration in windows operating system.

Elements of security tab

Object name c – view the object name c option enable you to detail name of current security name c:\ drives in windows 10 operating system.

Group or user names – group or user names option display you information about number of created user detail name all system default and manually created user account listed in this category you see authenticated users, system, administrator, users, detail in windows operating system.

Edit button – edit button option enable you to configure edit security of each created user in windows operating system, by default you get authenticated users, system, administrator, user, select anyone of given list or group or user names, add user for security, remove user security, change allow or deny user security related permission, according to need in windows 10 operating system, click on individual item to modify windows user permission related default setting if you allow some permission user to then click to allow or if you want to refuse or deny user control and permission in windows then click to deny user control option in windows 10 o/s.

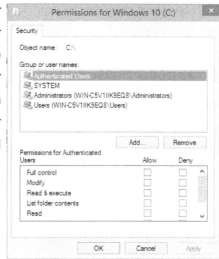

Permission for authenticated users – configure permission for windows based user account you may decide which user get which type of permission and control accessed by multiple windows user in windows 10 operating system.

Permission allow – permission allow option providing windows created selected user to allow resources or full control on active machine according to user need.

Permission deny – permission deny option enable you to deny permission of selected user account accessing resources during communication windows hard drive related control and information.

Full control – full control option provide user to full control for managing control, getting all windows resources, change hardware software setting, modify admin control, network services, and other control privileges allowed in full control mode.

Modify – modify option enable you to providing windows created selected user to providing control of changing in windows system files folder and related electronic document control in windows 10 operating system.

Read & execute – these option allow windows selected user to providing control of read and execute of windows related apps and information in windows 10 operating system.

List folder contain – configure or customize user permission related to access list of folder contain in windows 10 operating system.

Read – allow or deny windows created user account read permission depending on your check box selection category you may having permission to read or not information related to configure user account privileges.

Write – configure allow or deny write permission control of related user account information in windows 10 operating system, depending your selection user control apply in current mode.

Special permission – special type of permission option enable you to providing special permission by windows special user called authenticated users in windows 10 operating system, remember the special permission only provided to the special user of windows and its remain disable for all other user in this category, so you don't have option to allow or deny these category service to the other user account.

Advanced button

Permission tab – permission tab display when user click on security tab advance button to getting advance permission related detail and information in windows 10 operating system, in this dialog you will see name of permitted drive name, detail of owner permitted, view number of permission getting user, system, administrator user information, even change or view existing user system default permission according to need, click on anyone or a particular user account to customize their default permission settings whenever you need include define security related concept and issue related to user and particular hardware device.

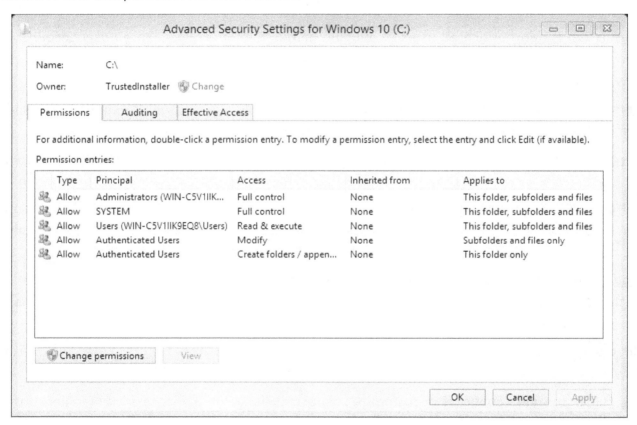

Elements of permission tab

Name – name title represents of configure security drive detail, you may see here which drive go to configure or customize related to security settings in windows 10 operating system.

Owner – getting owner security related information and detail include changing current owner from list of existing owner provider list in windows advance security configuration.

Permission entries – view detail information about permission entries user, type, define principal, access, inherited from, applies to, entries related to current user account in windows 10 operating system.

Add – add permission for particular user permission account in windows 10 operating system, configure principal, type, applies to, basic permission, customize other add user related information and detail in add option.

Remove – remove option enable you to removing permission entries of define user list in windows 10 operating system.

View – view permission entries related to permission entries user, you see how permission provided to the user or define in windows 10 user related settings and information.

Edit – edit button allowing you to customize editing detail of permission user entries in advance security user information.

Edit windows – edit windows display complete information about permission user account principal, type of allow mode, applied to effect on, customize basic permission like full control, modify, read & execute, list folder contents, read and write, by default basic permission check box uncheck but you according to need make them turn on whenever you need on click edit windows, whenever you want to clear all define basic permission on define windows user and client in windows 10 operating system.

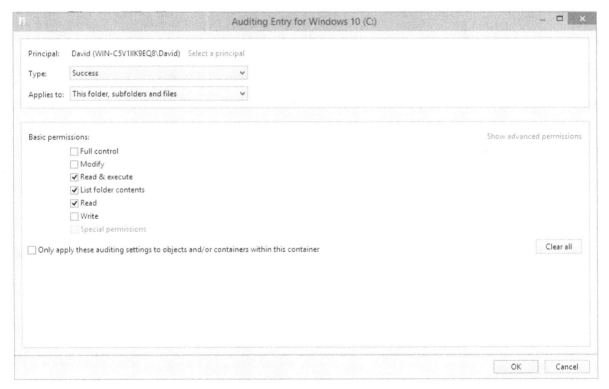

Elements of permission entry

Principal – view the define principal define for current or group of user permission entries in windows 10 operating system.

Type – type option allows you to configure user account security permission entries between allow or deny selection in windows 10 operating system.

Applies to – applies to option provides choice for users to apply setting on which item given choice in applies to option in windows.

Basic permission

Full control – full control option enable check box allowing windows 10 user to provide full control or not to the working user permission entries in window operating system.

Modify – modify checkbox allowing you to provide permission user to modify or not modify to the user account related configuration in windows.

Read & execute – read & execute check box permission entries option allow you to providing selected user to permission related to read & execute related permission or not.

List folder contents – providing or not list folder contents permission on selected user account in advance security category.

Read – decide configure user detail related read permission or not in windows 10 operating system.

Write – similar to read check box you decide permission configure user to permit write permission or not selected user in windows.

Special permission – special permission by default disable during editing mode, but some special permission provided by default to the existing user list in windows 10 operating system.

Share tab – configure sharing tab related setting for windows advance security setting in windows 10 operating system, view name of shared drive information, owner detail, detail about permission entries, add permission, remove existing user permission, edit or view provided permission related configuration in windows 10 operating system.

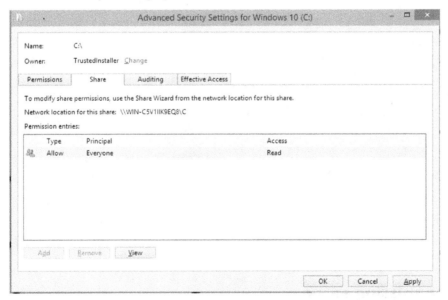

Auditing tab – auditing tab allows windows user to making desire auditing related changes for windows created user account, view default preview auditing entries, type of auditing, principal, access, inherited from, and applies to, add and select auditing user principal settings, provide user basic permission and control, along view and remove added auditing tab permission and entries.

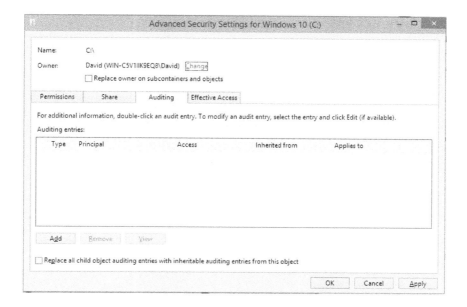

Elements of auditing tab

Add – add security auditing entries and control for adding new audit entries follow properly instruction of add new principal user entries settings.

Remove – remove option allow you to remove selected auditing entries on working auditing user, be carefully even don't delete some important user profiles auditing entries.

View – view auditing tab related entries and settings, know proper information about auditing profiles entries in detail view through this options.

Effective tab – effective tab display user provide special effective permission for existing windows user account, group of user account or individual user account, include configure effective access privileges user account settings along add group of user or user from select user option while click on select user type name of the existing user in active dialog after adding view user full effective access permission with privileges.

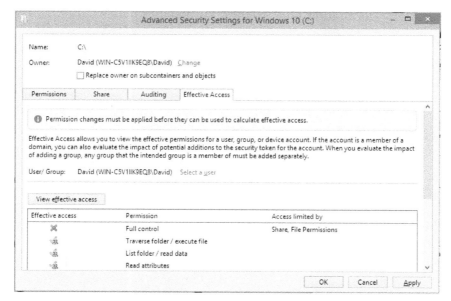

Elements of effective access

Select user – select user link option allows user to select user from existing group of user account type properly name of windows existing user and view their effective access and privileges on system security and other control.

View effective access – view effective access option describe or listed user account access full control or privileges on active computer system, check one by one all right provided of effective user through view effective access option.

Previous version tab – previous tab option enable you to restoring windows previous version of windows operating system, these options allowing to restore previous copy of installed windows operating system.

Quota tab – quota option enable to configure windows created user account hdd drive access permitted limit in windows 10 operating system, configure default behavior of disk quota status, deny quota limit after exceed quota condition, configure disk space limit, set or adjust quota warning level, when quote limits exceeds, view or modify list of quota entries in windows operating system.

Show quota settings – show quota settings option enable you to showing quota related setting, show quota configure user account quota status, enable disable quota management, deny disk space to users exceeding limit, configure do not limit disk usage, limit disk space, or other settings related in windows 10 operating system.

Elements of quota settings for windows

Status – show status of usage disk quotas are enable or disable in selected windows 10 hdd partition in windows.

Enable quota limit – enable quota limit check box option enable you to make check box turn on to turn off according to need in windows 10 operating system.

Deny disk space to users exceeding quota limit – deny disk space to users exceeding quota limit option enable you to make check box on or check turn off for controlling deny disk space during exceeding quota limits in windows 10 operating system.

Do not limit disk usage – do not limit disk usage option button enable you to don't allow to allocate disk quota limit for configuration in windows 10 operating system.

Limit disk space to – limit disk space to option enable you to configure how much limit for accessing hard drive partition size by each and every windows 10 created user account in windows, if you enable these option then you configure limit of disk quota usage by each user, you may set limit in kb, mb, gb, tb, pb, eb, select one of disk space usage size option end make them enable in windows 10 operating system.

Set warning levels to – set warning levels option enable you to setting a warning levels for user when quota limits are exceeding in windows 10 operating system, remember you can configure or set different quota limit warnings for individual user according.

Log events when a user exceeds their quota limit – log events when user exceeds their quota limit option enable you to report log events when user exceeds their quota limits in windows 10 operating system, by default these option remain uncheck in windows 10 you may need to configure these option to turn on with check on according to need.

Log events when a user exceeds their warning level – log events when user exceeds their warning level option enable you to generate log events report when user exceeds their warning level in windows 10 operating system, by default these option uncheck you may enable to make these option check on according to need.

Properties of dvd rw drive

General tab – general tab display general information about general used dvd rd drive information like type cd drive, file system, used space, free space, capacity, drive information hold by used optical media like compact disk, digital video disk, or other optical media that store and retrieve computer based information in windows 10 operating system.

Elements of general tab

Type – type title represent usage of optical media device information like use device is cd, dvd, or other optical media device category.

File system – file system title represent name of the current use optical device files system describe in current windows operating system.

Used space – used space option enable you to show detail about of used space of current using optical device, first of all view total space then check used with free space on current optical storage media.

Free space – free space title represents a free space of using optical media using in current optical storage media in windows 10 operating system.

Capacity – capacity option enable you to option enable you to show exact capacity of used optical media in windows operating system.

Drive name – show name of using optical media device in windows operating system.

Hardware tab – hardware tab displays information about using current optical storage media in windows 10 operating system, show all drives information, device properties, optical device using location include attach optical device status, even locate advance properties of using optical device.

Elements of hardware tab

All disk drives – view information about listed category optical and secondary storage media device like storage and optical media.

Device properties

Manufactures – view device manufacture detail of current using optical device media in windows operating system.

Location – view current use optical device location in active windows operating system.

Device status – view device status of current using optical storage in windows 10 operating system.

Properties – know exact working information about optical storage in windows operating system.

Sharing tab – sharing tab allowing you to configure sharing properties of using optical media device, if you share current optical device then somebody other client or user connect in your network also able to share optical media advantage on client machine, configure advance sharing option allow you to set right for individual client according to provided privileges in working operating system, configure individual client password protection when sharing current device.

Elements sharing tab

Network file and folder sharing – network files and folder sharing title represent you information about network file and folder sharing in windows 10 operating system.

Share – share button indicate sharing behavior of current use optical device in windows 10 operating system.

Advance sharing – configure advance sharing related to using optical device user in windows operating system.

Password protection – password protection option enable every windows 10 user to getting resources for accessing optical device in windows.

Customize tab – customize tab allowing you to customize default open behavior what kind of folder optimize folder you to get when start.

Elements customize tab

Optimize this folder for – select optimize drives for this folder option allow user to optimize drop down combo choice name documents, pictures, music, and videos, select one of them manually for optimize with defrag utilities.

Also apply this template to all subfolder – also apply this template to all subfolder option enable this check box for applying optimizing effect for this templates include subfolder according to need.

Folder pictures

Choose files button – select and browse option enable user to choose files for button in optical drives.

Restore default – restore default option discard all user made manually changes in working option.

Recording tab – recording tab option allows user to configure optical device recording behavior, view default multimedia disk behavior, include configure disc burning.

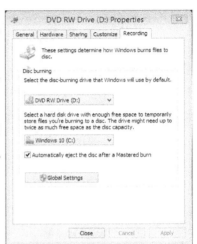

Elements of recording tab

Disc burning – select optimize drives for this folder option allow user to optimize drop down combo choice name documents, pictures, music, and videos, select one of them manually for optimize with defrag utilities.

Automatically eject the disc after a mastered burn – this option automatically sends eject after disk master burn, by default these features almost include with all windows operating system and when disk complete burn with desire data it throughout burn disk.

Global settings – configure global settings of optical recording devices, and other available check box settings.

Windows 10 every apps menu .....

App command – view app command of selected open active windows 10 apps, this command appear at the top of open windows apps, when user click on app command you see the related open active all app command listed and appear at below of working application.

Search – search command providing searching tool for searching windows 10 related item every in windows like it search find information at online or office sources, after finding search item just click to open it with supported apps.

Share – share apps allow you to sharing selected apps object and it content with share apps like microsoft outlook and other popular online share service or e - mail client.

Play – play option playing any kind of multimedia object with its supportive apps through playing option.

Print – print option allow user to printing selected apps content and information with supported apps in windows 10 operating system.

Project – display selected graphic multimedia object and other viewable content, but remember while you sending or display any output of media with attach projector device.

Settings – configure advance settings of working windows 10 apps these settings name are option, about, account, send feedback, term of use, and privacy statement now selected any sub setting of master setting for modification.

Full screen – full screen option previewing a full screen running windows 10 apps, in full screen mode it removes apps menu bar, toolbar, and other windows controls.

Windows 10 start menu properties

Elements of windows start menu

Open – open option enable you to open selected windows app, application, software and other selected program.

Run as administrator – run as administrator option enable you to running selected windows apps and program with administrative privileges.

Uninstall – uninstall option allowing windows user to uninstall/ remove selected windows app, program, and software category according to need in windows 10 start menu.

Pin to start – pin to start option pin selected windows 10 start menu selected app, program, software and control for showing in new windows 10 start menu include windows 10 start screen.

Pin to taskbar – pin to taskbar option enable you to pin to selected apps, windows program, software, application, and other windows control placed on windows taskbar location.

Remove from this list – remove from this list option enable you to removing selected apps, windows program, files and folder in start menu category.

Windows 10 start menu app properties

Unpin from start – unpin from start option allowing you to remove or unpin selected windows 10 apps from newt start menu category according to need.

Pin to taskbar – pin to taskbar option enable you to pin selected windows 10 apps at windows taskbar location.

Uninstall – uninstall option enable you to uninstalling windows 10 installed default application in windows operating system, be sure before uninstalling any windows 10 default apps in windows os.

Resize – resize option allow you to resize the default apps size in windows 10 operating system, resize default apps size in small, medium, wide, large, select one of apps size that one you need to be display in windows start menu.

Recycle bin – recycle bin option by default located at windows 10 desktop, you see microsoft continuously add recycle at windows desktop as important tools for storing windows electronic data and files, from any location item removal from windows hard drive, storage, software, application, deleted item automatically placed in recycle bin.

Recycle bin window

Recycle bin tools

Empty recycle bin – empty recycle bin option allowing you to remove or delete permanently recycle bin item in windows recycle bin folder located at windows 10 operating system desktop, remember while you empty recycle bin item it make free up disk space that used for storing another information data and information on computer hard drive location according to need.

Recycle bin properties – recycle bin properties option enable you to configure default properties of recycle bin contain files and folder, in these dialog you getting multiple option or settings to configure maximum size of contain deleted item list in windows, even modify both settings between two radio button choice, finally customize delete confirmation dialog when files and any electronic data and information removed for computer hard drive location, click on a particular option to modify according to need in windows 10.

Elements of recycle bin properties

Settings for selected location

Custom size – custom size option facilitate windows 10 user to manually customize disk space or size for containing deleted item files and data at computer recycle bin hard drive location, by default installed windows operating system automatically contain space reserve for containing deleted files and folder form various computer storage location in windows 10, remember you able to also customize increase or decrease maximum number of disk storage for recycle bing item in recycle bin properties according to need.

Maximum size (mb) – maximum size option enable you to configure or customize size of deleted item contain in recycle bin, remember during installation or configuration of windows by default windows recycle bin contain the size of storage deleted files and folder in windows, but if you necessary then you customize the size of default storage of deleted item in windows recycle bin.

Don't move files to the recycle bin, remove files immediately when deleted – don't move files to the recycle bin, remove files immediately when deleted option enable you to configure don't move deleted/remove files into recycle bin when user delete in windows 10 operating system, remember if you configure these second option then you don't need to have space on local hard drive partition for storing or containing deleted files and folder in windows recycle bin according to need.

Display delete confirmation dialog – display delete confirmation dialog check box option enable you to displaying confirmation dialog when deleted ore removing any electronic computer based information in windows recycle bin.

Restore all items – restore all items option restoring all recycle bin contain deleted files and folder move or restore them their actual deleted storage location in windows 10 operating system, even these option suddenly help full for user while immediately or by mistake deleted files and folder recovered through restore all item, even you manually restore particular deleted item from windows recycle bin location, or a one click restoring deleted item with restore all items according to need in windows 10.

Restore the selected items – restore the selected option specially working on those item that are you manually selected for restoring, pick manually desire one item from windows recycle bin windows in list of many more deleted item, after picking deleted item click on restore the selected option in windows recycle bin windows and wait, these option moves deleted files and folder to their actual storage location in windows operating system.

How starts command prompt

start – all programs – accessories - command prompt.

start – run -type – cmd - press enter.

Command prompt – microsoft disk operating system designed by microsoft company since 1983, microsoft dos is first microsoft operating system that launch by successfully run and tested on computer, microsoft dos work on cui (character user interface) base for everything we apply list of command, microsoft dos command trigger that meet certain condition and apply command mode, dos consist various category of command internal and external in past days most of computer program work on cui based company make program that support microsoft dos environment.

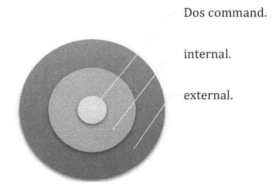

Dos command.

internal.

external.

Command prompt windows

Windows of command prompt

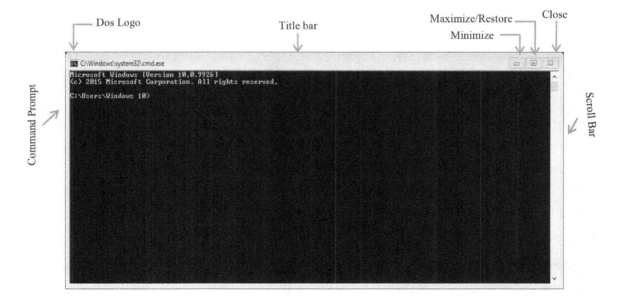

Internal command – all command supply from command.com file, internal command pre-stored in command, dos directory must remember all internal command apply without any external interface.

    Ex: - dir, copy, md, edit etc.

External command – all command apply in microsoft dos with any external medium like cd dvd or floppy called external command external command use to operate microsoft dos externally.

    Ex - format, disk copy, fdisk, disk comp etc.

Important microsoft dos file

- ⮑ Command.com.
- ⮑ I/o.sys.
- ⮑ Ms dos.sys.

Command .com – command.com microsoft dos file most use to support microsoft dos internal command in microsoft dos, it keeps all internal command and execute them according to trigger or action.

I/o.sys – input and output system file io.sys file work on all microsoft dos internal and external command or input output file processing generally microsoft dos process on many different file.

Ms dos.sys – microsoft disk operating system, file it keeps all microsoft dos system .dll exe and other system related file.

C prompt

    C:\> called c prompt in microsoft dos all command supply on c prompt.

Different c prompt

    C:\>

    C: - it represents current active microsoft root c drive.

    : - it separate root drive.

    /: backslash symbol.

    >: - grater then symbol.

Microsoft dos internal command

Dir – this command displays all active directory in microsoft dos windows operating system with show information about directory file name, date time, bytes, extension, and other detail.

    Syntax – c:\>dir

Dir/p – this command display directory and file in microsoft dos with page wise option, it displays remaining list of directory and file with press any key continue option.

    Syntax – c:\>dir/p

Dir/w – display all microsoft dos file and directory in wide horizontal order with specific column see all directory and file at same place, if many more of file then it will display press any key to continue order.

    Syntax – c:\>dir/w

Cls – command clear all microsoft dos previous run command output and clear screen for new command supply, it apply when need screen empty.

    Syntax – c:\>cls

Exit – exit command exit or quit microsoft dos operating system or terminate application software window.

    Syntax – c:\>exit

Date – date command shows active date of according current month day, month and year format, it represent date in us format mm/dd/yy but in india we use dd/mm/yy format for date preview.

    Syntax – c:\>date

Time – time command display active time according to bios setting, it display time that display by your mother board timer 3 volt battery time format in shape hh: mm: ss. S hour minute second and millisecond format.

    Syntax – c:\>time

Chkdsk – this command display status or health of your current hard disk drive, check individual partition of hard disk it shows all detail of partition table with used space free space file allocation table with bed sector information etc.

    Syntax – c:\>chkdsk

Scandisk – it similar to chkdsk but remembers, it works on window 98 o/s, it works similar to chkdsk but run in windows 98 operating system that became completely outdated now days.

    Syntax – c:\>scandisk

Tree – that command display hierarchical tree view of directory created file structure in tree structure/ manner order with directory structure in dos screen window.

    Syntax – c:\>tree

Pipe – pipe command combine and join two different commands in single command generally it used when apply two command action at a same time.

    Syntax – c:\>tree|more

    Syntax – c:\>dir|more

System info – it constructs the original information of each and every related to your computer like processor, ram, workgroup, net adapter, bios, operating system install date and other detail.

    Syntax – c:\>systeminfo

Vol – vol command show volume able information of active hard disk hard drive partition with volume label detail.

Syntax – c:\>vol

Label – label command display and change of exist hard drive disk partition label with new label name.

Syntax – c:\>label

Calc – show windows calculator for numerical calculation with additional effect normal and standard effect calculate ordinary and binary mathematical calculation.

Syntax – c:\>calc

Format – format command used when we need to format hard disk or hard drive partition, floppy zip disk, memory, pen drive partition, to clear track bed sector or cluster of disk and get again complete space for new storage.

Note – take backup your data or never apply on root drive otherwise you will loss stored data.

Syntax – c:\>format a:

Disk comp – disk comp command compare two floppy disk data programmed and file for comparison, remember two floppy drive must exist in computer while using and apply these command in microsoft dos.

Syntax – c:\>diskcomp a: b:

Disk copy – disk copy command copy data of floppy drive into empty floppy drive b, it simply work on copy and paste pattern to complete data of disk drive.

Syntax – c:\>diskcopy a: b:

Mem – mem command display amount of installed in current pc, it shows memory detail related to the operating system installed ram information.

Syntax – c:\>mem

Control – control command open active control of windows in window operating system, it simply open window control panel to configure windows different setting like add hardware or remove hardware and other setting, everybody knows about windows control panel its collection of windows settings includes command center.

Syntax – c:\>control

Attrib – attrib command work on different file properties, like it change attributes of file in different order, adding file attributes name read only, hidden file, add system and archive attributes, but in modern window command it allow show and display some limited attributes on created disk operating system file limited attributes.

Attrib attributes

+ r	Apply read only attributes
- r	Remove read only attributes
+ h	Apply hidden only attributes
- h	Remove hidden only attributes
+ s	Apply system only attributes
-s	Remove hidden only attributes
+ a	Apply archive only attributes
-a	Remove read only attributes

Example of attrib command in microsoft disk operating system.

Syntax – c:\>attrib + r file.txt

Syntax – c:\>attrib - r file.txt

Syntax – c:\>attrib +h file.txt

Syntax – c:\>attrib -h file.txt

Syntax – c:\>attrib +a file.txt

Syntax – c:\>attrib -a file.txt

Syntax – c:\>attrib +s file.txt

Syntax – c:\>attrib -s file.txt

Defrag – defragmentation command defrag specific hard drive partition with arrange in specific order ascending or descending, it increase or grow speed of your computer operating system.

Syntax – c:\>defrag

Find – find command find particular string and text or value in active file with few setting it work like search tool in microsoft dos.

Syntax – c:\>find name.txt

Finger – finger command work in network to find out no of user list in active networking environment

Syntax – c:\>finger

Logoff – it logoff your active window 10 operating system and again login with login command in windows.

Syntax – c:\>logoff

Ping – ping networking command it test reply connected multiple client in active lan (local area network) ping check network cable physical connection to share data and computer resources ping reply when request meet.

Syntax – c:\>ping 192.168.01.1

Print – print command print saves and exist windows and microsoft dos file with installed printer, printer must be installed before the printing any type of document and blank paper must be inserted for printing.

> **Syntax** – c:\>print readme.txt

Copy – copy command copy one or more file content with other file resources for copy here must should be two path source and destination.

> **Syntax** – c:\>copy file1.txt file2.txt

Wild card use with copy command

> ? – question mark
>
> * - asterisk

Md – make directory command create a new directory for storage directory, sub directory and file play role of container one directory keep one or more file in a root and sub directory.

> **Syntax** – c:\>md new

Create on or many directories in single directory

> **Syntax** – c:\>md one\two\three\four\five

Cd – cd command change or move into exist directory to view content of parent and child directory open directory and sub directory with change directory command.

> **Syntax** – c:\>cd one

Rd – remove directory command remove directory created by user if you want to remove directory and sub directory, first move into sub directory and remove one by one, remember you can't be remove directory with sub directory.

Condition

1. Remove directory must should be empty.
2. Remove directory one step should above.

> **Syntax** – c:\>rd new

Delete – delete command delete directory in microsoft dos win 98 operating system, it is remove directory and subdirectory.

> **Syntax** – c:\>delete new

Delete all – command remove directory and sub directory with additional directory, it removes directory and sub directory permanently with deletion, it asking if you finally delete directory then apply any key to delete all directory.

> **Syntax** – c:\>delete all new

Copy con – copy con command create new microsoft dos file, it allow us to create or manage one or more microsoft dos based file for text creation we create any type of extension file with primary and secondary name primary name must should 8 character and secondary name should be 3 character according to win 98 o/s.

> **Syntax –** c:\>copy con file.txt

F6/ctrl +z – both command use to save microsoft dos copy con created file with extension.

Type – command use to retrieve content of copy con created file simply type command display all the content file and information created in microsoft disk operating system.

> **Syntax –** c:\>type file.txt

Del – command remove created file in microsoft dos, it only removes all file one by one with file name and file extension.

> **Syntax –** c:\>del file.txt

Xcopy – xcopy command copy directory sub directory and file with complete path into another directory location with exact file directory format.

> **Syntax –** c:\>xcopy c:\ one\two*. * d:\two\

Shutdown – command allow privilege to shut down, restart, or abort, shut down, restart, abort within 30 second otherwise system will must reboot or shutdown so apply must within 30 second.

> **Syntax –** c:\>shutdown –s /*shut down active pc */

> **Syntax –** c:\>shutdown –r /*restart active pc */

> **Syntax –** c:\>shutdown –a /* abort shutdown */

Prompt – change microsoft dos prompt with many built prompt reserve prompt symbol, some listed prompt symbol is given below select desire prompt symbol and change default c prompt preview.

Prompt symbol is

> $a -& ampersand
>
> $b – lpipe
>
> $c – left parentheses
>
> $d – current date
>
> $e – escape code
>
> $f -right parentheses
>
> $g -gather then sign
>
> $h – back space
>
> $l – less than sign
>
> $n – current drive

$p – current drive and path

$q – equal sign

$s – space

$ t – current time

$v – window x pos version

   Syntax – c:\>prompt $d

   Syntax – c:\>prompt $t

   Syntax – c:\>prompt $l

Again c:\> prompt setting apply command below

   Syntax – c:\>prompt pg

Edit – change edit and allow us to add new text, paragraph, sentence, at the bottom, middle, and any were, at the created file microsoft dos created file for implementation edit is a microsoft dos based small cui editor that manage store new or edit open save file.

   Syntax – c:\>edit

Compact – display list of compact file in order of file compression mode default it show compressed file and also show non-compressed status of file.

   Syntax – c:\>compact

Ipconfig – this command shows the status of connected file with default ethernet setting or know the condition of active ethernet connection.

   Syntax – c:\>ipconfig

Reg – show status of active installed windows operating system with some default setting or customize and put query related to registry.

   Syntax – c:\>reg

Telnet – open telnet virtual terminal for telephone network communication in client server at cui based environment and share data file folder etc.

   Syntax – c:\>telnet

To open window application with ms dos based service

   Syntax – c:\>notepad

   Syntax – c:\>write

   Syntax – c:\>mspaint

   Syntax – c:\>prompt pg

TOPIC

02

Window 10 Apps & Overview

- Notepad apps.
- Microsoft paint apps.
- Remote desktop connection.
- Run.
- Snipping tools.
- Sound recorder.
- Sticky not.
- Sync center.
- Windows explorer.
- Mobility center.
- Word pad apps.
- Ease of access program.
- Windows magnifier.
- On screen keyboard.
- Windows speech recognition.
- Control panel.
- Disk cleanup.
- Disk defragmenter.
- Resources monitor.
- System information.
- Task scheduler.
- Windows journal.
- Windows power shell ise.
- Dvd maker.
- Windows fax and scan.
- Windows media player.

About notepad – notepad a small text editor especially used to creating html web page, web site with, small read me, serial text file, notepad prefer to started level beginner user, it's a simple basic small level formatting, editing, application software, which is created and continuously supported by microsoft company, notepad text editor by default installed during windows 10 and other previous version windows loaded, installed by any hardware software basically now days most of user, programmer, and developer, use notepad++ version for creating's basic script writing program with source coding generate, notepad allow formatting and editing any application at 64 - bit level capacity remember notepad doesn't support higher level formatting and editing.

How to reach notepad

start - all programs – accessories – notepad.
start - run - type – notepad – press enter.
start – run – cmd – type – notepad.

Basic windows of notepad

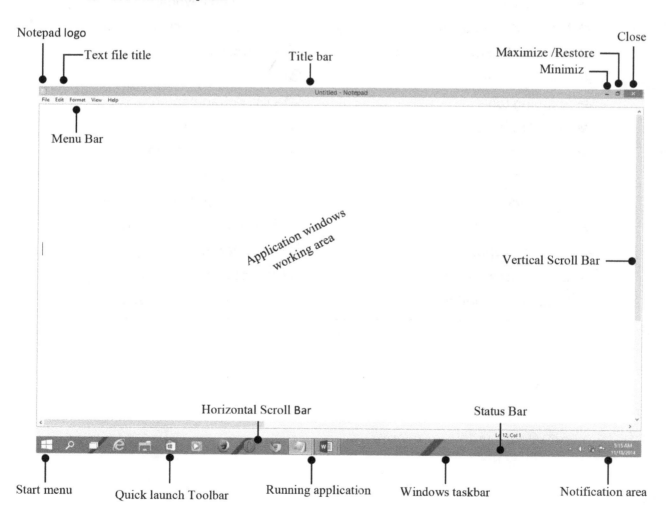

Notepad logo – show at the top left corner of open notepad application software, notepad logo indicates software information with logo easily recognize its belong to notepad file and content.

Text file title – by default it show open file title near to notepad application software logo, file name added by text file creator.

Title bar – it display in color of blue if windows 10 theme, changes notepad title will changes automatically title bar, display many control on it like file title, logo, minimize maximize, restore, close, control etc.

Title bar control

Minimize – minimize active application in task bar windows in minimize application will store in task bar, again you can maximize, restore and close it.

Maximize – maximize minimize windows from taskbar in maximize application will display full screen, of running text file and its content.

Restore – restore active notepad software in small windows middle of desktop screen preview, you see all text and file content show at middle of windows desktop screen for preview its content.

Close – close or terminate active run open application software temporary, if need start again then click on windows accessories and open it for desire purpose.

Menu bar – display five menus in notepad menu bar, four menus will control notepad text file operation like new, open, save, print, cut, copy, edit, active notepad file, fifth menu display help and product description.

Application windows – a blank white space area inside of notepad windows use to create, edit, delete, customize, notepad written text and information file.

Vertical scroll bar – move your notepad text from top to bottom with scrollbar, but text must more than one page then it automatically appear in right side of notepad application software windows.

Horizontal scrollbar – it appear when you write text more than right alignment, it appear automatically along horizontal scrollbar move your text direction from left to right direction, drag these text till then it created or placed on current text file window.

Status bar – appear at the bottom of notepad application software, it is a last bar connect with notepad application software, generally status bar show or indicate application line and column information in status window.

Notepad menu

File menu

New – create new .txt (text) empty document for new task creation, simple create new text file write down desire text inside it then save it.

    Shortcut - ctrl + n

Open – open previous saved and existing notepad files for editing, appending, customization, according to need, even while working on programming script open existing scrip and making some desire changes in it.

> **Shortcut -** ctrl + o

Save – save active open created notepad file for future need or reference, if file save and exist then edit any time anywhere, even save helping user to keep/store text file as secondary purpose.

> **Shortcut -** ctrl + s

Saves as – save previous active open notepad text file with new name, new location, as secondary backup copy, if first lost then secondary copy will play role of first copy.

Page setup – set active notepad file margin from left, right, top, bottom, alignment along change, default file orientation from portrait to landscape order etc.

Print – print active exist notepad document with attach printer customize printer configuration, print size, orientation number of printer pages etc.

Exit – exit terminate active running notepad application software and turn back window on desktop screen.

> **Shortcut -** alt + f4

Edit menu

Undo – undo last three actions in active notepad text file, undo reappear remove text that can be cut, delete, or suddenly destroy removed etc. Use undo option while application action get back or undo while user need.

> **Shortcut -** ctrl + z

Cut – cut unnecessary, unwanted, unrequired, text selection form active notepad text file, generally cut text will be paste and place at new location.

> **Shortcut -** ctrl + x

Copy – copy repeated duplicate text, information file content, matter, letter, etc. That be similar or place new location with same content without avoid recreate similar text, but always remember copy create copy for buffer, it doesn't work till then apply paste command.

> **Shortcut -** ctrl + c

Paste – paste copy text file content at desire location in open notepad application software windows remember copy text will be placed many time new locations with paste command.

> **Shortcut -** ctrl + v

Delete – delete unwanted selection from active notepad document, along delete menu in active notepad software deleted text will be recover with undo command.

> **Shortcut -** del

Find – find a particular word, alphabet, numeric, text, content, information, current notepad selection, active open notepad file find help while some search information quickly get and view.

    Shortcut - ctrl + f

Find next – refined find text information value text content with last find activities, find next only work on find last values in active text file.

    Shortcut - f3

Replace – replace find text word, alphabet, numeric, content, symbol, numeric, or may other but find text must be existing in active notepad documents paragraph.

    Shortcut - ctrl + h

Go to – go to or jump any line number in current notepad documents file with go to command, it works when we create one or more line with go to command quickly reach at desired line number.

    Shortcut - ctrl + g

Select all – select all portion of notepad documents for editing formatting without selection, we can't able to edit any particular or individual portion of notepad documents without selection.

    Shortcut - ctrl + a

Time/date – insert current date & time in default system format, select the location where you want to be insert current date and time then click date & time option for insertion date and time.

    Shortcut - f5

Format menu

Word wrap – word wrap active notepad text page line from horizontal margin line will be automatically move in next line paragraph and user view or create continuously horizontally in notepad file.

Font – change font of selected notepad text file with available font dialog apply font style like, bold, italic, regular bold, with italic, and increase decrease font size between 8 to 72 of selected text file content.

View menu

Status bar – make visible invisible status bar appear in current notepad application, working of status bar in notepad to display status of active of line or column in current text file.

Help menu

View help – display help about notepad application software like what is notepad how, it functions how to control menu operation which company is create it, and many more guideline about notepad.

About notepad – it is digital certificate which is display product specification like product info, copy right act, license agreement, installer detail version info, os detail and many more.

How to start paint

    # start – all programs – accessories – paint.

    # start – run – type – paint.

    # start – run – type – mspaint.

About microsoft paint – microsoft paint special drawing image drawing, editing, graphic generating, software, which use to draw, sketch, diagram, sceneries, map, cartoon, graphic, 3d movie posture, colorful, text, behind, wallpaper, background, and more, commercially used microsoft paint now days for designing graphic for hollywood or bollywood movie for animated movie create with microsoft paint graphic and effect added every graphic created in paint save .bmp(bitmap) extension, microsoft paint mainly operated by kids to drawing graphic for school project.

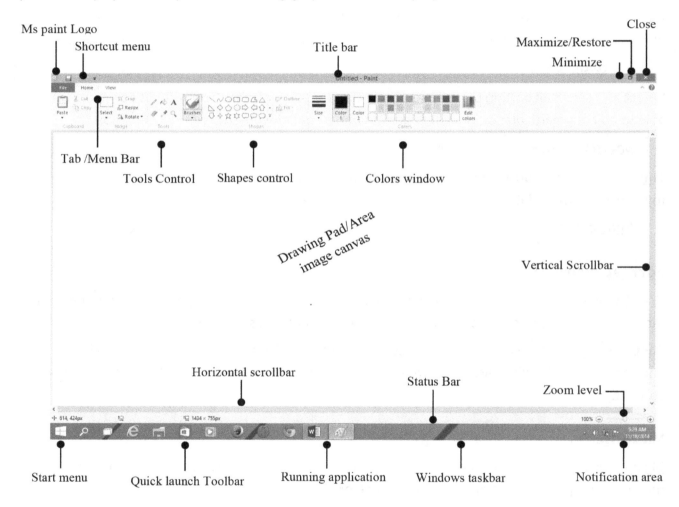

Microsoft paint logo – microsoft paint logo small icon display left corner of paint title bar, paint logo represent microsoft paint application created graphic icon.

Shortcut menu – it is just display near to the microsoft paint logo, shortcut menu show save, undo, redo, default preview and some short cut will be display they are manually enable by user.

Image title – small bar in color default blue bar show the title of active open microsoft paint image, here image title indicates name of open microsoft paint file.

Title bar – show at the top menu bar or application software, it holds different control like paint logo, short cut menu, image title, minimize, maximize, restore, or close, control for application controlling.

Paint menu

New – create new bmp image drawing pad for drawing, sketch, diagram, snap, logo, cartoon etc. New is just similar draw desire panting content on bank paper in your drawing book.

    Shortcut – ctrl +n

Open – open pervious created save and existing image graphic sketch image for editing improving adding new formatting effect, paint control etc. Even open helping its user to making some desire changes in working drawings/images.

    Shortcut – ctrl + o

Save – saving of bmp image is refer to store image documents for future need or reference, if image bmp picture saved then it can be edited any time/anywhere with new effect or attributes.

    Shortcut – ctrl + s

Saves as – saves current bmp image with new name, new reference, new location, for secondary copy, if primary copy damage, lost, or corrupt, then save as secondary backup copy will be used.

Different save as format

Png – save current microsoft paint image graphic in png file format commonly used in internet browse links, png abbreviated as portable network graphic.

Jpeg picture – abbreviated as (joint photographic expert group) mostly prefer common graphic offline and online graphic extension in image editing or computer graphic.

Bmp picture – default extension provided and saved by microsoft paint all picture created added with bmp file format.

Gif picture – gif stand graphic interchange format is another type image background wallpaper format which is commonly for image saving.

Other format – save active bmp image with available file format may some different above discuss image file format.

Print – print current bmp image with attach printer and change printer setting like print order number of copy printed print, image orientation, from portrait to landscape order.

    Shortcut – ctrl + p

Print control

Print – print open microsoft paint graphic image background sketch information etc. With attach printer, printer is a commonly used output device which produce hardcopy in softcopy order.

Page setup – set open microsoft paint image margin from all direction like left, right, top, bottom, image orientation in portrait to landscape order.

Print preview – display print preview of printed microsoft paint image and think for customization from printed image all direction orientation etc.

From scanner or camera – direct input image graphic from attach scanner or camera device, capture live footage snap even get previous capture image in microsoft paint program, for editing improve picture performance but the condition external media like handy cam or camera must be connected with machine.

Send in e-mail – send current microsoft paint image at unique e-mail address with attachment to the defined person type one two and three persons at same time but your internet connection e-mail account should be configuring before sending e-mail.

Set as desktop background – set current microsoft paint created image in shape of your desktop background with this set as desktop background format, after applying these option you will see the created or working bmp image us or set as current desktop background.

Fill – set current microsoft paint image as desktop format as fill order.

Tile – display current open microsoft paint image as tile format in computer desktop order.

Center – preview current desktop background as center of your machine.

Properties – display properties of active paint object like created, modify, access, date, image location allocate byte, consume space, file name with file extension.

About paint – about microsoft paint digital certificate which show current product specification configuration and other detail like that product name, version, and other essential information will be show.

Exit – terminate open microsoft paint drawings application software, and move back at windows desktop area.

Microsoft paint home menu

   Paste – paste microsoft paint bmp image content form same location to another location, pasting refer to generate same object at new location without modification.

     Shortcut – ctrl + v

   Cut – cut selection image portion background any selected object from selected location remember cut text object will be place with new location with paste command.

     Shortcut – ctrl + x

Copy – copy repeated image background portion copy avoid rewrite process any object, we can copy any object place copy object new location with paste.

   Shortcut – ctrl + c

Select – select current microsoft paint object for editing formatting and any other operation, without selection no possible modification selects current object different method.

   Shortcut – ctrl + a

Different selection tools

Rectangular selection – select any microsoft paint current object in rectangular shape selected shape will be cut in square or straight rectangular selection mode.

Free from selection – select current microsoft paint object in desire shape cut select, wherever you want choice may be anything use free from selection.

Select all – select complete microsoft paint object for formatting or editing change view apply new effect after select all.

Invert selection – apply invert selection effect on current microsoft paint selection, it inverts effect and condition on current paint object.

Delete – delete active selection in microsoft paint windows with delete command, apply delete command for removing and deleting some unnecessary portion of current drawings, image.

Transparent selection – enable transparent effect on active selection in current bmp image or other background, graphic, in transparent selection selected object will be transparent so you view in both side during editing or modify it.

Crop – crop active microsoft paint image till then you want set level size margin of crop image then release crop image, these option helping paint user to show specific are in complete image portion or area.

Resize – resize image size or margin new set elements, even resizing option helping its user to configure all size and object orientation.

Rotate – rotate microsoft paint object, picture, graphic, background, at rotate left and right 90 – degree angle, similar rotation drawings rotating at 180 – degree, flip vertical, flip horizontal, direction according to its user need.

Microsoft paint tools

Pencil – draw your own desire shape with pencil shape pencil tools used everywhere for design and construct any shape, sketch, create text, title, and many more.

Fill with color – small down box tools which used to fill color in any shape, image, background, text, snap or may be anything.

Text – create new text article heading word art object with style shape and attractive look we may use text tools for text creation.

Eraser – eraser another useful tools which erase remove any image portion, text, graphics content, selection.

Color picker – pick any color form any image text background and use for new object color picker work similar fill with color tools.

Magnifier – zoom magnify active bmp image size from 10% to 800% percent set level which you want to be best meet your requirement.

Brushes – brushes microsoft paint control small collection of different kind of painting drawing tool, that may be selected by image or painting creator, while created brushes image in paint, click on drop down arrow located below brushes control and pick desire one brushes for creating paintings.

Shapes – insert various kind of readymade shapes at working drawings, just you need to click on shapes gallery now pick desire one shape for your drawings drag or draw these shape at desire location, by default it provides user line, curve, oval, rectangle, start, callouts, triangle, arrows, pentagon, hexagon and other remaining shapes available for insert.

Outline – change default outline of draw object shapes at working drawings image object, first of all select desire object now click on outline and apply desire shape outline from outline gallery, remember these outline located outside of selected object and shapes in microsoft paint.

Fill – fill the selected shape outline object color from available fill color choice or you may be get other colors from colors available choice, while apply these operation shapes and object must be selected.

Size – change the size of selected shape placed or draw in microsoft paint program, after selection of shapes you may get choice of shape size from minimum to maximum just click and apply desire one from available choice.

Color 1 – color 1 represent foreground color in paint program, color 1 and color 2 will be change depending on user selection for foreground include background color display in selected object, color 1 always used as object foreground insertion.

Color 2 – color 2 represent background color these color used as fill background color in working paint program selected object.

Colors – color option represent huge collection of important and remaining color combination that are necessary for insertion in microsoft paint selected object, user just need to user fill with color tool for insertion desire color in a selected object from available color gallery.

Edit color – edit color control provides liberty of paint user to select or create own customized modify color combination for insertion in a selected microsoft paint object, select base color and moving slider control to own desire modified color added in color group as a custom color these added custom color can be inserted one or more time in a desire picture or object.

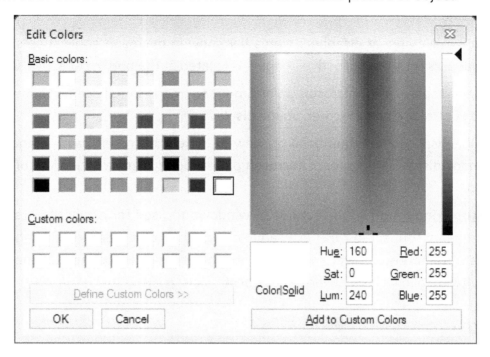

Microsoft paint view tab

View tab/menu

Zoom in – zoom in active bmp image size 12.5% minimum 800% maximum, click continue on zoom in button increase size of active image.

Zoom out – zoom out size of current bmp image 800% to minimum 10%, 12.5% according to need set desire zoom level for active bmp image.

100% - set the default 100% image margin level for current bmp image by default image display in their actual size may be original size when clicking 100% image display in 100% view.

Ruler – enable disable ruler bar appear in microsoft paint ruler display horizontal vertical across the open microsoft paint image.

☐ **Gridlines** – display small rectangular horizontal vertical gridline across the open microsoft paint image gridline can be show or hide from view menu with view we can just make enable and disable it according to need.

☑ **Status bar** – make appear disappear status bar show in microsoft application software status bar stats bar present status of active image it is located at the bottom of active software.

Full screen – display open microsoft paint bmp jpeg image in full screen mode hiding all bar menus tab control during full screen image display.

Thumbnail – display small thumbnail preview of current microsoft paint image in thumbnail preview image display left corner of microsoft paint drag or increase size width of current image according need.

Remote desktop connection – this features of windows 10 used for established remote network connection between connected lan (local area network) in office, same building, organization, campus, firm, etc. Remotely connect and control attach network client computer, manage resource install client software allow client privilege control etc.

How to reach

start – program – accessories – remote desktop connection.

start – run – type – mstsc.

Remote desktop connection (fewer windows)	**Remote desktop connection (full windows)**

Run – run is command executer which execute any application, software, program, from its storage/ installing location directly without follow manual step or guide, run any program command from you may browse program application or then press ok run play role to start execute any application from every from your machine, so it's called command application executer some program or application only start load by run method.

How to start run

start – run

start – all program – accessories - run

press toggle key - windows + r

Basic windows of run

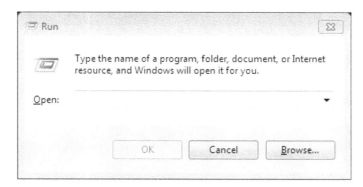

Snipping tool – snip tool small application software which used to cut any graphic, picture, dialog control, menu shortcut, from run open application software, program this features only added in version of windows 7 and later operating system, it by default loaded along windows 10 with sniping tool cut any shape in free from snip, order rectangle windows snip, or full screen snip choose best meet your requirement save cut image edit store for other use.

How to start snipping tool

start – all program – accessories – snipping tool.

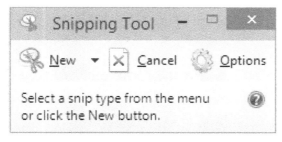

Snipping toll control

Free from snip – cut any shape application in desire shape with snipping tool.

Rectangular snip – cut any picture shape application rectangular order with rectangular snip tool control.

Windows snip – cut shape application dialog in straight rectangular fix order shape, these option cutting and taking snapshot of picture in windows snip.

Full screen snip – cut shape in fix full order shape without modification windows of snipping tool, use these option while you want to capture a full screen window.

Sound recorder – multimedia application software used to record direct human voice with connected microphone headphone receiver, speak whatever you want to be speak, start record function then speak record till then you want, now stop open location of storage recorded sound file, now you can listen voice or you can make audio video presentation for any project store .wma, .wav format for sound for record any sound microphone must be connected or sound driver must be install.

How starts sound recorder

> \# start – all program – accessories – sound recorder.
> \# start – run – type – sound recorder.

Windows of sound recorder

Sticky notes – create add sticky notes write information whatever you want to be store in format of sticky notes, sticky notes small square shape notes window, which store something you like to store for routine purpose text, information, notes and other small text keep store in shape of sticky notes.

How to start sticky notes

> \# start – all program – accessories - sticky notes.
> \# start – run – stikynot.

Windows of sticky notes

this is a example of stikynot in windows 10

Sync center – sync center is place where you can sync/synchronize files, folder, and other computer content, share among your personal computer or network or other computer path, you see a sync device location, activity, during sharing or communicating between offline files in network, you connect you cellphone, smart phone for sync files, folder, image, graphic, audio, video, contact, calendar, notes, and other electronic content between smart phone to your computer, but remember you must need to configure even install sync software for collaborative information sharing among connected device.

How to start

start – all program – accessories – sync center.

Windows explorer – in windows 8.1 you getting new better enhance multi features file explorer previously called windows explorer in windows 98 to windows 7 operating system, but in windows 10 windows explorer rename with file explorer with new features and support, in file explorer you preview recent files, file, folder, image, audio, video, zip content, even any other electronic content/ item you used folder in computer, last time you working on them easier get from file explorer it show them always when it start, new file explorer contain new tittle bar, browsing windows, user interface, arrange item sequentially in ascending order.

How to start

start – all program – accessories – windows explorer.

start – run – type – explorer.

Windows of windows explorer

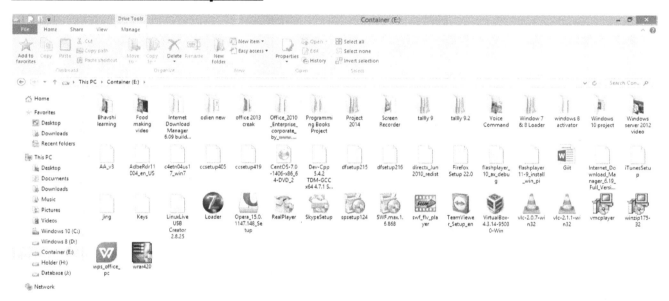

Windows mobility center – microsoft windows 10 mobility center features option, gives you configure important windows control without go anywhere you save time during processing, no need to located individual setting at different place, configure laptop brightness level minimum to maximum, windows media player sound increase decrease mute sound, also change windows power saver scheme, make it balance power saver or high performance, according to use on off wireless wi-fi connection on/off, connect laptop to external display like duplicate, extended or projector display, sync windows with other mobility device turn projector features on for connect with projector presentation.

How to start

start – all program – accessories – windows mobility center.

Windows of mobility center

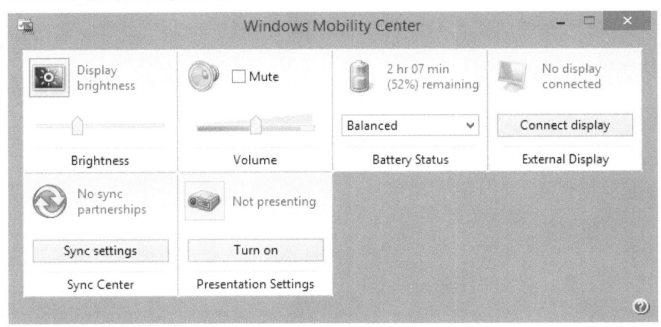

Word pad – word pad is small documents text editor which is by default loaded along windows 10 operating system, current version popular in windows is word pad 6.0, word pad allow more formatting, editing, controlling, and manage current documents, in word pad create rtf(rich text format)format in previous release of word pad we create also .txt(text file), unicode text file format, commercial use of word pad to create small but larger than notepad file, creating word pad allow more formatting tool, editing color, font effect, small letter, matter, application, resume, report, information can be easily created with notepad and also manage it function also.

How to start

start – all program – accessories – wordpad.
start – run – type – wordpad.
start – run – write.

Windows of word pad

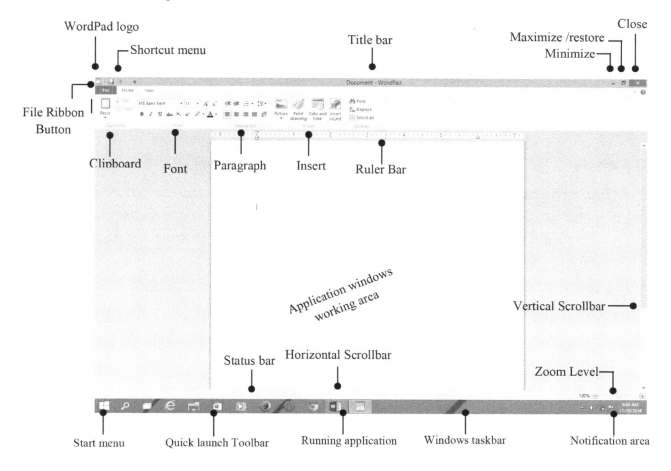

Title bar – appear at the top of word pad application software display word pad logo quick shortcut menu documents title windows control minimize maximize/restore close button.

Title bar

Menu bar – menu bar contains special menu list in pull down order with quick access shortcut toolbar menu bar help to manager rtf documents operation like cut copy paste format edit new save editing and many more operation word pad display two common use menu name home and.

View like as a tab

Menu bar

Ribbon button – ribbon button display front of home tab/menu in wordpad it consist wordpad common operation like new save open print etc like a pull down menu use and select which operation you need to be apply on active wordpad documents.

WordPad Ribbon Button

File menu

New – create new rtf, txt unicode text, document for new text information letter, matter information, biodata, creation, new provide empty document windows like new pages in copy/register after complete full of previous pages just similar that there is no limit you can create how much number in rtf documents in wordpad.

> **Shortcut** - ctrl + n

Open – open previous store wordpad rtf documents for print editing, editing formatting, even appending some additional matter in previous paragraph, senction matter letter, if rtf documents exist then it can be modify any time.

> **Shortcut** - ctrl + o

Save – save active rtf documents for future need reference, if documents save and exist then it can be reopen modify but first condition it must save saving, just like similar keeping record and information keep for future requirement, generally saving refer to store copy of current documents in disk may primary or secondary purpose.

> **Shortcut** - ctrl + s

Save as – save current wordpad documents in saves as with new name, new address, new location, saves as refer to store secondary copy as a backup of primary data copy, if primary copy lost or misplace then saves copy use as a purpose of primary copy.

Other save format

Rich text documents – save as active wordpad documents in rtf(rich text format) which indicate file belong to wordpad application software automatically wordpad save file in rtf format.

Office open xml documents – save wordpad document in xml(xtensible file format) which manly used in internet world wide.

Open document text – save rtf document in text file format which belong notepad application software text file open and edit with notepad application software.

Plain text document – save rtf documents in plain text file formating with less formatting editing with no major effect.

Other format – store wordpad rtf documents in many availabe choice format, on click drop down combo box drop down selection choice.

 Print – print rtf wordpad save exist documents with attach printer, for printing documents rtf documents must open printer must connected empty paper also install/inserted in printer then finally press print menu to produce hard copy of softcopy.

 Quick print – allow quick print withought display print preview or page setup print in as it is same look like with no set orientation or margin from all side etc.

 Print preview – display print preview of printed rtf documents and see modification, editing point line, with orienatation, and margin page size etc. Whatever we see in print preview that's final for printing.

 Page setup – set rtf documents page margin from left, right, top, bottom, documents orientation between portrait or landscape order or customize page size in a4, a3, a5 legal tabloids custom size etc.

 Send in e-mail – send current rtf document to the related person at unique e-mail address open previous documents configure outlook express connect internet then send e-mail click send button to confirm send e-mail.

 About word pad – about wordpad ist is digital certificate which display wordpad version, copy right, licence, free memory, used resource information, etc.

 Exit – exit or terminate current open wordpad application software.

Word pad home menu

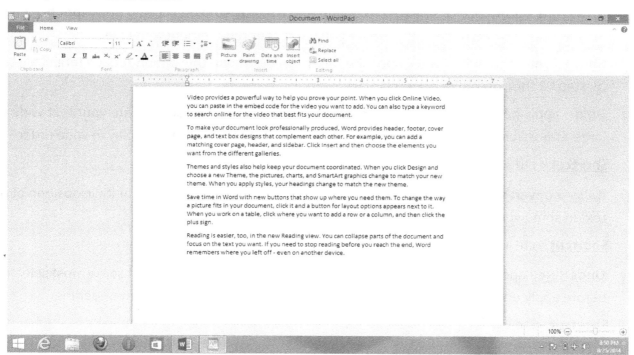

Word pad home tab

 Paste – paste rtf documents content at desire location remember before apply paste command you must need to be copy repeated information then place copy text with paste command.

Shortcut – ctrl + v

Cut – cut unnecessary, unwanted, rtf text selection, from word pad documents windows cut text place at new location with paste command.

Shortcut – ctrl + x

 Copy – copy repeated similar common information used at many place many time copy avoids process of rewrite similar text.

Shortcut – ctrl + c

Font family – change font of selected rtf documents from available font family dialog, first of all your text must be selected then choose desire font form font list like arial, mono type corsiva, elephant, comic sans ms, weddings bookman old style, etc.

 Font size – increase or decrease font size of selected rtf documents among minimum 8 to maximum 72 but you can grow size of current rtf document text from 1 to 1638 font text size.

A **Grow font** – grow size of selected rtf documents step by step on clicking grow font button to increase desire level of font stop where you meet your requirement font level.

A **Shrink font** – shrink font work opposite the grow font menu this option reduce font size step by step till then user click on it manually.

B **Bold** – apply bold text effect on selected rtf content, remember bold create your text wide or large as possible as, even add bold effect while current text ready for display in wide order.

Shortcut – ctrl + b

I **Italic** – convert selected rtf documents italic order text must be selected for italic position of rtf text in some vertical down preview order.

Shortcut – ctrl + i

U **Underline** – apply underline below the selected word pad rtf text your text same must selected before apply underline effect, you see underline text display above current underline.

Shortcut – ctrl + u

Strikethrough – apply strikethrough effect on selected word pad rtf documents first of all select word pad documents then click on strikethrough in strike through text will be covered with middle horizontal straight line continuously it used to indicate some specific information highlight/notice.

X_2 **Subscript** – convert selected text word pad text in subscript order, subscript display selected lower radix above of normal text.

X^2 **Superscript** – convert selected text word pad text in superscript order, superscript display upper radix of normal text.

Text highlight color – apply different list of color behind of selected rtf documents first of all select rtf documents then click on text highlight color choose color then click for apply as document background.

A **Text color** – apply automatic standard or more color even edit your required color then apply selected rtf word pad documents.

Decrease indent – decrease indent moves selected rtf documents form right to left direction step by step according to need.

Increase indent – increase indent move your selected rtf document text form left to right according to need stop where you want to be stay your text.

Start a list – apply bullets number alphabet roman number as a bullets front of selected rtf documents, paragraph, section, heading, etc.

Line spacing – apply line spacing effect on selected rtf documents set your requirement choose space margin between number of selected line add space 1.0, 1.5, 2.0 or at least.

Align text left – align active rtf documents letter, matter, paragraph, content, in default left direction.

Align text center – align active rtf documents in center direction, first select rtf text now click on align text center option for setting text in center direction.

Align text right – align selected rtf documents in right direction, whatever of rtf document text and information will be selected use align text right button for set or align text in right direction or preview.

Justify – justify option equally justify selected rtf document text and information from both side even show in equal direction during preview its content.

Paragraph – set paragraph indention from left, right, first line direction, even align text in left center, or right direction, with spacing effect also.

Picture – insert graphic in working rtf document inserter picture may be jpg, gif, bmp, png, may be another extension, insert picture where you want to be insert select browse your desire background picture then insert it in current document.

Change picture – change active inserted image, picture, wallpaper, with available another picture or choice new picture will place at old picture inserted.

Resize picture – if picture modify or increase decrease size, then click resize this will move current picture in actual previous order.

Paint drawing – this is odbc(object database connectivity) features of word pad it allow to move rtf content information in ms paint for editing now we edit word pad content with all ms paint tools and features.

Date and time – insert current date & time in various available format in different mm/dd/yy, yy/mm/dd, yyyy/dd/mm, format choose desire date & time format and click ok to insert time format is hh:mm:ss.s.

Insert object – insert linked with embedded application software features and function, now insert object provide many application merge with word pad edit existing application with word pad.

Find – find word, alphabet, numeric, string, content, symbol, in current rtf letter, matter, documents, with find quickest get information or reach at required find/search information along find tool.

Shortcut – ctrl + f

Replace – replace word pad, rtf documents, letter matter, information, with find word, alphabet, string character, symbol, numeric, etc. Replace quick made changes in rtf documents at large level with using replace option.

Shortcut – ctrl + h

Select all – select all word pad documents for editing, customization, modification, without selection rtf documents no possible to make change any part of rtf document editing.

Shortcut – ctrl + a

Word pad view menu

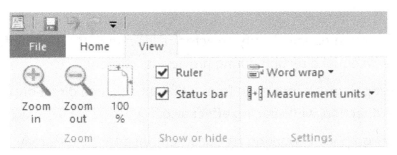

Zoom in – zoom in word pad documents size form 100% to increase 500% maximum, set your zoom level where best meet your requirement by default it will set on 100%.

Zoom out – zoom out work opposite of zoom in it will reduce remove zoom level form 500% to 10% set minimum zoom level is 10% and maximum zoom level 500%.

 100 % - set zoom level at default 100%, it will remove all zoom level previous setting zoom be in or zoom may be out 100% will set default level.

 Ruler – show or hide ruler bar appear in rtf document ruler used to change align margin of rtf documents from left to right direction.

 Status bar – same as ruler bar but it, displays at the bottom of rtf documents status bar display status of word pad documents, you can show or hide status bar visible in word pad application software.

 Word wrap – wrap rtf documents from different angle wrap move rtf documents according to ruler wrap to windows or no wrap option.

Different wrap option

No wrap – this option work on no wrap windows move windows will not wrap in rtf documents.

Wrap to windows – wrap rtf documents according to word pad windows rtf text will set according windows ruler.

Wrap to ruler – set rtf documents according to wrap to ruler text will not move more than word pad ruler windows.

Measurement units – change rtf documents measurements in picas, inches', centimeters, points, etc.

Ease of access center – ease of access center collection of important windows utilities and software, that make easier windows function and activities during using mode, by default you getting ease access center control is, magnifier, narrator, on screen keyboard, set up high contrast, select any one of them for configuring a related property in windows operating system.

How to reach

start – all program – accessories – ease of access.

Magnifier – magnifier tool increase visibility of present character paragraph size from 100 % zoom to 1600 % percent zoom level, read any type of character, word, picture, map, diagram, control and other tool menu, dialog, features in enlarge with magnifier tools + (plus) increase level of zoom but – (minus) reduce the level of zoom.

How to start magnifier

start – all program – accessories – ease of access – magnifier.

start – run – type – magnify.

Views magnify windows 10 object

Full screen – magnify object in full screen order.

Lens – magnify object in lens order.

Docked – magnify object in docked windows.

Preview in full screen – preview magnify object in full screen windows.

Windows of magnifier

Narrator – windows narrator word, character, paragraph, documents, sheet presentation, reader tool, which is read offline written text information, generally narrator display microsoft voice for text reading reader listen himself, or his audience, student, staff, member, etc.

How to start narrator

start – all program – accessories – ease of access – narrator.

start – all program – run – narrator.

Windows of narrator

On screen keyboard – on screen keyboard is ordinary and special type of keyboard, used for when installed keyboard computer will not work properly or in touch device on screen keyboard use necessary with touch device, you access all key in on screen keyboard name function keys, alphabet keys, numeric keys, special keys, arrows key, space bar, will not work properly then on screen keyboard play role of internal external keyboard, it work completely function like any keyboard attach external keyboard.

How to start on screen keyboard

start – all program – accessories – ease of access – on screen keyboard.

start – run – type – osk.

start – run – cmd – type – osk.

Windows of on screen keyboard

Windows speech recognition – speech recognition option enable you to record dictate your voice with your laptop desktop computer, first of all you configure your voice according to your computer than you given command to your computer for create speech text or document, before apply these operation you must configure your computer speech recognition program set up microphone level, take speech tutorial, finally train your computer to better understand your configure voice command all these above setting properly and you dictate/supply voice command for your computer without any keyboard connectivity but you must be configure these all thing properly before apply these operation, big advantage of speech recognition is it permitted windows user to control windows with voice command and create text, open application, include all other computer keyboard mouse task easier do with windows speech recognition program.

How to start

start – all program – accessories – ease of access – windows speech recognition.

Windows of windows speech recognition

Set up microphone – setup microphone option enable you to configure your windows microphone, how it communicate or work with speech recognition program, in set up microphone dialog you configure which type of microphone you have to be installed it may be headset microphone, desktop microphone, or other type of microphone you configure manually in this process set up microphone sound level installed hardware configuration, finally your computer microphone properly installed and you can ready to record or given speech command in speech recognition mode.

Headset microphone – configure and dictate your sound with headset microphone with speaker, in this kind of microphone you have choice of hear/listen or speak or dictate voice command for control windows and its apps through speech recognition program.

Desktop microphone – configure windows desktop microphone major changes between headset and desktop, microphone is that headset microphone portable even it move between many electronic gadgets, but desktop microphone used as fixed purpose no movable purpose text creator speak voice command in desktop microphone for create electronic document.

Other – configure other kind of portable or fix kind of microphone with microsoft speech recognition program, remember microphone installed here for fix purpose name record and listen sound direct from computer user, follow step to install and configure other category microphone with speech recognition.

System tools

Character map – windows system tools character map which is mainly used for insert any symbol, character, numeric, roman number, bullets, space, font, word, special character, function key, small graphic symbol, front middle left and center of current documents, select character from character map then copy place with paste in any documents windows.

How to start

start – all program – accessories – system tools – character map.

start – run – type – charmap.

Windows of character map

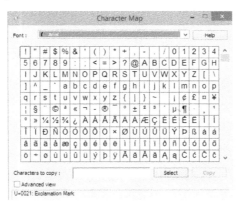

Control panel – control panel is also describe in previous chapter, go to control panel and get each and individual features about windows 10 control panel features, now again i will explain about control panel features control panel main control of windows application hardware software will be managed, control and operated by control panel windows control panel is heart control of windows for each and every setting, related to windows operating system will be configure by control panel menu till then, release of windows different flavor all windows hold its own control panel.

How to start control panel

start – start menu – control panel.

start – run – type – control.

start – run – cmd – type – control.

Windows of control panel

Disk cleanup – windows 10 system utilities is calculated how much space ready to free, from windows selected hard drive every time we work with windows so many time prefetch, system temporary, backup, internet cookies history, recycle bin, download cookies, uninstalled installed application, system restore file store in different of partition of windows, disk clean up utility wizard permanent clear them one time they will automatically create after some time so you need to regular clean up them for fast system process respond so start use disk clean up every two three or regular day for better system performance.

How to start disk cleanup

start – all program – accessories – system tools – disk cleanup.

start – run – type – cleanmgr.

Disk defragmenter – disk defragmenter is another system utility, it arrange selected system hard drive partition file folder and data in sequence order, so they can easily fast secure access without delay one by one, select windows hard drive partition, if you just want to analyze partition track, sector, cluster size, on disk or disk defragment hard drive data information defragment make better fast performance of hard drive.

How to start disk defragmenter

start – all program – accessories – system tools – disk defragmenter.

start – run – type – dfrgui.

start – run – type – cmd – type – defrag – a c:.

Windows of disk defragmenter

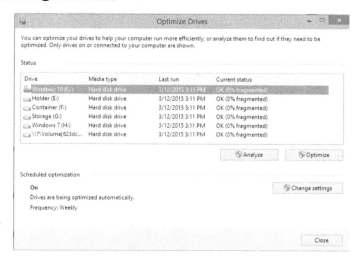

Resource monitor – windows 10 resource monitor is system tools, which display which computer function hardware resource used and allocate by computer display report, of usages of cpu memory hard disk, network client, server performance, overview you can see with resource monitor allocation of your machine hardware resources.

Main elements or resource monitor

Overview – display overview of cpu memory hard disk network performance.

Cpu – view cpu usages resource allocation and allotment by resource monitor use frequency.

Memory – display use memory resources available free use memory and number of total memory.

Disk – display hard disk partition resources used free space in active hard disk.

Network – display attach client server network performance network activity tcp/ip connection etc.

How to start resource monitor

      # start – all program – accessories – system tools – resource monitor.

      # start – run – type – resmon.

Basic windows of resource monitor

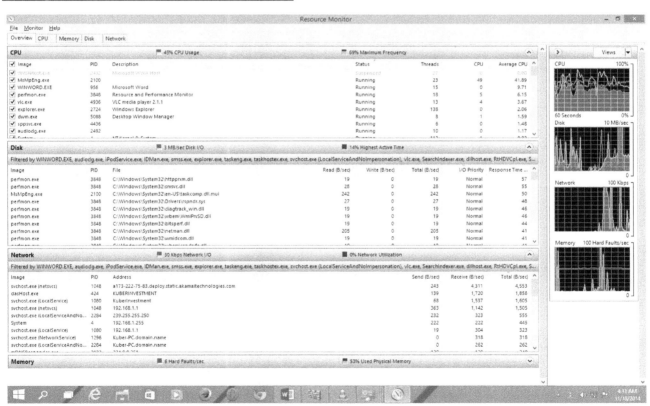

System information – display system information like install operating system name, system information, operating system version, device manufacture, bios version, hardware resources device, computer detail, ports detail available physical memory, display system irq, dma memory, hardware setting, driver information, detail of installed device, installed component input, output, network, modem ports, usb, printer ports, display sound card, bluetooth, infrared, usb, and other remaining hardware, completely detail or view software resources information system drivers running task services network connect etc. Generally system information is only tools which is tell you everything about current running system.

How to start system information

start – all program – accessories – system tools – system information.

start – run – type – msinfo32.exe.

Display windows of system information

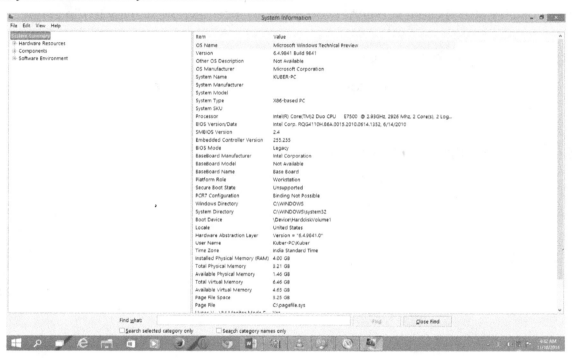

System restores – system restore is best system tools which restore your system in previous date and month, system restore point will create automatically or manually, created by you in any date or month after windows installation, with system restore utilities you can restore your machine with accurate date and time format in which case system restore work, if system hang program not access, software, hardware failure, installation software hardware not working proper, order then go to system restore remember system restore work in case that system restore point must be exist, otherwise it will not work so always set system restore point then follow system restore dialog start set original system installation date & time then go to system restore.

How to start system restore

start – all program – accessories – system tools – system restore.

start – run – type – rstrui.

Windows of system restore

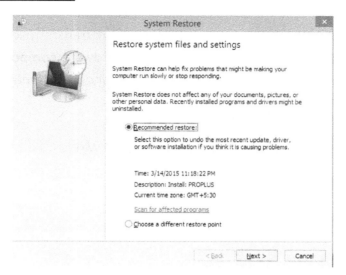

#**Note** – once system restores start then can't be stop or interrupt so restore only when you seriously start system restore function.

Task scheduler – task scheduler is another popular system utility, which manage handle your routine system default and self-created task, task scheduler starts each task events in system in define time edit, enable, disable, run, edit, delete, previous created task in task scheduler with task scheduler you can create basic task, create task import, task enable, disable running task set trigger action condition setting for created system task.

How to start task scheduler

start – all program – accessories – system tools – task scheduler.

start – run – type – taskschd.

Windows of system task scheduler

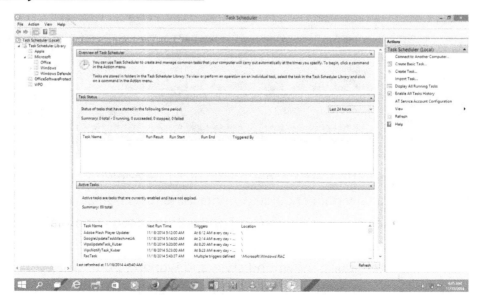

Welcome to windows easy transfer report – windows easy transfer application design for those user they want to be share locally windows created user account, computer apps created document files and information, user store music files and information, transfer user e-mail, videos, pictures, with connected electronic gadgets and other computer hardware component, this became easier while user need to share of transfer particular category of windows elements object.

How to start windows easy transfer report

start – all program – accessories – system tools - windows easy transfer report.

Windows of windows easy transfer report

Tablet pc – tablet pc input features add windows tablet pc or tablet supported windows 10 operating system device, direct input keyboard command and function from touch keyboard in windows operating system, now if you have touch device then you may enter all character command from touch input keyboard device it make easier of entering text direct without from touch input device in windows 10.

Tablet pc writing pad window

Personal handwriting recognition – personal handwriting recognition features allows specially windows tablet user to personally train or guide your machine to recognize your voice and character while you interact with machine or computer, in handwriting recognition dialog configure target specific reorganization errors option to recognize errors during system communication, include tech the recognizer to know better your handwriting style and working pattern, if everything configure properly then it will properly recognize your system properly during handwriting communication.

How to start personal handwriting recognition

start – all program – accessories – table pc.

Tablet input panel – using application name tablet input panel allows its user to using a touch sensitive device with pen, stick or human finger to create text or information and touch device or tablet input panel device, using touch keyboard for correcting and creating text information, edit create text correcting, deleting, splitting or joining table input panel text information.

How to start tablet input panel

start – all program – accessories – tablet pc

Windows journal – windows journal program automatically installs along windows 10 operating system installation, windows journal allows you to create hand written, self-modified, customize notes, task, paragraph, and other textual content according to need, create new note use light pen input device for create desire text information even use touch screen laptop tablet to write text information in your hand writing.

How to start windows journal

➲ Click on windows 10 start menu choose all program click on accessories choose tablet pc and click on windows journal to open it.

➲ Start click on run type journal.exe.

Windows journal window

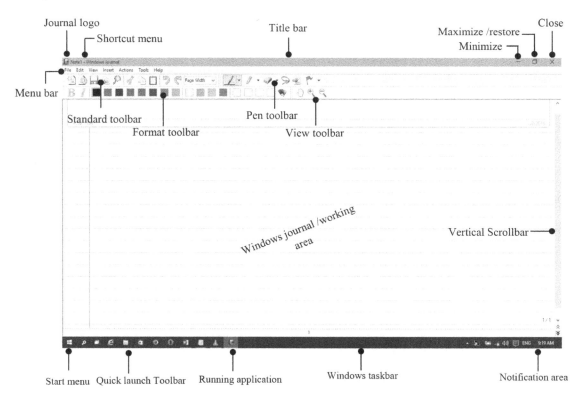

Windows journal menu

File menu

New note – click on file menu choose new note option, by default windows journal place new note while you open window journal and write desire information in it.

New note from template – new note from template option provide you built category of attractive template choose desire from category and select them for handwritten text information.

Open – open previous existing store windows journal task note, and edit information add new content remove previous content according to need.

Import – import windows journal file information from existing storage unit, select and click to import in current journal note.

Search – search required information from current design or existing open windows journal notes, click on search type search keyword and click on find for search text in previous and next order continuously.

Save – save current windows journal notes in hard disk storage location, remember if any information save or store it can be access or modified any time anywhere.

Save as – save as save current windows saved journal with new name new location new identity as a secondary copy or primary save copy, if primary copy lost secondary used as purpose of primary copy.

Export as – export current existing saved windows journal notes information in web archive (.mht, mhtml) file format or tagged image file format save format support web browser.

Move to folder – move current design windows journal note in existing folder or create new created folder for move desire notes in it.

Delete note – delete note option used while you really don't need current note in required list, click on delete note and apply delete note option to delete permanently.

Page setup – set page of printed windows journal note customize paper size orientation style background and title information, according to need.

Print – print current existing windows journal content with attach printer, customize printer dialog setting before printing.

Send to mail recipients – send current windows journal note as mail recipient's journal note, web page, black and white image tif file format attach and send to the required e-mail user.

Recently notes – view list of recently access used journal, click on any recent note list open it make any changes print it edit it quickly.

Exit – exit windows journal window, it like stop working after done work.

Edit menu

Undo in stroke – undo given stroke apply before few moments ago, it like remove unwanted editing effect action in active journal note.

Can't redo – can't redo option reverse undo in stroke effect, redo reappear undo effect action in windows journal notes windows.

Cut – cut unnecessary unwanted windows journal paragraph text content information from new windows journal note window, cut journal note paste at new location.

Copy as text – copy as text windows journal control enable you copy only journal note text exclude all other information placed in windows journal notes.

Copy – copy repeated similar information, copy placed copy content in clipboard a temporary area where placed copy content and paste it at required location in windows journal.

Paste – paste option paste windows journal content at required location in windows journal windows, remember copy contain paste many time.

Selection tool – selection tool enable you to select, select windows journal text content area according to need.

Select all – select all windows journal note for editing custom changes, remember after selection possible to make desire changes.

Select page – select page option enable you to select complete page for editing custom changes, cover all page from all side.

Cancel selection – cancel selection option deselect all selection in windows journal note, cancel selection remove selected windows.

Delete – delete page delete current open windows journal windows, delete unnecessary unwanted windows journal information or complete page.

Find – find required text information content in open windows journal windows, find journal text in previous or next direction continuously.

Go to page – go to page directly move cursor location at required page number in number of pages display in current windows journal.

Format – format selected windows journal text information, formatting windows content according to need.

View menu

Toolbar – toolbar windows consist common use toolbar list, click on toolbar menu check on check off available choice of toolbar in windows journal, on off standard, pen, format, view in windows journal software.

Page bars – show or hide page bar show at bottom of windows journal windows note.

Recent notes – view recent viewed list of windows journal note, click recent note view by list, by folder, by creation date, by modification date, by flag order.

Refresh – refresh current windows journal notes information.

Page width – view current windows journal note according page width size, page width increase full size of page margin from all side.

Whole page – whole page option display windows complete in single windows, text size paper size automatically reduce.

Two pages – display windows journal in two page if, display windows in two pages while multiple pages display in current windows journal.

Reading view – reading view allow you to display windows journal note in reading view.

Zoom – zoom windows journal note size between 15% minimum to 200% maximum, set zoom level between these given ranges.

Full screen – full screen windows enable you to display windows journal note in full screen view remove unnecessary bar menu and toolbar.

Insert menu

New page – new page option allows you to create new windows journal pages, new pages automatically add new windows journal pages in sequences.

Insert/remove space – insert and remove space between current windows journal text information, first add space and remove space.

Text box – insert text box anywhere in windows journal windows note, text box allow to create text information in rectangular windows.

Picture – insert picture at required windows journal location, picture provide commercial meaning for any windows journal.

Flag – insert red, green, blue, purple, and flag at current cursor location, stretch inserted flag location and make large size of flag.

Action menu

Convert selection to e-mail – convert windows journal notes in e-mail format, it mean send select journal note as e-mail to the recipients client.

Convert handwriting to text – convert windows journal note in handwriting text format, handwritten display odd from computer script written method.

Group – group selected object in windows journal, first of select desire object in windows journal now try to make group in windows.

Group as one word – group as one word option group all object as one word in windows journal, first of all arrange all object as a single object.

Ungroup – ungroup all windows journal selected object for ungroup order, it detach all attach group object in windows.

Change shape to – change shape selected journal shape into available shape format for windows journal in windows 10 operating system.

Tools menu

Pen – change windows journal note pen color in black, red, black fine very fine pen format, click and select desire pen format according to script requirement.

Highlighter – display color full highlighter in background of windows journal text, select highlighter from highlighter choice are medium yellow, bright green, pink, turquoise, light orange etc.

Eraser – choose eraser for removing unwanted background color text drawing shape from eraser, select eraser size in small, medium, large, stroke, click select eraser and erase windows journal text.

Pan – pan option display hand sign to you select hand sign to move windows journal text in top to bottom direction continuously.

Option – customize option setting of new format, view and order tab, journal font, pen, measurement, journal note page view, language, automatic save, and many other essential setting configure related journal note.

Install or repair journal note writer – install windows journal print driver for printing journal individually from attach printer, now you can print journal with journal note writer.

Help menu

Windows journal help – windows journal help describes or guide you how to operate basic function of windows journal, how to create save print and other journal information.

About windows journal – about windows journal dialog describe you, product version, copy right information, license agreement, and install operating system information.

Windows power shell ise – windows power shell is cui(character user interface) and gui(graphical user interface) command based shell scripting programing language, it is object depend microsoft, net framework through power shell user manage automation services include automation task even develop power shell based system management tools, in work with microsoft .net framework as scripting language all power shell task execute in cmdlets called(command lets) is a group collection of .net classes, even we say that windows power shell is command prompt even more then command prompt because user create command module script or apply command in power shell .

How to start windows 10 windows power shell ise

start – all program – accessories - windows system - windows powershell.
start – run – type – powershell.

Windows power shell

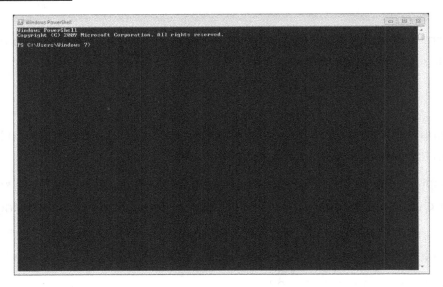

Windows dvd maker – windows dvd maker install automatically while windows 7 operating system install in any computer, it may be laptop, desktop or notebook, commercial and entertainment use of windows dvd maker tool to create video, picture, slide show, of adding video, movie, picture add dvd maker effect to make attractive provide commercial effect on selected video, picture gallery, and view them on computer, laptop, television, tablet pc etc. Change menu on video picture slide show, menu style, menu text, include font, add dvd title, and configure other detail and finally burn it, before burning insert new blank cd dvd finally press burn button to burn dvd.

Start windows dvd maker

- ⮞ Click on start menu in windows 7 click on all program click windows dvd maker to open it.
- ⮞ Click start select run type dvdmaker.exe.

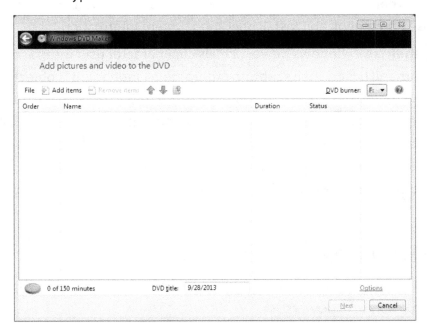

How to make dvd video picture

➲ Click on add items option in windows dvd maker.

➲ Browser video/picture whatever you select in this category.

➲ Select video/picture one by one or all at time click add to continue.

➲ Remove item any video/picture from video picture collection.

➲ Move up down video picture location.

➲ Click next configure ready to burn dvd dialog and configure menu text, customize menu or display slide show edit before preview menu style select menu style best meet your requirement now finally burn it for making in process of dvd.

Windows dvd maker window

File menu

New – create new dvd audio video picture project, çombine your digital handy cam, camera, web camera video add item and configure other setting in complete process of making new dvd video viewing on your laptop, desktop, or television set.

Open project file – open previous storage save dvd project for editing preview custom changes, add new effect, remove previous unnecessary effect from current project.

Save – save current windows dvd picture project for future reference use, remember if project save than increase chances to modify or editing.

Save as – save as option provide facility to save current working project with new name or new location, save as similar to save but it shows you again save windows dvd maker project with new strategy.

Exit – exit windows dvd maker software.

Windows fax and scan – windows fax and scan program enable you send and receive fax from your computer, even scan document, image, text, graphic from attach scanner device, but you must have installed before fax data supported modem properly configure according to need.

How to start windows fax and scan

➲ Click on start menu click on all program choose windows fax and scan application to open it.

➲ Click on start choose run type wfs.exe.

Windows fax and scan windows

Title bar – title bar display at the top of windows fax and scan application software, it indicate title of open or using current fax and scan object in application, you know name or title of using current object through title bar, you see here fax and scan logo include minimize, maximize or restore button also on windows fax and scan title bar.

Windows Fax and Scan

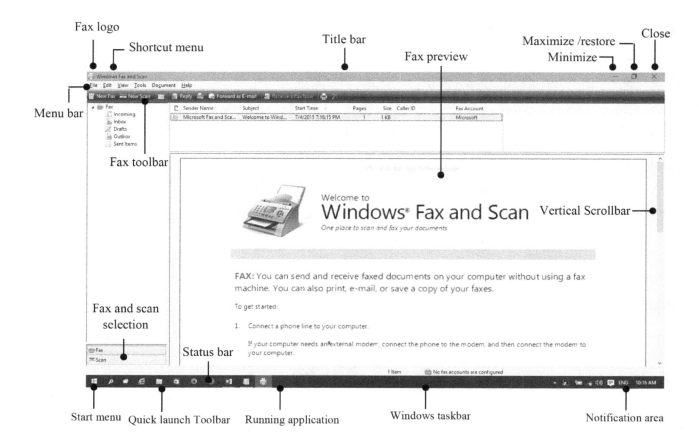

Menu bar – menu bar located after title bar in windows fax and scan software, by default menu bar display 6 default menu for controlling windows fax and scan operation, they allowed you to manage and control scan and fax related routine activities easier from using help with menu bar.

Toolbar – toolbar display below menu bar in windows fax and scan application software, generally every toolbar contains most routine application most/more usable shortcut for direct access with help of toolbar you can perform routine application important task easier or faster.

Status bar – status bar displays at the bottom of the windows fax and scan software, every status bar shows current show application status, by default it is ocated at the bottom of current windows fax and scan software, you know about working activities through status bar.

Preview bar – preview bar important bar in windows fax and scan software, it shows preview of using current object in windows fax and scan software, you view complete display of created fax or scan object through preview bar, now you decide about making some changes in current design object through preview pane in simple, it show overall structure of using or created object in fax and scan software.

File menu

New – new option gives you three different choices for creating new items for windows fax and scan application, it allow you to create new fax, create new scan or use fax from scanner, select your desire choice from given option and continue to create it, here you select proper your new choice elements for fax and application software.

Fax – create new fax option enable you to deal with new fax creation procedure, follow step by step involve during creating new fax, remember before apply these option you must configure before your fax and scan hardware properly to communicate with new fax creation wizard, it giving you to connect with internal fax modem or fax server, enter proper new fax created and follow its instruction.

Creating new fax windows option

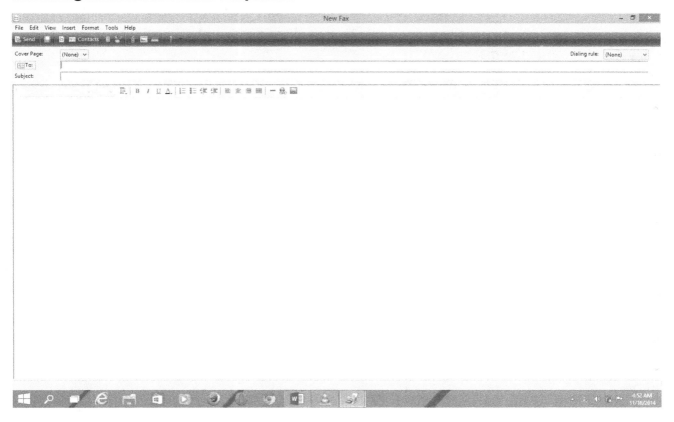

File menu

New fax – new fax option allow you to create new fax for windows user, now after creation new fax option it will represent you new fax windows here you enter receiver/recipient information, subject of compose fax, in new fax body area type the fax information content or detail, now format current design fax content with adding font attributes include font, font size, font color, bullets, hyperlinks, image, increase or decrease indent effect on it.

Send fax – send fax option enable you to start process of sending current design new fax, before apply these operations you must remember your network internet phone line connection must be connected even fax installed pre-configured, now click to send fax option to send it at recipient's address, if everything is proper than fax sending at recipient's address properly.

Save – save option allow you to save current send or design fax at local hard drive partition for future reference, remember, if fax saves on local partition than you can access, it according to need, even save option preserver your content.

Delete fax – delete fax option allow you to delete current working fax immediate, if you really don't want it, but if you need it than carefully apply these option because it removing your fax content.

Print – print option enable print option enable you to print current design fax, it produces hard copy of fax created content, configure properly fax setting and apply print command to print it.

Properties – properties fax option enable you to display you properties about current using fax detail like message type, location of current design fax, size, attachment, priority, sent, and received detail view through properties dialog box.

Close – close option in new fax windows immediate terminate new fax design windows.

Edit menu

Undo – undo last three fax use operation in windows fax dialog, it enable you to undo last using action or text type by you and suddenly erase, in simple it move back in previous situation.

Cut – cut option is a common option used in many windows based software application software, now we see cut option in reference of windows fax and scan option, here it only used for cut any unnecessary unwanted text from newly design windows fax, even cut text can be placed at new location through paste option.

Copy – copy option enable you to copy similar repeated content in windows fax and scan software, copy option save your time and money, if similar or common text information used one or more location than, it simple used with copy and paste command, copy command keep copy value in buffer called temporary space of computer memory some time called clipboard.

Paste – paste option work after copy option it enable you to paste copy text content one or more time at same or different location, paste option paste copy fax content at body in new fax design windows.

Select all – select all option enable you to select all text appear in new design fax window, remember without selection you can't able to making desire modification in created fax content or material, after selection a normal white fax text windows text immediate turn in blue selection mode.

Find – find option also used in most windows application, these option immediate enable us to find required text, content, numeric, string, or other information in current design new fax windows, with the help of find dialog box you quick search required information in newly design fax text.

View menu

Formatting bar – formatting bar contain some important fax software routine most usable control that quickly access with formatting bar, by default formatting toolbar display below of the menu bar, form view menu you enable to make enable or disable formatting toolbar in new fax design windows.

Status bar – status bar display the status of current using application features, by default it is display at the bottom of any windows application software, form view menu in new design fax windows you able to making appear of disappear status bar in new design fax windows.

Preview – preview windows display preview of new design fax content output, form view menu in new design fax, now here you able to making enable or disable preview windows from new design fax option.

Insert menu

File attachment – file attachment option in insert menu enable you to add or attach file along send fax in new fax design windows, click on file attachment you getting insert attachment dialog now pick desire attachment files or content one by one or more, then apply send command to send attach content along newly design fax content.

Picture – picture option enable you to adding or inserting picture graphic image or other visual graphical content in newly design fax windows, you can insert one or more picture in fax according to need, finally click on send button to send all included content with send fax.

Text from file – text from file option enable you to adding text from belong to windows notepad application software, attach or browser required text from file content in newly design fax, finally click on send button to send along attach text from file content along new design fax content.

Pages from scanner – pages from scanner option direct allow you to insert pages from windows fax attach or installed scanner device, first of all picture document or other visual content you want to insert in newly design fax insert in installed scanner device and click on scan even page from scanner, now properly insert or scan image from scanner in design fax, finally you ready to deliver or send design fax at recipient's address.

Horizontal line – insert horizontal line at required location in new design fax windows, inserted horizontal line divide current new design fax into two or more section, click at the position wherever you want to be insert horizontal line in design fax, remember you may insert one or more horizontal line in new design fax windows.

Page break – page break option enable you to insert a page break in current design fax windows, a page break option start new section in design fax windows, you may insert one or more page break in design fax windows according to need.

Format menu

Font – font option enable you to making attractive commercial or standard look appearance of your design newly fax content, it allow you to change font, font style, font size, font color, font effect etc. On selected newly design fax content according to need, font dialog contain many font script that change your computer paragraph script in various format select desire one and make it permanent with send fax.

Paragraph – paragraph option allow you to set alignment for selected paragraph text from left, center, right or justify direction select one of and your new design fax selection will be moved or place according to paragraph alignment selection, even it allow you to adding bullets front of selected new design fax content remember bullets may be number or bullets front of selected fax text.

Increase indent – increase indent format menu option enable you to moving step by step selected new design fax selected text from left to right direction according to need, now it depends on you wherever you want to be see selected text with increase indent option.

Decrease indent – decrease indent option in format work opposite increase indent option, it enable you to revert action of apply by increase indent option, now it allow you to move text from right to left direction easier with decrease indent option in windows fax and scan.

Tools menu

Sender information – sender information option in tools menu enable you to adding all sender or display send information about sender detail like sender name, fax number-mail address, title, office location, home phone, address, company, department, work phone etc. view in sender information easier getting from tools menu.

Check names – check name of send fax user, if any name of fax sender user will be incorrect then more chances to go on wrong route of network path in network location.

Select recipient's – select recipient's option in new design fax option enable you to selecting contact from select recipient's list, these dialog contain list of common or routine recipient's detail pick one of them your recipients and client to ok, even it allow you create new recipients from new contact option, finally apply send fax command to deliver design fax at destination address.

Contacts – contact option immediate moves you in contact folder appear in windows 8 contact group, here you import contact, create new contact group, import, export contact, even create new folder according to need, here you pick contact from contact to in new design fax.

Set priority – set priority of design fax between low, normal, or high, set your category from given option and configure according to your fax requirement, given priority option decide nature of created fax in fax list.

Options – option dialog enable you to configure option setting related new design fax, here you configure about delivery reports, e-mail configuration, priority, fax schedule or other remaining fax related configuration customize, if really need to customize it otherwise it works by default in good condition.

Help menu

About windows fax and scan – about windows fax and scan option describe you detail about using current microsoft application product like product name, version, copyright information, license agreement, operating system version etc. It is called digital certificate which complete tell about using product specification related query.

Scan – scan fax and scan option enable you to scanning fax object through installed scanner software, must remember these option work proper while you already installed scanner software and configuring properly it, now you able to scan document, picture, graphic, and other visual graphical visual material for new fax created services.

Fax from scanner – fax from scanner option enable you to send additional item through fax from scanner object, it direct send scanner object through fax service you must insert fax attach content with installed scanner now click on fax from scanner option to done these procedures well.

Open – open command allows you to open existing created or received hard drive storage fax and scan material according to need, first of click on open command now select the hard drive path and choose open object between fax and scan to work with now.

Save as – save as option enable you to save current created fax and scan object with different name and location, it also helping you to creating new file with new name with another copy at new location on local hard drive.

Print – print option enable you to print current or existing fax and scan content from local hard drive partition, open my document select fax and scan folder now open it and apply print command configure print dialog properly and finally apply print command to producing a new print hard copy.

Exit – exit menu enable you to terminate current windows fax and scan software immediately.

Edit menu

Delete – delete option allow you to delete existing or current windows fax and scan object according to need, first of all click on delete option now select the local hard drive path for deleting windows fax and scan object, browse and select fax and scan object finally click on delete button to delete fax and scan object according to need.

Select all – select all option enable you to selecting all current object content, object content may be windows fax and scan material remember, select all option allow you to making desire modification on current using object in windows fax and scan material, without selection no possible to make desire modification or changes on application using object.

Select none – select none option allow you to deselect previous apply select all command effect revert position, while you applying select none command than all previous selection discarded even text blue selection will be turn in normal white text color.

Invert selection – invert selection windows fax and scan windows fax and scan option enable you to making invert selection in current windows fax or scan selection.

Mark as read – mark as read command mark windows fax and scan content for reading for user, you manually selection which fax and scan elements ready for user read or not, if you mark for reading than you able to read any time of windows fax and scan object.

Mark as unread – marks as unread windows fax and scan option make mark for unread windows fax and scan object from local hard drive location, if you marking any fax or scan object for unread than you don't read it in category for mark as read.

Refresh folder – refresh folder option allow you to making refresh folder for windows fax and scan, every time when you click on refreshing folder option you will wait and it receive new fax from modem or fax server.

View menu

Arrange by – arrange by option enable you to arranging received fax and scan content in specific order, arrange by option provide you various category of choice for arranging fax object in desire given choice from available option.

Status – status option enable you to arranging received fax content in according to status order, after applying the status option for arranging you see all received fax content would be display as status order.

Fax account – fax account option arrange all received fax from sender side, whenever arranging all fax in fax account order these show first fax account wise detail of received fax content.

Number of pages – number of pages' option allow you to arranging all received fax content as number of pages' order display.

Csid – csid option allow you to arranging all received fax according to csid inbox order, it display all fax content in csid preview order.

Tsid – tsid option also arranging all inbox fax content in windows fax and scan order, tsid show all fax according to tsid order.

Size – size option enable us to arranging all received inbox fax content according it its size order, now you can see also size of all received fax with incoming fax in windows fax and scan.

Dialing attempt – dialing attempt option arranging all inbox received fax content according to dialing attempts, you see them according to need.

Jod id – job id fax arrange option enable you to arranging all received inbox fax according to job id, now you see them according to job id order.

Broadcast id – broadcast id arrange by option all received inbox fax according to its broadcast order id mode, now you can see them as broadcast id wise preview mode.

Caller id – caller id option allow you to arranging all received inbox fax content according to caller id order, now you see them as caller id wise in windows fax and scan view.

Transmission start time – transmission start time option enable you to arranging all received fax content according to transmission start time order, now you see them as transmission wise.

Transmission end time – transmission end time option arranging your all inbox received fax content in transmission end time preview, now you see them as transmission end time preview mode.

Transmission duration – transmission duration arrange by option enable you to arranging all received inbox fax according to transmission duration wise, now you see them as transmission duration wise all received fax content.

Subject – subject arrange by option enable you to arranging all inbox received fax content as subject wise, now you see all inbox fax in subject wise preview.

Receipt name – recipient's name option arranging your received fax content according to all receipt name wise display, now you see them as receipt name.

Receipt number – receipt number option arranging all received inbox fax as receipt wise, now you able to view them to view them as receipt number order.

Other – other option is also allow you to arranging all received inbox fax content in various other order, the other option differentiate choice between normal arrange by order and other arrange by method.

Device – device option enable you to arranging all received fax content and device wise display, now you able to view them as device category view.

Routing information – routing information option enable you to arranging all inbox received fax in routing information wise display, now you able to view them as routing information wise.

Document name – document name option enable you to arranging all received fax content as document wise, now you able to view all received fax content as document name order.

User – user option allow you to arranging all received fax according to user setting wise, now you able to view all fax content as user wise display.

Priority – priority option allow you to arranging all receive inbox fax content in priority wise order, now you able to see all inbox received fax as priority wise.

Original time – original time option allow you to arranging all received inbox fax content as original time wise, now you able to view them as original time.

Submit time – submit time option enable you to arranging all received fax content as submit information wise, now you able to view them as submit time wise fax content.

Billing code – billing code option arranging all fax content as billing code wise, now you able to view them as billing code wise display or fax content.

Send time – send time option arranging all inbox received fax content as send time wise display, now you see them all arrange fax as send time preview order.

Extend status – extend status option arranging all your received fax content as extend order wise display, now you see them as extend preview wise order.

Current page – current page option enable you to arranging all received fax content as current page wise display, now you able to view all fax content as current page display.

Sender name – sender name option allow you to arranging all received fax content as sender name detail wise display, now you see them as sender name wise detail.

Sender number – sender number option enable you to arranging all received fax inbox content as sender number detail wise information, now you able to see all fax as sender number preview order for display.

Toolbar – toolbar option allow you to making enable or disable current show windows fax and scan standard toolbar from windows fax and scan application view, by default it show in windows fax and scan these toolbar contain important fax and scan quick shortcut you can immediate execute them or perform desire task.

Status bar – status bar display at bottom of windows fax and scan program, generally it show status about current application using object, here you able to making enable or disable status bar in windows fax and scan software according to need.

Preview – preview option allow you to making show or hide preview windows in windows fax and scan software, you just click on preview check box to show or hide it according to need, main role of preview option to show overall structure of design windows fax and scan object in windows fax and scan software.

Go to – go to enable you to selecting choice between go to selection of fax view or scan view choice, select one of them that currently display in windows fax and scan in display.

Fax view – fax view option display all fax related menu control toolbar and dialog that are necessary to manage fax related control and activities in windows fax and scan software.

Scan view – scan view option moves fax view to scan view generally scan view show all scan fax document picture or other electronic content that are necessary to use along with send fax.

Zoom – zoom option enable you to fix size of zoom windows fax and scan document, you can increase minimum to maximum size of windows fax and scan elements it gives option choice between 25% to 200% zoom size of view fax and scan content, even you display it fit to page or fit to width according to need.

Add/remove column – add remove column option enable you to adding or removing column for windows fax and scan elements in windows fax and scan application package you can move available column into displayed column according to need.

Tools menu

Sender information – sender information windows fax and scan elements display all windows fax and scan sender detail during send any scan fax content to the recipient's address, you can add sender name, full name, address, contact, e-mail, office location, work phone, home phone etc. Remember these information telling receiver about sender detail information.

Cover page – cover page decorate your fax and scan documents, it allows you to modify existing cover page create new cover page, open existing cover page, copy, rename, or delete cover page of fax content.

Contact – view or move direct in contact folder where you store your recipient's contact, with them you communicate for exchanging regular fax and scan document every day these contact may be your business partner or business colleagues or business associate, even all these contact keep regular update about your company related group of people, company, or individual.

Fax status monitor – fax status monitor option enable you to view status about using or sending fax in windows fax and scan menu, status represent you about the detail information about using or designing fax content in windows.

Receive a fax now – receive a fax now option allow you to receive a new fax from recipients from fax server through modem, periodically these process repeat for every day for checking new fax from its server, it automatically download all new fax from fax server.

Fax setting – fax setting option enable you to configure current install fax modem configuration, these setting allow you to send as well as receive fax from windows fax server location, by default these setting configure properly if you really want to edit or modify than click to modify or edit it according to need.

Fax account – fax account enable you to create new fax related setting, now here you configure your fax server setting you can connect your system to fax modem or you able to connect fax server on my network configure both setting properly and follow instruction properly till than fax setting not properly configured.

Options – option dialog allow you to configure default fax related setting, if you don't want to change it than leave it default or want to change than you can change general, recipient's, send, or compose fax related configuration again configure but you need detail knowledge before do this.

Document menu

Reply – reply document option enable you to reply of any received scan fax document from user side, reply belong to response about received query from our client side, select the fax content now click on reply button to done these procedure.

Forward – forward option enable you to forwarding any received fax from another client or company, it direct allow you to forwarding any received microsoft fax to the another windows client, forward option important while some common fax content send one or more individual at a same time, than we use forward option to done it.

Forward as e-mail – forward as e-mail option enable you to sending or forward any received windows fax and scan content to another windows fax received user, before apply these option you must pre-configure you installed microsoft outlook software because while you ready to send or forward current fax as e-mail option than it direct moves in outlook application software.

Pause – pause windows fax and scan document operation during running mode, even it stop user created task immediately while user press pause button to control windows fax and scan operation, when you want to resume windows fax and scan content again press on pause button to resume it.

Resume – resume button work opposite pause button these option enable you to resuming pause button operation, it works when you already pause any windows fax and scan operation, you click on resume option to resume pause operation.

Restart – restart option of document menu enable you to restart and pause or resume windows fax and scan operation in microsoft windows and fax operation, it start any process from beginning mode.

Help menu

View help – view help option show all well define collection of each topic in sequence describe properly related to window fax and scan description, click on view help option and select desire topic from it now explore required content in it.

About windows fax and scan – about windows fax and scan option describe you detail about using current microsoft application product like product name, version, copyright information, license agreement, operating system version etc. It is called digital certificate which complete tell about using product specification related query.

Windows media player – windows media player is entertainment, multimedia application software, it allow you to run audio, video cd, dvd file format, play movie of bollywood hollywood listen mp3 song view moview play other movie, supported extension, use windows media player application software, while you free form official work, insert cd dvd double click and run it, burn cd dvd multimedia file view picture play recorded tv video display list of playlist starting sync media information with attached device.

Windows media player window

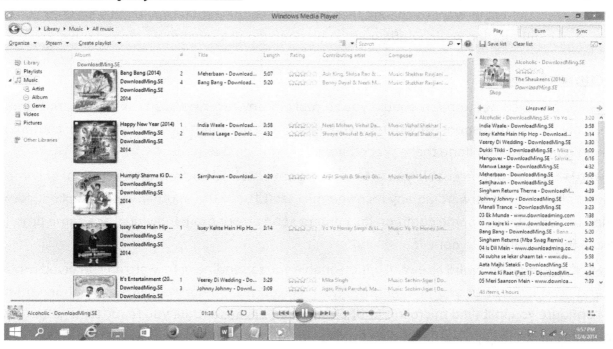

File menu

Open – open media file mp3 supported movie extension, click on open menu browse storage location of movie audio video finally click to play them one by one.

Open url – open url media file form website, click on open url now type web address browse streaming audio device file in windows media player software.

Save as – save option allow you to save current media format content in disk, for future reference.

Close – close option close open windows media player mp3 song video or other any media streaming format.

Create playlist – create playlist and group your favorite multimedia object in it, for routine play listen song or watch video.

Create auto playlist – click to create auto playlist option to click combo box and add windows media player library elements for creating auto playlist.

Save now playing list – save now paying playlist now option add all video audio save as playlist, you can play it any time again and again whenever you need to be play.

Save now playing list as – save current media player media file as different format like .wpl, m3u, asx, and any file format.

Manage libraries – manage libraries of windows media player in file menu for windows media player.

Work offline – work offline mode play all media stream from local hard drive, all playing media play from local hard drive, your network connectivity automatically would be disabling.

Exit – exit from windows media player multimedia software.

View menu

Library – default view of window media player is library view library view display library, playlist, videos, picture, recorded tv and other libraries all media album listed as thumbnail view from top to bottom click and play any video and audio format.

Skin – change library view to skin view skin view display multimedia in small skin format, play selected object in skin view window media player.

Now playing – now playing mode option play windows media player supported file format, now playing mode play supported format.

Skin chooser – skin chooser window media player option allows you to choose skin play for window media format.

Show menu bar – show menu bar in windows media player, even show or hide menu bar according to need in window media player entertainment software.

Plug-ins – view windows media player plug in list, even install online plug ins from microsoft website.

Dvd features – view inserted dvd features in windows media player, first of all insert desire dvd and check its features according to need in windows media software.

Switch to other program – switch current windows media player program to another program windows media program for user in windows.

File markers – file markers option enable you to view file markers related information in windows media player.

Statistics – view statistic related play multimedia object and information in windows media player, click on statistics to view them properly according to need.

Choose column – choose column for display along windows media player, these setting manually allowing you to selecting a desire number of column need to be display in windows media player.

Full screen – full screen mode display video in full size remove all, menu bar toolbar and other windows media player unnecessary dialog windows.

Refresh – refresh current playing media player format, refresh reactivate current playing version.

Video size – increase decrease windows media player playing format size between 50% to 200% according to need.

Play menu

Play/pause – play windows media player video film mp3 audio file, even pause windows media player elements.

Stop – stop current window media player supporting multimedia object format, stop video play again click on play menu play option.

Play speed – change current windows media player playing speed set between fast, medium, slow, default play multimedia object in normal mode.

Dvd vcd or cd audio – play dvd vcd or cd audio format from cd dvd driver directly, from dvd drive insert any multimedia audio video play with windows media player.

Previous – play previous audio video window media player format in previous order continuously, click on previous multimedia object continue.

Next – play next group of arrange multimedia object in multimedia media player format continuously next one by one.

Rewind – rewind multimedia object format continuously.

Fast forward – fast forward current multimedia object.

Shuffle – shuffle current multimedia object.

Repeat – repeat option repeat continue selected multimedia object continuously, whenever you want.

Audio and language track – play audio and language track it tag or list in windows media player, just click and play these audio track with supported apps.

Lyrics caption and subtitles – view playing media object lyrics caption and all subtitles include information through this options.

Volume – set multimedia object volume up down and make it finally mute, up increase volume of media down decrease level of volume current media format.

Eject – eject current cd dvd from dvd cd drive, these option ejecting immediate use multimedia audio/video compact disk form its location.

Tools menu

Download – download new plug ins, visualization, skin from microsoft website, you must should be online now download required content from website.

Apply media information changes – apply any media information changes in current media player entertainment application software.

Plug –ins – install or download windows media player additional plug ins to update windows media player elements.

Options – configure option related windows media player different tab setting, click any default setting if necessary to need to be customize.

Advance – configure advance setting related windows media player library setting,

Help menu

Windows media player help – get windows media player offline help to better understand working method of windows media player.

Windows media player online – connect windows media player online to get new advance features of windows media player.

Check for update – check for update option add on new advance updated features in existing installed windows media player software.

Privacy statement online – view windows media player related privacy statement from microsoft web site, read all privacy related information before using windows media player.

About windows media player – about windows media player describe you product version, license agreement, copy right information, end user license agreement.

TOPIC
03

Linux Overview and Introduction

Linux- an overview of linux

<u>Linux</u> – linux open source versatile multiprocessing, multitasking, multimedia, network capable, database connectivity, client server, operating system, developed and design by linus torvalds in before year 1990 at helsinki bell laboratories california, linux inspired from unix operating system, but unix and linux both individual different operating system both foundation on open source based, but pattern of working different form each other, linus torvalds create clone name minix than after some rename it linux o/s, linux completely free operating system but some condition commercial use it would be chargeable operating system, linux do everything do by other popular operating system like windows, unix, mac, android, linux created by many company organization or hundred thousand open source developer across the world wide online community, now linux used by many company, developer, organization, and it would be leading open source free operating system, linux provide user everything function and features other operating system like features.

What is a linux – linux is type of operating system like windows, unix, androids, and apple macintosh but these are pay operating system, but linux is completely free from client and commercial use, because linux developed by world developer community from different region and location, linux operating system iso freely available for downloadable or distributable along linux magazine, unix is a mother of linux operating system most linux features control application similar to unix but now days unix became completely outdated operating system, but linux still developed by many company and individual user developer worldwide for client and computer user, linux operating system available for install desktop, laptop, notebook, palmtop, smart phone, tablet, video game, client and server operating system, a special thing about linux operating system is it is highly performance service provide operating system that support any type of platform include hardware and software for its user, linux project started by mr. Linus torvalds when he was student of helsinki university (finland) in year 1991, linus torvalds work on unix clone called minix that time and finally he created clone of unix called minix and this is beginning of linux operating system, now many individual developed created own customized linux operating system on the base of linux kernel, linux kernel source available for free of cost for download across worldwide, even linus torvalds regularly maintain kernel of linux operating system, kernel is a core or heart of linux that manage relationship between linux services, hardware, and software.

Linux distribution

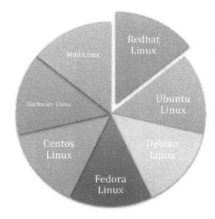

Other listed linux operating system list

Linux operating system name					
Debian linux	Open suse linux	Megia linux	Zorin linux	Puppy linux	Lubuntu
Kubuntu	Free bsd	Pc linux	Ultimate	Knoppix	Pc- bsd
4mlinux	Chakra linux	Ghostbsd linux	Sabyon linux	Mandriva	Suse
Vector linux	Solaris	Androids	Scientific linux	Fedora linux	Centos linux

Idea of a open source – idea of open source developed by open source apps creator, many advantage of open source application for those user they unable to buy license software product in category of operating system, open source office, database, web programming, open source programming language, other apps and manipulation software easier to access and learn with open source technology, online open source find equivalent license software open source software category without paying anything for using and accessing these application, run open source application on many supportive platform operating system to access and control these application features.

Why linux is not popular between ordinary – some people still think is linux is tough command line operating system, and need extra advance knowledge to learn linux operating system, but now day's linux developer company develop linux operating system with graphical environment like windows operating system include step by step dialog guide to complete any task like windows and mac os, but in past day linux access only by computer professional, developer, engineer, programmer include unix power user, and designer, it remain hard to learn for ordinary user, even old linux accessed from command line mode, and most of people access windows operating system, so they feeling difficulty during accessing linux operating system, but i telling you to about linux is a simple user friendly operating system that can do everything for you whatever does by other operating system available in market, so you try to started learn linux on basic step.

About unix operating system – unix operating system popular long time ago between computer professional and individual, even unix became father of modern operating system, when microsoft windows, and linux, operating system not popular or not developed in world of information technology, unix operating system developed in year 1970 by ken thompson and dennis ritchie (developer of c language) in bell laboratories, the source code of unix kernel written that time high level language called c programming, it make unix modern and different operating system during using, unix allow user to graphical environment, multi user, multi-tasking interface, and many more thing that make unix versatile operating system in that time.

Unix distribution

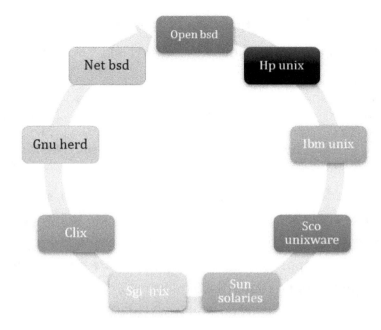

Difference between now days and traditional linux – linux and unix both are separate operating system, but most people and professional understand is a linux is complete clone or based on unix operating system, but we shall clearly sad about linux is a completely different operating system then unix, linux os inspired from unix but its basic structure completely different then unix os, linus torvalds written linux kernel code different from unix kernel.

Advantage of linux

Special linux advantage/features			
🖥️ Stability.	🖥️ Efficiency.	🖥️ Security.	🖥️ Networking.
🖥️ Flexibility.	🖥️ Open source.	🖥️ Free of cost.	🖥️ Multi user.
🖥️ Multi-tasking.	🖥️ Technical support.	🖥️ Console/graphical environment.	🖥️ Office productivity.
🖥️ Internet.	🖥️ Server.	🖥️ Free office suites.	🖥️ Accuracy in performance.
🖥️ Tough environment.	🖥️ Modern hardware support.	🖥️ Faster speed.	🖥️ Global advantage

Why use linux operating system

🖥️ Open source.	🖥️ Free of charge.	🖥️ Multiuser.
🖥️ Multi-tasking.	🖥️ Multiprogramming.	🖥️ Client server support.
🖥️ Multimedia support.	🖥️ Database server.	🖥️ Internet support.

⌨ Strong foundation.	⌨ Security.	⌨ Robust environment.
⌨ Windows similar application support.	⌨ Install windows os and application with wine package.	

Hardware specification for installing ubuntu linux

Sl. no	Minimum requirement	Recommended hardware
1	700 mhz processor (about intel celeron or better).	Intel 2.4, 2.6 microprocessor better intel i3, i5, i7 better performance recommended.
2	512 mib ram (system memory).	Ram 2 gigabyte or more.
3	5 gigabytes of hard-drive space.	500 gigabytes or 1 terabyte.
4	Vga capable of 1024x768 screen resolution.	Hdmi dvi based resolution.
5	Either a cd/dvd drive or a usb port for the installer media.	Wi-fi capability with ethernet.
6	(internet access is helpful).	Must be broadband.
7	Cd, dvd, bootable usb drive.	

Where to get ubuntu

- ➲ Buy ubuntu license dvd from ubuntu linux store.
- ➲ Download ubuntu latest version iso from its web site – www.ubuntu.com.
- ➲ Burn iso cd/dvd.
- ➲ Create ubuntu bootable usb flash drive.

Step during installation of ubuntu 13.10

- ➲ Restart computer press del, f2, f10, in entering bios.
- ➲ Select first boot device cd/dvd drive if boot from usb set first boot device usb drive.
- ➲ Ubuntu welcome screen appear follow instruction carefully.
- ➲ Must remember if multiple simultaneously installation of windows and linux ubuntu must keep backup secure, before formatting any windows partition, linux swap partition during installation so data can be lost for better prevention keep data back in secondary media device.

Linux ubuntu 13.10 installation procedure 1

- ➲ **Welcome screen** – welcome screen firstly appears while ubuntu booting from cd/dvd or usb flash drive, welcome windows provide you option for installation language choose, your country region language from subcategory, remember selected language used during and after installation.

- **Try ubuntu option** - enable you to try ubuntu latest distro/version without installing used new version features function menu application and control directly from cd or dvd.

- **Install ubuntu** – option permanently reside ubuntu in selected hard drive partition permanently, it is better option if you regularly used ubuntu from local hard drive even store data information and manage all ubuntu features.

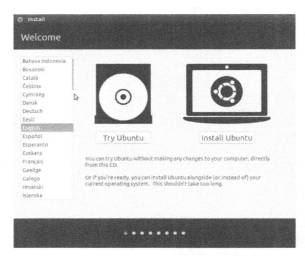

Preparing to install ubuntu – preparing to install option ready to install ubuntu, from inserted media, confirm reserve hard drive partition for installation for ubuntu client, at least 10gb partition necessary for better installation storage and os performance, always connect personal computer while install linux ubuntu and other operating system, it add install new version software update and other resources from ubuntu software center website, keeps you always update.

Download update while installing – these features enable you to get newest update, latest release of existing version from build date to today's till date, network connection properly connected even high speed broad band connection need for these otherwise installation time will be increase.

Install this third – party software – install third party resources from third party resources website, latest updates sources automatically update from ubuntu and other third party web site during installation, keep check mark on while installation continues.

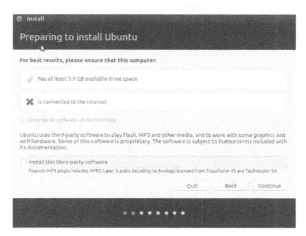

Installation type – select installation type during ubuntu installation ubuntu offer you multiple installation type choice, install latest ubuntu version with many criteria.

Install ubuntu alongside windows 10 – install ubuntu alongside windows 10 option appear while you install ubuntu along existing windows 7 with dual ubuntu installation, these option enable you to dual booting with lilo(linux loader) or grub linux boot loader after installation, you select windows 10 or linux ubuntu from both one at single time.

Replace windows 10 with ubuntu – replace windows 10 only appear while ubuntu installation begin with existing windows 10 installation, if you click it one remembers existing windows 10 operating system replace with ubuntu and it remove from installation drive, so carefully apply this, apply only while really you don't need windows 10 operating system with ubuntu, if click yes ubuntu installation single boot option

Erase disk and install ubuntu – erase disk and install ubuntu option enable while fresh single linux ubuntu installation started, if you are using 80 gigabytes or 500 gigabytes, 1 terabyte hard drive, it will convert all hard disk space size in single ubuntu installation partition.

Encrypt the new ubuntu installation for security – encrypt the new ubuntu installation for security installation method enable you to install ubuntu with encryption security for files and folder, encryption protect files and folder in online/offline communication mode.

Use lvm with new ubuntu installation – use lvm with new ubuntu installation type enable you to use partition with logical volume management for existing linux windows partition resizing, select existing partition that are resizing for new lvm ubuntu installation type.

Something else – something else option enable you to manually convert create resize partition of existing hard disk according to need, select hard drive is already partition created in windows version choose existing one else manually create new partition from menu choice, by default ubuntu support ext 3, ext 4 partition type where windows support fat, ntfs, partition type, create how much new ntfs, or ext 4 type partition for ubuntu installation, select first ext 4 partition for ubuntu installation and continue for next step, be strictly/careful if existing drive contain precious data and information take backup before any linux version installation.

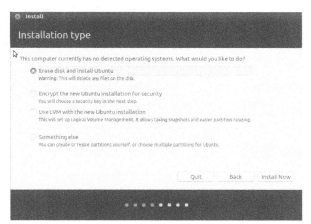

Where are you – where are you option allow you during ubuntu installation, select you country gmt/ist location in world map, even manually select country location on clicking word map automatically ubuntu set ist/gmt time zone according to your country/region, time zone display in ubuntu panel windows show current date and time according to select your continent zone.

Keyboard layout – select keyboard layout connection during linux installation, default selected english (us) common language during default ubuntu installation type, if you are form different region or country select french, germen, japanese, chinese, thai, hindi and other common keyboard layout from given subcategory, keyboard layout decide your working country language method.

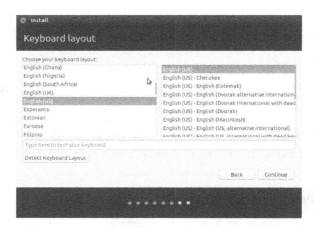

Who are you – who are you option allow you to create linux ubuntu user account, one account must essential created during installation, fill your name, computer name, pick a user name in given text box window, choose password method strictly restrict unauthorized, user access in ubuntu os, password protect your machine from illegal computer user even make secure your data and information, password should be strict alphabet, number, special character, small capital cap lock on/off, during password enter, remember never share password with all user you not trust them, enter password two time in who are you windows, select required my password to log in enable it, if you choose log in automatically it don't ask password during log in process, even encrypt my home folder with password protection.

One account to log in to everything on ubuntu – these are new features added in ubuntu latest version installation process, create ubuntu one account if you want to access all latest ubuntu related information, new releases of software, apps, photos, music, cloud, game, multimedia object, os version and other information, click to enter e-mail and password be member of ubuntu one linux services,

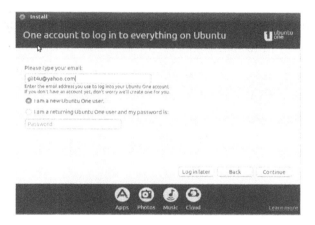

Install – installation begin and view installation screen application and other features, flashes in installation windows, at bottom you see installing system slider increases and install installation services till then completely install, you wait for a moment till then all installation files copies in dedicated hard drive partition.

Installation complete – installation complete dialog indicate ubuntu linux completely set up on your local hard drive remove all external bootable media and restart machine form configure all installation files or boot ubuntu from local hard drive partition, it gives you two option continues testing test install linux ubuntu version and restart again ubuntu version form local hard drive partition.

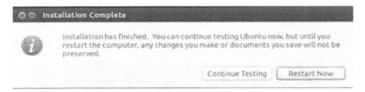

Basic linux

How to start linux ubuntu terminal.

Note – explain below some linux command need administrator/super user privileges for command successful execution.

Note – while you apply some linux command you see blue and white information where blue belong to the directory and white belong to file.

Df command – df command used for now complete information about how much free space available in current hard drive partition, df print report of free space, block space, even allocated space in current hard drive partition.

Output windows

    Syntax – # df

    Syntax – $ df

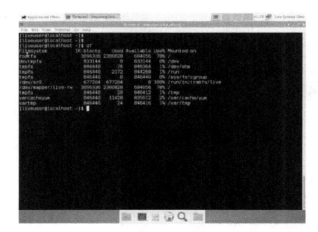

Du command – know information about current hard drive partition how much disk contain occupy, by file directory and other storage data in active mount drive these command list all file drive.

    Syntax – # du

    Syntax – $ du

Output windows

Ls command – ls command display complete information about current mount hard drive partition contain like file directory subdirectory, it completely similar to windows command prompt dir command.

Switch used along ls command

Switch	Description
L	Show owner, link, file size, access, and modify file information.
T	Show according to last modification time.
A	Show hidden file in current mount drive.
D	Show directory content information.
I	Show directory inode information.

Syntax – $ ls

Syntax – $ ls –a

Syntax – $ ls –i

Output windows

Note – all above ls command along switch display directory and file information.

More command – more command display remaining information of file and directory, it used with multiple switches.

    Syntax – # ls –a l more

Output windows

Shutdown – shutdown command allows you to immediately move back computer in shutdown mode, it force close all running application software and running task, similar in windows command prompt like c:\>shutdown –h.

    Syntax – # shutdown now

Output windows

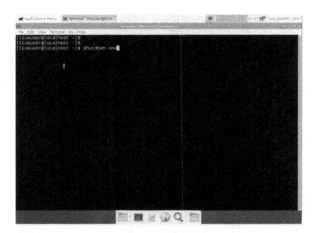

Note – above command shutdown computer immediately.

    Syntax – # shutdown now

Note – above command shutdown computer and restart immediately.

    Syntax – # shutdown -h +10

Note – above command shutdown computer after 10 minute.

Logout command – logout command terminate user console shell session on which shell user working type logout command to terminate or logout session window

   $ logout

Tar command – tar command extract zip files and folder in linux console location, some file zip or compress with compression utility software using tar console command to extract or revert compress data in their original condition.

Pwd command – pwd command display or print working directory information, if you want to know where are you in linux terminal directory type pwd command it will show you all detail about working directory structure.

   Syntax – # pwd
   Syntax – $ pwd

Output windows

Gzip command – gzip linux compression utility command that allows linux user to compress linux files to take less space and hard disk partition size so easier to carry and travel between network, using these command to compressing one or more linux platform created files and information.

   Syntax – # gzip filename.txt
   Syntax – # gzip myfile1.txt myfile2.txt myfile3.txt

Unzip command – unzip linux command unzip linux and other source created zip files format into unzip or extracting zip file in full format compression effect removes after applying unzip command.

   Syntax – #unzip data.zip

Ps command – ps command describe detail information about running process in active machine, you know which process running in current session.

   Syntax – # ps
   Syntax – $ ps

Output windows

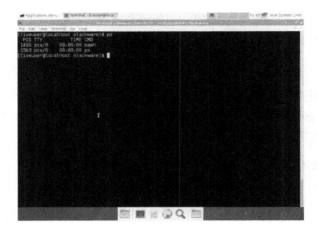

Kill command – kill command allow you to directly kill any background running process immediately, if you want free space for new process then terminate process with kill command.

> **Syntax** – # kill [job name]

Cat command – cat command used in linux console for creating as well as displaying content existing console created file information even display two or more information at a same time, it is similar to copy con command used in windows command prompt (ms dos).

Switch used along cat command

> **Syntax** – # cat > [filename]
>
> **Syntax** – # cat > first.txt
>
> **Syntax** – $ cat > one.doc

Output windows

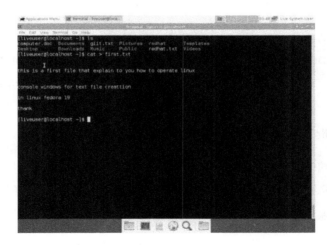

Note – remember after adding file information in cat command created file save file with ctrl + d.

Display file content with cat command

> **Syntax** – # cat first.txt one.doc

Output windows

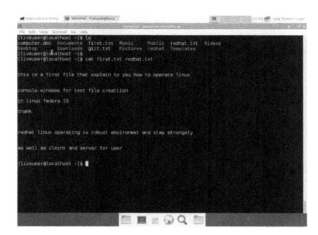

Note – the above given syntax display simultaneously two file content at a same time in console/terminal/root linux windows.

Rm command – rm command used in linux console for delete file from linux directory storage location, remember apply only really file doesn't need.

    Syntax – # rm first.txt

Output windows

Chmod – change mode command using linux console to providing user permission and rejecting user permission related to particular file name.

    $ chmod permission file

Cmp – cmp command used in linux console for making comparison between two different consoles created file find out line, paragraph, character, difference between two individual file.

    Syntax – cmp [first file] [second file]

    Syntax – # one.txt two.doc

Note – two file compare with line by line finally display difference between both of them.

Output windows

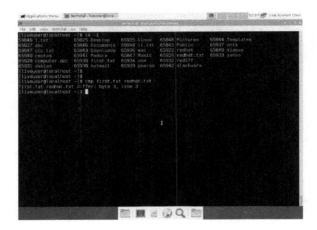

Cp command – cp command used for copy content of existing cat command created file, two file needed during cp command file approach file must already exist in disk second file that copy content of first file.

    Syntax – cp [source file] [destination file]

    Syntax – # cp one.txt two.doc

Output windows

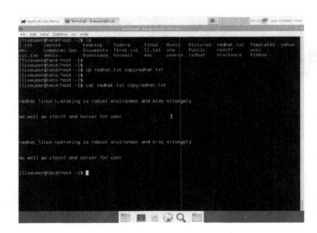

Note – above command copy one.txt file content in two.doc file even change one.txt extension from txt to doc extension.

Mkdir command – mkdir command allow us to create new empty linux console terminal directory for storage any information data file or sub folder, mkdir create new empty directory you can store desire resources in it, mkdir command similar to md command used in windows command prompt.

    Syntax – mkdir [directory name]

    Syntax – # mkdir ubuntu1

Output windows

Note – above command created new directory name ubuntu, you can graphically view it from linux home user directory location, now store desire information in it.

Cd command – cd command used for change working directory even view open linux created directory file sub directory information with cd command, same apply in windows command for change directory.

> **Syntax** – cd [directory name]

> **Syntax** – # cd abc

Note – above command open/change directory abc for view information.

> **Syntax** – # cd..

Note – above command moves you on root drive location you immediately exit from working directory.

> **Syntax** – # cd ~

Output windows

Note – above given linux console command moves you on home directory.

Rmdir command – rmdir command allow us to delete remove console based created directory and subdirectory, it very similar to windows rd command apply in command prompt for deleting existing directory.

    Syntax – rmdir [directory name]

    Syntax – # rmdir ubuntu

Output windows

Note – above command delete permanently ubuntu name directory previously created, be sure before delete any directory apply while really don't need directory.

Mv command – mv command used for dual operation in linux console window, mv command rename existing file name even move existing directory in another existing directory location, it is very similar to windows move command.

    Syntax – mv [old file name] [new file name]

    Syntax – # mv one.txt two.doc

Output windows

Note – above command rename file one.txt with two.doc.

> **Syntax** – mv [source directory] [destination directory]

> **Syntax** – # mv ubuntu redhat

Output windows

Note – above mv command move ubuntu directory in red hat directory, remember source directory must be exist destination directory automatically created even you manually created it.

User add command – user add command in linux console/terminal/root shell allow you to add a new user of existing list of user, but remember you must have privilege of administrative user for do this, it mean if you have power of root/super user facility than you can do it otherwise guest user don't possible.

> **Syntax** – # useradd amit

Output windows

Add user in graphical view windows

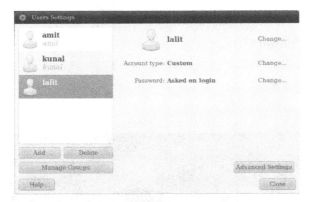

User del command – user del command use deleting existing client user from user group, while any user account unused and necessary to delete it permanently apply user del command with carefully, remember for deleting any user account must log in as administrator/root user otherwise no possible.

> **Syntax –** # userdel amit

Output windows

Del user in graphical view windows

Usermod command – user mode command used while existing user information needed to change type usermod command with given user name for making user account changes.

> **Syntax –** # usermod lalit

Groupadd command – group add command similar to add new user for current use account same these groupadd command allow you to add new group add in list of existing user group.

    Syntax – # groupadd admin1

Output windows

Groupadd in graphical view windows

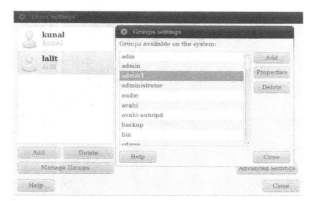

Groupdel command – group del command work opposite of group add command, while you really don't need to existing any group apply group del command to delete existing group permanently.

    Syntax – # groupdel admin1

Output windows

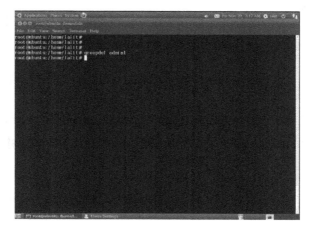

Groupdel in graphical view windows

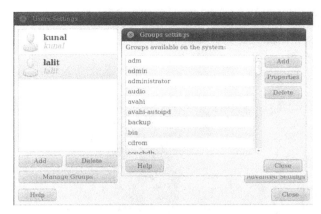

Wc command – wc command used to count line, word, byte, newline, from start to end file, apply wc command with given file and view wc report at bottom.

> **Syntax** – # wc redhat.txt

Output windows

Cksum command – using cksum command to check file input bytes count for particular input file, with cksum command you may know about corrupt data information during communication.

> $ cksum file.txt

Nl command – nl command using in linux to know actual number of lines in working file, these command very helpful while user ready to know the count of number of using file line number and other detail.

> $ nl file.txt

Time command – time command used in linux to know how much system or command take a time to find out result and perform calculation during supply command and string.

> $ time pwd
>
> $ time du

Uptime command – uptime linux command explain how much client currently working or log in in linux session even view information about log user.

> **Syntax** – # uptime

Output windows

W command – w command display information about log in user in current session show user information like user name, tty name, login time, and other essential detail.

> <u>**Syntax**</u> – # w

Output windows

Users command – users command print information about currently log in user name in active linux root/terminal/console session.

> <u>**Syntax**</u> – # users

Output windows

Whoami command – whoami command similar w command, it will also print information about current session log in user information.

   Syntax – # whoami

Output windows

Sudo command – sudo stands (super user do) sudo provide ordinary linux terminal user grant access of system privilege access and manage by root or admin user he can able to interact linux interface.

   Syntax – # sudo [option]

Sort command – sort command arrange your created existing file in ascending order, if you want to change file character sequence in descending user – r switch along sort command, it will sort complete file line in descending order.

   Syntax – # sort [filename]

   Syntax – # sort redhat.txt

   Syntax – # sort –r redhat.txt

Output windows

Vi command – vi stands visual editor unix/linux text based editor, allow you to create, edit, save, text file in linux, console/terminal session, but you must learn some command for operating visual edition while you open it, finally close vi editor: q command exit from vi editor.

     Syntax – # vi [filename]

     Syntax – # vi first.txt

Output windows

Chmod command – chmode command allow you to change mode of file access reading and writing permission control, alter modify permission with chmod command of linux files and directory.

Term used with chmod command

U – indicate about user.

R – provide read file permission.

W – provide user write permission.

<u>X</u> – enable user to execute permission.

<u>O</u> – other user provides privileges.

> **<u>Syntax</u>** – chmod u=rwx

> **<u>Syntax</u>** – chmod u=rwx, g=rx o= rw file.txt

<u>Chown command</u> – chown command allow you to change ownership of existing file directory in console windows, remember these command allow administrator privilege before logging you must log in as root user before apply these command.

> **<u>Syntax</u>** – # chown amit abc.doc

<u>Note</u> – above apply command change ownership of file abc with amit.

<u>Passwd command</u> – password command allows you to change password of your and other administrator sub category user, for these operation you must log in as root user otherwise you can't change password of created account.

> **<u>Syntax</u>** – #passwd

<u>Output windows</u>

<u>Note</u> – after applying above command enter current password type new account password again, type new password for confirmation now restart machine and type new password for linux log in windows.

<u>Ifconfig command</u> – ifconfig command display overall information about installed lan card/ ethernet card detail description quickly, even you know nic (network card interface) configuration overview.

> **<u>Syntax</u>** – #ifconfig

> **<u>Syntax</u>** – #ifconfig eth0 111.112.113.1 up

Output windows

___

Note – above command manually assign ip address to working installed ethernet card name eth0, if two or more ethernet card installed than type correct ethernet name properly.

___

Su command – su stands super user who get administrator privilege for accessing and allocating resources of active machine, apply su command with user name and became ordinary user to super user in this list.

   Syntax – # su username

   Syntax – #su lalit

Output windows

___

Note – now above command make lalit as super user access.

___

Man command – man command display help information about given linux terminal command, type man command along console command, you get basic help guide of about applying linux command.

   Syntax – #man mkdir

Output windows

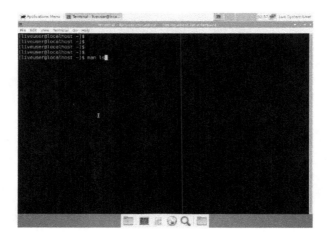

Note – above command display information about mkdir command in linux console.

Yum command – install windows services other program server program with yum (yellow dog update manager) utility.

> **Syntax** – # yum service name

Rpm command – install linux red hat supported rpm (red hat package manager) software application program in active linux red hat, centos and fedora linux operating system easier, remember never install .deb (debian)package along rpm because software package produce separate.

> **Syntax** – # rpm application name

Ping command – ping command check network connectivity between client and server machine, generally while apply ping command, it call server while server reply it mean network connectivity is in proper shape order with network connectivity.

> **Syntax** – # ping www.google.com

> **Syntax** – # ping 111.112.113.1

Output windows

 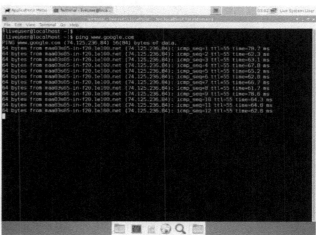

Date command – date command display print current system date include current date month and year, same apply in windows 8 command prompt for display date.

> **Syntax** – # date

Output windows

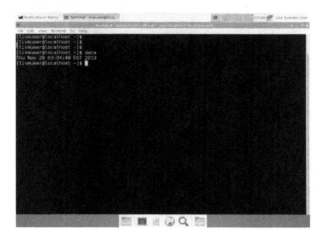

Dir command – dir command display list of all files and directory create in root drive linux console windows, but it can't filter difference between directory and file but ls command filter directory as well as file separately, similar command prompt used dir command in windows.

> **Syntax** – # dir

Output windows

Fdisk command – linux fdisk command to create new fresh linux based hard drive partition, view existing partition, delete, modify existing partition size, using multiple switches with fdisk command to know actual status about installed hard disk information by user.

> **Syntax** – # fdisk

Output windows

Bc command – bc command used in linux console windows for apply mathematical operation like addition, subtraction, multiplication, and division, similarly used in windows for calculator calc command for arithmetic math operation.

> **Syntax** – # bc

5+5

10

Output windows

Chgrp command – chgrp linux command used to change user group permission for using file, folders and directory, move user group into other linux user group mode,

> **Syntax** – $ chgrp mygroup file1.txt

Note – change group of file1.txt into my group in linux root location.

Clear command – clear command used to clear screen output of given command, it erase or clear all previous command apply output in terminal/console window, it very common command cls used in windows command prompt.

> **Syntax** – # clear

Output windows

Cal command – cal command using in linux console for displaying or view current month calendar information, you can view previous and next year month calendar as well as.

Option used along cal command

Switch	Description
1	View current month display
S	Start sunday first day of week
M	Start monday first day of week
Y	Show current year calendar

Syntax – cal option month year

Syntax – # cal 10 2013

Output windows

Halt command – halt command shut/turnoff computer immediately, closing all running linux application, it is similar to windows command prompt shutdown – h command.

Syntax – # halt

Syntax – $ halt

Output windows

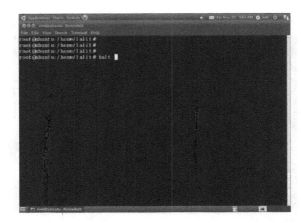

Power off command – these command immediately power off active running linux red hat, ubuntu and other linux flavor based computer machine.

   Syntax – # poweroff
   Syntax – $ poweroff

Output windows

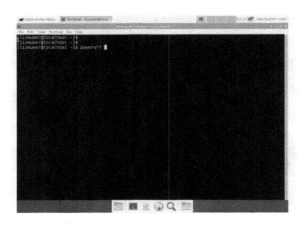

Reboot command – these linux console command immediately restart linux based install operating system machine, apply these command while need to reboot machine with root or terminal.

   Syntax – # reboot
   Syntax – $ reboot

Output windows

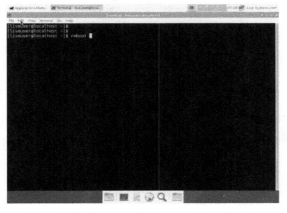

Host command – host command used to find information ip address of require url domain, display information about current domain name along internet protocol address.

> **Syntax –** # host

Output windows

Hostname command – hostname command describe the hostname description.

> **Syntax –** # yum service name

Jobs command – jobs command specially apply while you exactly know how much jobs/process running in background even foreground in current session, apply jobs command it will display list of jobs running in active session.

> **Syntax –** # jobs – l

Netstat command – netstat command display network status report port, protocol, socket and network device information.

Restore command – restore command using in linux to from its dump file location, generally restoring allows linux user to restore some required or necessary files from its default location.

> **Syntax –** # restore if – mybackupdata

Who command – who command display information about user who are currently log in working linux terminal session, even you know how much user actually working in current session in client server connectivity.

> **Syntax –** # who

Output windows

Whois command – whois command specially used in linux terminal for knows about any url domain owner information, type any url with whois command and see owner information.

> **Syntax –** # whois google.com

Output windows

Traceroute command – traceroute command explain description about how much packet are incoming and outgoing with traceroute process, you find out actually what network done in active session windows.

> **Syntax –** # traceroute www.google.com

Output windows

Nslookup command – ns lookup command used in linux console to find out information any url/ website domain ip(internet protocol)server address.

> **Syntax –** # nslookup [urlname/website name]
> **Syntax –** # nslookup google.com
> **Syntax –** # nslookup 192.168.1.1

Output windows

Finger command – finger command show you everything about current session login user information about like name, terminal detail, login time, and other essential detail along it.

    <u>Syntax</u> – # finger

    <u>Syntax</u> – #finger – amit

Output windows

Telnet command – using linux telnet protocol to connecting other linux installed telnet computer or terminal, both computer run simultaneously to connection and making telnet session, after connecting telnet session using its services and control.

    <u>Syntax</u> –# telnet

Pine command – pine command linux based e-mail program allows linux console user to check, view information about e-mail, news, and message broadcast updates, include other e-mail information, create new mail, view folder list, message index, and quit from pine e-mail program.

    <u>Syntax</u> – # % pine

Ftp command – ftp command used for connecting ftp (file transfer protocol) server for command line session, for these type ftp command along ftp server ip address.

    <u>Syntax</u> – # ftp 111.112.113.1

Output windows

Free command – display status about free swap memory in working linux terminal windows.

    Syntax – # free

Output windows

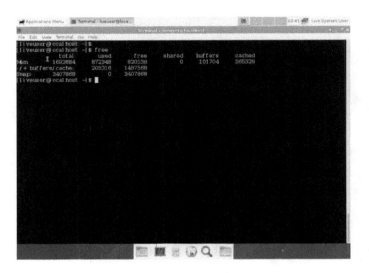

Basic linux elements

System features

Linux ubuntu software features – linux ubuntu software features allow you to download linux ubuntu software third party software even individual software, click on all software and select category software select accessories, developer tools, education, fonts, games, graphic, internet, office, science & engineering, sound & video, system, theme & tweak, universal access, category software listed and wait till permission ask enter password and wait till than software download, remember high speed broadband connection needed during installation selected software sources from software ubuntu software site, even here you view list of installed software, history and all software, search required application and directly installed in active operating system.

Popular linux ubuntu software features describe

Explore Ubuntu's features and apps

Web browsing   Office applications   Social and email   Music and mobile   Photos and videos   Games and apps   Personal cloud

Accessories features – accessories in linux ubuntu it contain basic accessories software utilities that are basically used application, these application are general purpose software package that normally used by any linux user these are listed here archive manager, calculator, character map, disk usage analyzer, terminal, screen shoot, text editor, panel notes and other application features you just compare, it with windows accessories you found many similarities with that and most application exact same like windows.

Game features – game features in linux it provides you collection of built in linux ubuntu card game that automatically loaded during linux ubuntu installation, click open and play game remember you must know how to play you found some similarities between windows and linux ubuntu game windows also provide you game application enjoy and play game while you relax mode on machine.

Developer tools features – developer tools contain development application package include c, c++, java, eclipse, neat beans, jdk, php sql, my sql, python, apache server and other online programming development tools download from third party software web site even main from ubuntu web site.

Education features – education features provide you collection of huge amount of various kids learning game application for your kids you can access the easily even download it from given software center website easily.

Font's features – font's features allow you to add install manually fonts in linux for open office, libre office, sun office, apache office, king soft office, download added fonts change script text appearance during display in related application software package, it is similar in windows control panel where we can manually install fonts according to need.

Graphic features – graphical feature provide graphical application that allow you to view edit photo, pdf document, manage photo operation, scanning images include, image viewer, just similar in windows image viewer or google picasa, acdsee and similar software package, download new graphical many online package from given url with high speed broadband connection.

Internet features – internet features allow to browse surfing online www content in linux environment linux provide many open source web browser for surfing like firefox, google chrome, safari, conqueror and many other with instant messenger, torrent client, remote desktop, internet chatting package, ftp package, net meeting/web conference package, terminal connection and many other manually downloadable from ubuntu software center, remember i again discuss you must have high speed internet connection for this, microsoft windows provide default browsing software name internet explorer but in linux you got lots of more choice for that.

Office features – office software package automatically install during most of linux operating system linux provide you many office choice like open office, libre office, apache office, sun office, kings office, abi word, calc, spreadsheet and many individual office application software package in modern linux distribution office package provide you everything that provide for windows user, many online office package available for your os download them from software center a collection of office package name.

Different name in linux office or microsoft office		
Sl. no	**Linux**	**Windows**
1	Dictionary	Spelling & grammar
2	Evolution	Microsoft outlook 2016
3	Evolution mail and calendar	Microsoft outlook 2016
4	Open office/libre office presentation/impress	Microsoft power point 2016
5	Open office/libre office spreadsheet/calc	Microsoft excel 2016
6	Open office/libre office writer/word processor/abi word	Microsoft word 2016
7	Open office formula	Microsoft equations
8	Drawing/tux paint	Ms paint

Programming features – in programming features you can view list of automatically programming software package manually added or automatically during linux operating installation even if you download manually installed programming listed in this category.

Science and engineering features – science and engineering option allow you to install download online science or engineering student related application software package linux software provider provide you many designing 3d automation 3d art and craft free software download and display in category of science and engineering, pick software package with root user privilege and install in your current machine.

Sound & video features – sound and video linux ubuntu features allow you to play listen music video burn data audio video dvd cd, record sound with sound recorder these are default loaded include linux operating system even if you want to install many multimedia application click on ubuntu software center pick sound and video category now you download desire audio video player and other multimedia utilities like vlc player, m player, banshee player, totem player, connect with high speed broadband internet and quickly download ubuntu automatically set download software in related category now you click ubuntu panel menu select application and launch it according to need.

System tools features – system tools feature allow you to configure system root related privilege configure any system related setting easier with system tools apply root command cui operation with root terminal window, even customization cd/dvd creator, configuration editor, file browser, root terminal etc. From system tools, it is similar to windows control panel administrative operation.

Theme & tweak features – theme & tweak features allow you to download new latest theme that change view of your installed linux appearance like menu, control, icon, desktop, panel, windows, right click menu, apply decoration attraction to your commercial look desktop, lots of more online theme and tweak available online for all linux distribution you can download them according to need.

Universal access features – linux universal access features allow you to operate internal onboard keyboard while internal keyboard don't work properly hit any key to type print text in open application windows, terminal easily type desire text in text editor, writer, impress, even enable magnifier for reading text in enlarge mode with orca application include speech recognition, pronunciation, text attributes, all these are more similar with microsoft windows on screen keyboard, speech recognition, magnifier, negotiation etc.

File structure

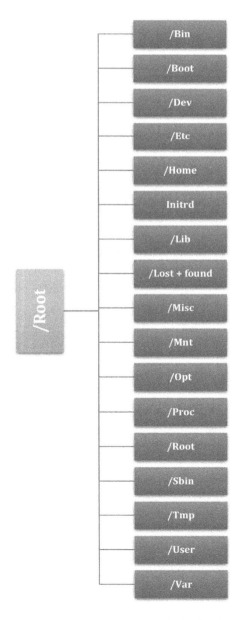

Explanation about linux roots and files structure

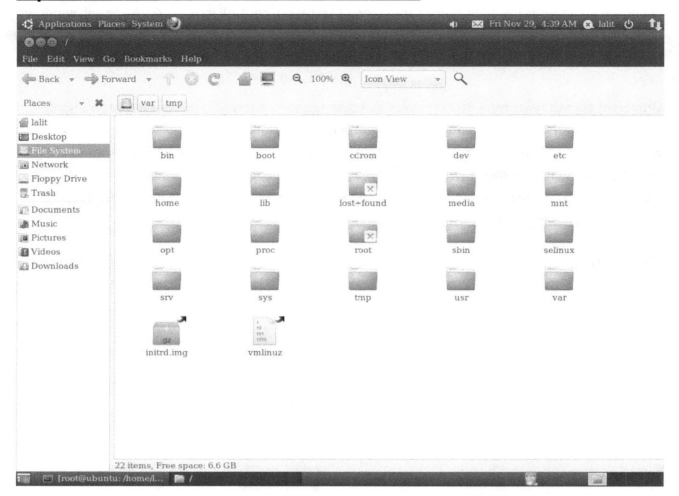

/root directory – root directory manages and control another directory created in linux operating system, root play role of group all linux directory management, every single file start from root directory location even root provide data access modification privilege, generally root directory store contain administrative task related directory that are not to be easier by any ordinary user for access theme must have root/super user privilege.

/bin directory – bin directory contain ubuntu linux binary command that are executed on terminal or root command prompt/terminal it in executable binary program running in linux environment, each command design for specific task from root location, it gives you control to manage administrative and network related task perform easier, it store most command executed in terminal these are ls, ping, grep, mkdir, pwd, cat, date, kill, ip, df, dd, log in, mv, su, tar and other command.

/dev directory – dev directory contain linux installed attached device directory information like installed disk, cpu, fdd, cdrom, net, terminal device directory cpu directory contain information about installed hardware software special properties, all device working manage related device task from device directory.

/etc directory – etc directory in linux operating system work like windows control panel that allow you to modify device system properties administratively, configure edit linux operating system startup shutdown password related script manually customize according to need, if you need to be customize any linux console/gui based services/etc directory contain related configuration click and custom with administrative access.

 /home directory – home directory similar windows 10 user where number of administrative guest or ordinary user list created each and every one access their terminal from user name and password, similar that in linux environment home directory contain information created in linux operating system, even it display list of number created linux user account include ordinary or administrative account view each user access desktop used application document download working directory files, store and access information even placed automatically manually installed application view from home directory.

/initrd directory – intird directory automatically created during linux operating system installation, it contains information about linux booting, in modern linux operating system you can't find it.

 /lib directory – lib directory contains linux operating system library file like kernel shared library bootable linux operating system image all library file access and used by linux user for proper linux functioning, even supported bin/sbin for each linux user.

 /lost + found directory – lost + found linux directory contain information unexpected error broken file during linux installation, you can easier recover lost file from here generally, it stores file that are failure even store corrupted file during disk check access them and restore at proper location.

/misc directory – these directory created for ordinary system miscellaneous target.

 /media directory – media directory store information temporarily mounted device information like floppy, cd rom, dvd rom, pend drive media file created automatically while using any installed or attach media device in linux operating system environment.

 /mnt directory – it contains mount device directory file that are connected in linux operating system mnt directory may be like cd rom, digital camera etc.

 /opt directory – opt directory automatically created in linux root drive/file system, it contain optional software installed from third party software from any linux distro website for installation, you must connected with high speed broadband internet service and finally view list of additional manually install linux third party software like java, neat beans and other, many online open source developer company created software package for client it may be rpm(red hat package manager) or deb(debian)package remember rpm package supported in red hat, centos, fedora, and deb supported in debian, ubuntu, kubuntu, lubuntu, and support other debian ubuntu based operating system, third party vendor provide free access download open source software for customer/company use no need to pay or take nay license.

/proc directory – proc directory hold information about system resources used as virtual file system process id contain information store information of unique system process id.

 /root directory – root directory created while any linux administrator created user account these root directory personal created for each root user who access own root directory service, now you must learn difference between user root and linux root directory these both are different nature, these root directory created for each home user separately.

 /sbin directory – sbin directory contain binary executable program information essential for linux system administration maintenance linux system services, like init, iptables, reboot, fdisk, ifconfig, ip, tc etc.

 Srv directory – srv directory stands service hold file that are necessary for server specific service linux files easier configure server related configuration file from srv directory, it work and activated while you communicate with server or making server.

 Sys directory – sys directory appears in newer linux operating system releases you can't found these previous linux release but modern linux distribution support, it sys directory provide virtual file system configure and customize system related service task.

 /tmp directory – tmp stands temporary similar in windows temp which store information about file directory and other services information as temporary by user as a gust ordinary or root user these files store unnecessary space on disk, it reduces system startup speed effect system application speed during run time.

 /user directory – user directory contains binaries, libraries, documentation, source code for user program, it contains binary files for system administration and other user necessary program.

 /var directory – var abbreviated as variable directory store temporary file and directory created by user such system file, log file, mail, printer spooler area, even online download content form internet even stores buffer image also, all these variable file release/delete after computer reboot.

File handling in linux: h/w

Booting a linux system

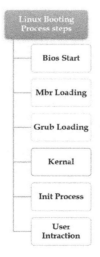

Explain each step briefly during linux startup

- ⊃ Switch on linux operating system install computer.
- ⊃ Bios program starting.
- ⊃ Bios start all hardware and other post (power on self-test) service.
- ⊃ Search boot device loader location.
- ⊃ Start loading boot loader may be (grub/lilo) linux boot loader.
- ⊃ Start os from mbr(linux master boot record) where actually os installed.
- ⊃ Start interaction with linux interface.

Describe briefly linux operating system startup process

Bios startup – bios stands basic input output system a special program written by computer manufacturer while computer motherboard and component design/manufacture, bios contain bootable instruction that are necessary for normal booting linux and other operating system, bios search and load boot sector from floppy drive, cd rom, or hard drive installation.

Master boot record (mbr) – mbr stands as (master boot record)mbr is master boot record that contain information that are necessary for booting proper linux system linux os have two basic boot loader one is grub and second one is lilo, it depend on choose linux os boot loader responsible for loading all services and application necessary for proper booting linux system, mbr placed on disk 1 sector of bootable disk while booting start t search boot program from it hdd fdd or other optical device minimum or less than size of nay boot loader is 512, so finally boot loader program like grub load mbr and bootable linux system.

Grub/lilo linux boot loader – grub stands as (grand unified boot loader) same as lilo stands (linux loader) grub boot loader program automatically load while, if you install two or more linux window and other os kernel now you can choose desire os from given choice grub startup screen gives you minimum amount of start operating system select in that time otherwise linux start automatically selected operating system automatically, you can edit startup time and other grub boot loader configuration with administrator/root user privilege.

Kernel – kernel is heart of any linux windows operating system which actually deal with system while computer communicate with hardware services, main responsibility manage by kernel is that manage root file system kernel execute program, it start initrd abbreviated as initial ram disk kernel mounted initred as main root file system mounted even, it control and manage other necessary hardware related services.

Init – init find/etc/inittab file for start linux boot run level after that you get many choices for run linux operating system with many level these are describe below better.

- ⊃ 0 – halt
- ⊃ 1 – single user mode

- ➲ 2 – multiuser mode
- ➲ 3 – full multiuser mode
- ➲ 4 – don't use
- ➲ 5 – x11
- ➲ 6 – reboot

While linux startup process begin it automatically search run level and load required program automatically.

User interaction – user interaction started after all above process completion, now log in with command prompt called terminal/console/root with username and password, now you able to access linux services features and application function according to need.

Linux ubuntu desktop description

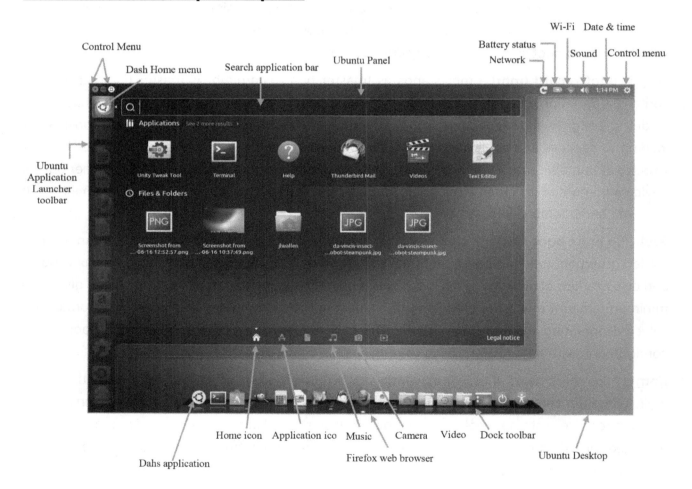

Ubuntu panel – ubuntu panel like windows xp, vista, windows 7, 8 task bar here you can application menu notification icon like wired ethernet network, wi-fi connection volume control, date & time calendar, and command system start, restart, control menu, ubuntu panel display or contain common ubuntu desktop operation like opening application closing application you can place ubuntu panel in left, right, top, bottom position according to need.

Ubuntu desktop – ubuntu desktop like other operating system like windows, macintosh, unix, android and other popular operating system, ubuntu provide everything even more than other commercial operating system like application launcher, dash menu, panel control provides working surface area for controlling ubuntu operation related working or navigation application.

Dash home – dash home menu similar windows 8 start screen, where you get all software application menu and function installed in dash home menu, in dash home you get home, application file, music, camera and video choice select and pick your category choice which one you want to run or execute application from its apps category choice.

Home – home windows return you where homework done in ubuntu desktop environment all application executes access manipulate by you automatically listed in home menu of ubuntu 13.10 windows, you can access them easier according to need.

Application – application menu similar windows 7 menu even in windows 8 look like metro style apps menu program, listed as thumbnail view similar that application menu, display in dash home windows where you get all automatically install or manually installed application listed here pick desire application software and execute them according to need, you get here application like accessibility, accessories, developer, fonts, graphic, education, internet, game, media, office, science & engineering, and system application click and execute according to need.

File – view ubuntu dash board located file information and query through file option, click to control open and operated selected file behavior and other features according to your need.

Music application – music application windows display you all executed music listed here even online music album for playing click anyone from list and play with supported music player application software, remember some linux distribution need music codec plug in while first time launch music with installed software.

Camera – view installed camera taking picture even other watch view image picture gallery in camera folder, remember it display only while your camera must plug in, otherwise you can't view any picture attach camera while fresh linux os installation even manually install with supported debian software package.

Video – view video player play video even list of online video that one you play in category, play with installed media player like mplayer, vlc player totam and other related supported software.

Application launcher – application launcher displays in left vertical corner position of ubuntu linux 13.10 or later desktop, application launcher just like windows quick launch where you set quickly access application list here, in application launcher shortcut you get shortcut like libre office application like writer, impress, spreadsheet, mount hard drive, flash card, pen drive, cd/dvd, workspace, multiple desktop, home, web browser, trash (recycle bin) etc.

Search bar – search bar allow to quickly search required application element quickly without delay in dash home menu just type name of required element and wait till search element listed below in search windows, it common similar to windows find or search features.

Wired network – wired network display connection status of installed ethernet wired network, while you begin installation of any linux distribution, it checks all installed computer mother board hardware specification include eth0 configuration, if you access wired internet connection than wired network option enable you to access internet service through broadband service.

Battery status – battery status option displays in only if you are using linux on laptop/notebook/ ultra - book/tablet, battery status shows how much portable/handy device remaining battery than you plug it in portable computer device with main electricity.

Wi-fi connection – wi-fi connection represent wireless network service, if you are using wireless router for accessing broadband internet service, then wi-fi connection appear in your laptop desktop ubuntu desktop panel windows, now you can make it enable disable according while you accessing wireless internet services.

Bluetooth – bluetooth represent wireless device connectivity among your desktop/laptop and other side any wireless device like cellphone, digital camera, handy cam and other wireless portable media, pair bluetooth device and share data resources among two connected wireless device easier.

Sound – sound represent status of installed sound card in active computer here you can play sound animation, audio song, video song, even control sound volume mute volume fast forward previous next audio song according to need.

Date & time – date & time ubuntu panel option enable you to access current date previous date even future date with view current time, click date and time panel notification windows for customize date & time related configuration, change date time, time zone and relevant information.

Control menu – control menu in linux ubuntu and other linux application to control open working application into a close, minimize, maximize and restore open working application window, include using ubuntu application shutdown control to shut down, restart, logout, or switch user features use to control operating system behavior.

TOPIC 04

Information Technology and Society

- Introduction of information technology.
- Application of information technology.
- Cost time reduction.
- Business competitive age.
- Business globalization benefit
- Control business houses environment.
- Database management.
- Work efficiency.
- Importance of information technology in communication.
- Computer.
- Cellphone/smart phone.
- Internet services.
- E-mail.
- Fax machine.
- IPad.

Information technology and society

Information technology and society – todays information technology made tremendous change human and society, every one use information technology for perform ordinary commercial and non-commercial task, like create letter matter, store database, search database, accessing and providing record and information, search online provide online connectivity connect virtually with remote desktop for sharing resources and commercial task, in every office, organization, industry, department, collage, school, hotel, departmental store, shopping mall, workplace, even other all remaining sector where information technology application use for routine purpose, now information technology be essential part of human life like sharing thought do official job, online meeting, conference, sharing resources, and database are easier communicate along information technology, information technology completely impact on affect social and traditional working method, it improve human work efficiency living standard communication style and behavior.

Impact of information technology on society

🖥 Business environment.	🖥 E-commerce.	🖥 Market behavior.
🖥 Workplace communication.	🖥 Multimedia industry.	🖥 Social life.
🖥 Education.	🖥 Working style.	🖥 Reliability & stability.

Business environment – traditional/cultural business houses run business at their regional level while information technology developed, it make tremendous changes in traditional business environment, now many things became online buy online sell online choose desire product online view 360 degree angle of selected product choose variety of product pay online even discuss online about business product and deal maintain business product inventory get immediate query about selected product, old business houses adopt new information technology invention for improving traditional business structure and performance.

E-commerce – e-commerce replace traditional/cultural business platform, at e-commerce service anybody go online, any e-commerce service product provider web site select product view specification and other detail, finally make request for buy product online, all system process under superior supervision, now day's many online e-commerce (electronic business) service provider available online for buying and selling online product, from everywhere anywhere across the global, market make possible e-commerce service today's without internet e-commerce not possible now day's many company make online their company goods/product catalog for their online/offline client, client buy sell any product online form company web site and pay payment through debit/credit/master/visa/or atm card even online net banking facility include, e-commerce save your time money energy.

Market behavior – market behavior helping information technology to know the exact mood of consumer product buyer which product and technology demanded now days between specific country consumer, it helping to big companies and industry to know more about these customer/

consumer, many industry, organization, companies, ngo include government agencies create seminar, group meetings, survey to know about actual fact and market mood.

Workplace communication – information technology change workplace communication modern employee share online e-mail, video, chatting, online messenger, for communication, they send each other online letter, e-mail, fax, what's aap, used skype, yahoo messenger, windows net meeting, line, we chat text/video messenger team viewer, ammy, remote desktop connection for connection in virtual world communication, possible for everywhere from home or workplace information technology taught everyone to work with efficiency and dignity.

Multimedia industry – multimedia industry big industry across the world in different continent and region, using multimedia in information technology include social life to create special movies, create learning video, design electronic web site, post some news and broadcast news live through radio, television, or e-mail, making some school higher school learning education material design or easier to created using multimedia application, on large level kids animated movies, cartoons, and animated stories created worldwide for different kind of user and consumers using these techniques.

Social life – computer generated application and software helping computer consumer to create and manage social application for connectivity across worldwide network, using face book, we chat, skype, one drive, twitter, linkdln, and other social web sources to connect and share social message, text, photos, video, animated content, attach and share with connected client, create voice message, made video conference, using voip technology to make international internet calls and conversation, include using computer videos, software, games, learning materials and many other social content be part of technology somebody access and use these features according to need.

Education – all modern school and collages having computer equipment for their student, teach student with visual, graph, chart, smart, organization chart, using tables, picture, animation, 2d, 3d animated object audio, video slides, database, document and other kind of material used to teach and describe elements of information technology in reference of computer education, learn through online teacher, view online web sited videos to learn and explore some new technology, create research some new and old topics, created suitable document books, design own project content, control many student from single location, solve issues, problem and student query through online connectivity, provide video conference learning, meetings, and learning communication made easier using education with computer technology, provide student learning material run in computer, force student to making some digital notes and information, include many other opportunities to using computers in education field.

Working style – using computer technique to improving working behavior with using these technique, use cad(computer added design) application, computer application, software, multimedia application, social application, management control software and other special features reduce human efforts, computer control and manage thousands of user work, use auto pilot in aviation industry to control jumbo jet, planes, using embedded system to control self-control operated learning software program to control electronic gadgets and hardware device, control account with inventory, keep record of organization industry, process computer generated records and manipulation computer process data and electronic information include several advantage you will find online using network.

Application of information technology

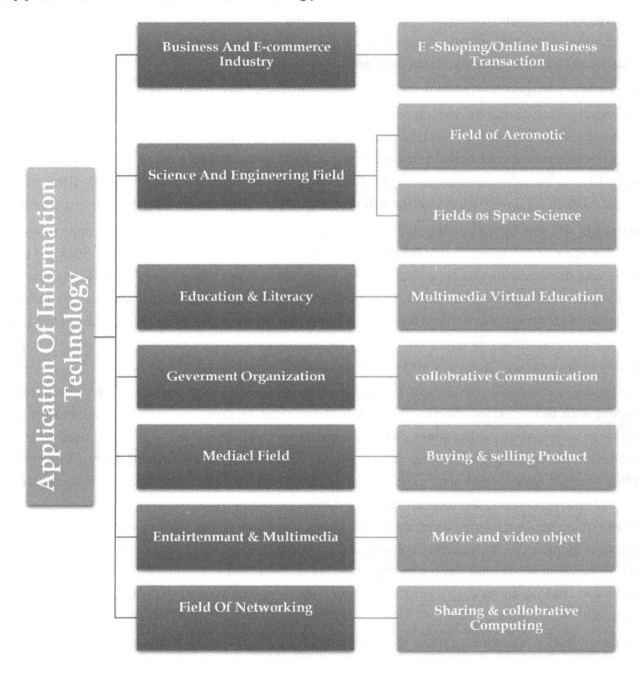

Importance of information technology in education

- ➲ Now in control of user getting online resources from web.
- ➲ Immediate response of information.

- No foundation of learning anywhere anybody can learn.
- Sharing collaborative attitude.
- Online education.
- Connectivity worldwide.
- Global advantage of data and resources.

Importance of information technology business

- Analysis design and development of business product.
- Integrative/collaborative business environment.
- Work efficiency improvement.
- Cost time reduction.
- Business competitive advantage.
- Business globalization benefit.
- Control business houses environment.
- Improve business work method and performance.
- Management of business inventory data.
- Database management.
- Customer relationship would be easier.

Importance of information technology in communication

- Computer.
- Cellphone/smart phone.
- Internet services.
- E-mail.
- Fax machine.
- Ipad.

Indian it acts – indian it act 2000 passed by indian parliament, this act protect it related rules regulation terms and condition developed by indian government for controlling protecting information technology, related task and function these act describe all function behavior related information technology, generally.

Intellectual property rights – intellectual property right describes some right of world community any user, these right helping user to make their product more secure and effective in global market, these intellectual property right keep secure your right product in across the globe market, anybody able to getting intellectual property rights of their invented, created product, software, games, music, book publishing, company trademark and other, default you have to right under intellectual property rights name patents, trademarks, copy rights, geographical indications, some design, photos, and other kind of unique and special invention be part of these.

Application of information technology

Railways – information technology spread everywhere in field of computer science and other relevant area of technology we just describe here, it in reference of railway, now days most of online offline task easier perform by information technology user.

Advantage of information technology in railway

- ⮯ Make online reservation request from home.
- ⮯ Book online e-ticketing from own terminal at home office.
- ⮯ Cancel ticketing from home.
- ⮯ Automated ticket vending machine.
- ⮯ Train schedule time table information easier to access.
- ⮯ Get information about each and every train individual passenger.
- ⮯ Distance ticket price and other station information access easier.
- ⮯ Railway new vacancies announces other news access.
- ⮯ Know about all indian railway system.
- ⮯ Get detail information about train route distance and how much take time.
- ⮯ Railway database management/quick information retrieval.
- ⮯ Future project plan management overview.

Airlines – airline are also travelling services that are responsible to travel their passenger from source destination to reach destination of information technology in reference of indian and other airlines system it forces.

Advantage of information technology in airline

- ⮯ Make online reservation request from home.
- ⮯ Booking online e–ticketing from home/office own terminal.
- ⮯ Get airline route ticket journey start end how much take time and other detail.
- ⮯ Manage multiple aero plane schedule time fare.
- ⮯ Manage airport services client database, flight database.
- ⮯ Control air traffic while busy airline route.
- ⮯ Control flight database manage flight database with database management technology.
- ⮯ Flash plane route time cancellation detail.

- Post every day latest update on connected online terminal in airport.
- Announce any services immediately.
- Flight management system/auto pilot flight management system.
- Flight simulator control management.

Banking – bank are register with government agencies and provides services for you financial insurance, loan, and other similar services bankers running, firm of money making processing like deposit money, withdrawn money, loan scheme, online offline money transaction, customer service, and many other customer related services provide by any banker company, in india or across india people going to take bank service for complete their business routine task and banking firm used information technology software for making payment, atm machine online e-transaction, e-money facility provider device, include debit card, credit card, master card, visa card, atm card and other plastic currency card provide by their own client who have related banks account, online client database information easily maintain store and retrieve even global branch connectivity across the world, now day's many banker are online for routine bank and customer service communication.

Advantage of information technology in bank

- Bank manage multiple client database like client name address contact amount withdrawn deposit taking loan amount fixed deposited payable or getting interest on deposit and many more information in special customize banking software.
- Perform easier computing communication retrieve information and banking knowledge easier.
- Information technology manage easier relationship between client bank employee and bank officer staff.
- Banking provide best service infrastructure reliable fast services to their client with online information technology connectivity.
- Client self-inquiry facility home/remote banking/online banking any time/anywhere banking, telephone banking, e – banking.
- Bank employee/staff analysis of financial statement chart bank statistic and other detail.
- Bank control online their atm, tele banking, online banking, provide customer online service from connected their terminal.
- Bank post online proposal, new plan, bank scheme, policy customer related material online vacancies and other detail with information technology online on bank web site.

Insurance – insurance sector wide sector in field of information technology where policy creator hold and create or issues new policies its user or client, store insurance staff, employee related all detail store in computer, keep policy holder term and complete record hold in it, create customer attractive advertisement, manage client risk portfolio, providing necessary information and data, getting policy holder claim information, maturity detail, paid premium detail, show term and condition sign by customer while policy taking and other rules regulation followed by policy holder during policy period, these database connected nation wise it mean anybody access these centralized information through connectivity with lic offices, bajaj finance, and other similar services provides company.

Inventory control – inventory control system allow you to store and maintain inventory of buying selling product like, electronic goods, clothe, food, books, hardware equipment, software product, buy and sell by retailer, hole seller, and consumer store all database with inventory control software is a collection of hardware and software that keep up to date, commercially inventory control system operated by retailer who store many versatile product keep tracking selling of product detail, inventory data base immediate describe about remaining product quantity selling quantity selling price, selling unit, selling customer detail and many more other relevant information.

Financial systems – using computer technology in financial system to manage and keep financial database system record information, database query, create communication between various company branch connectivity, store and access company records and database query information, view detail about user made transaction, show status financial system information, and other hidden advantage you will getting using financial system in information technology worldwide.

Advantage of information technology in financial systems

- ➲ Manage financial project plan and cost information.
- ➲ Manage plan/project related budget/funding.
- ➲ Manage online offline billing.
- ➲ Estimate project costing.
- ➲ Control financial environment.

Hotel management – hotel is place where people guest or traveler or traveler group stay at for night for getting food, meal, or relaxation and other services now day's hotel became place where people or group of people enjoy their meal do party seminar conference and other business related meeting and task, hotel provides you all type luxury that you accept, now turn in reference of hotel management and hospitality industry make easier their guest work experience they provide you everything that you ask like water, meal, telecommunication service, conference hall, all type of business arrangement and related service, hotel staff manage employee guest request, process request arrange meal process billing room detail guest detail with the help of information technology software.

Advantage of information technology in hotel management system

- ➲ Manage guest information like name address contact where to come and where to go how long stay room number identification document detail like pen card, voter id card etc. Store in hotel computer software.
- ➲ Store and process client request demand and relevant information.

Education – information are very essential in field of education, e-learning, computer science, online home workplace e-resources material, browse information objective material for every one with the of information technology, learn online education, pay online bill, view and surf www content, provide visual literacy those who illiterate play online video and teach many more student from home or office, provide online video meeting/video conference online e-education from anywhere the world.

Advantage of information technology in education

- ➲ Online accessibility of www learning resources.
- ➲ Easier understand of any topic learning material with visual graphic audio video material.
- ➲ Learning and teaching easily possible with information technology.
- ➲ Expend new idea plan project overview easier in education with it technology.
- ➲ Multimedia learning object/online learning material that provide globalize access of information and resources.
- ➲ Portability online learning material can be access globally from anywhere any location.

Video games – video games most of like by kids who want to play always 2d and 3d highly game with lots of more action and stunt even entertainment game learning game, racing game and other category of game play by mature of kids, game help everyone to refresh memory and relax sit back with some happier moment, game create student kids memory sharp and they easily understand the virtual world 3dimensional animation video even cartoon animated image game impact kids nature and affect his/her work performance, now days after lots of more invention information technology engineer making newest technology for their client/customer every day, buy online free game for your kids.

Telephone exchanges – telephone exchange established by government organization private limited company for spreading telecommunication services like wired landline, wireless network internet service high speed broadband internet service, tele message sending std, isd, video conference service provide at regional or global level telecommunication make possible to everyone to talk each other from anywhere anytime without interference, telephone exchange control their server client machine with the help of information technology it control client cellular landline operation even manage client company employee/staff database with online connectivity software, information technology design individual software for telecommunication field for client or server operation.

Mobile phones – mobile phone became essential gadgets for everyone who is the technology lover, cellphone shrink human life work experience at home workplace or any virtual world, cellphone technology improve human life and living standard now everyone talk and walk buy sell any product complete office work and collaborate with staff community, perform commercial non- commercial task with video conference, voice chatting facility send and compose message from cellphone take picture, play audio and video or other multimedia object from cellphone get direction map route use internet broad band services store required data in available storage media, store contact watch and surf online e-commerce product perform banking financial task from cellphone, each cellphone contain small rectangular chip call sim(subscriber identification module) just like ip address in internet each cellular/cellphone user assign unique single sim, remember it can't be two or more never.

Information kiosks – information kiosks called a small terminal contain computer cpu and screen contain computer device that enable its user to get retrieves some necessary information according to user made query and request, any user or people making request for required information through using information kiosks service or platform these information kiosks you find in a corporate house, company, shopping mall, and government agencies these structure organization keep data information about some important people, organization, firm database that help new user to solve some query and issues.

Special effects in movies – computer using in hollywood and bollywood movies to adding some special effect, modify movie scene, adding movie additional visual effect, adding movies sound, audio, visual, 3d animated effect, include create some impossible movie scene effect easier using computer technology, hollywood movie create some unrealistic movie sequence and scene that not possible to manually shoot, after invention of computer technology and it application using computer added effect to make movies some tremendous effect possible in movies.

TOPIC 05

Introduction to Internet

- Introduction to internet.
- Different kind of internet.
- Internet characteristic.
- Benefit of internet.
- Losses of internet.
- Application of internet.

Topic covers in internet sections

1. Introduction to internet
2. Internet protocol
3. Internet connectivity
4. Internet network
5. Internet service
6. E – mail

Introduction to internet

Internet definition

Internet – in term of simple language internet is interconnected networked of network connected via telephone line spread across the world wide, different server and domain connect regional national or international server for information resources access.

Internet – internet is huge collection of worldwide information shared across the world wide in a shape of lan man or wan information are posted updated or loaded by world separate different domain for different purpose now days internet would be more popular among people for it service or application like e-mail, surfing, navigation, downloading, uploading, web/video conference e-transaction, web page, website or another use purpose.

Internet – internet is collection of information database web pages web sites linked together as shape of html web pages include graphic multimedia animation 2d 3d animated effect object contain in it.

Internet connectivity world wide

Let's describe history about internet

Arpanet – arpanet stand as (advanced research project agency network) is first network of world work on packet switching method after some modification it invented with new name internet, arpanet project started by us defense service for connection local or global computer.

Nsfnet – nsfnet abbreviated as national science foundation network nsfnet design by us national science foundation network after some time nsfnet will be merge (replace) with arpanet that days nsfnet connect government organization, universities, and research laborites, and government department, nsfnet are now backbone of today's popular internet in mid-1970 to 1980 nsfnet provide high speed data communication between connect super computer and regional center, in mid-1980 computer engineer, analyst, scientist, or developer access services of nsfnet for resource sharing and network collaboration nsfnet is base or foundation now days popular network services.

Internet – internet started by us defense services in early year of 1960 when us defense decide to protect their data information secret code while second world war they invented computer machine for purpose share their secret information among regional head member, now days internet us by government agency university official department or organization, after long journey renamed with arpanet, nsfnet, and finally introduce in year 1990 internet, after invention first graphical browser by mark anderson name mosaic, mosaic is first graphical browser which one capable to view display or browse first time web page in complete graphical view it display graphic wallpaper image and sketch and greater power ability then lynx browser used that days in unix operation system.

Now day's internet affect everybody life in every days in different sector region domain country may be social commercial or ordinary life, every day we access many application trigger many control with the help of internet. Like e-mail, video conference web hosting chatting, e-commerce, online transaction or different sector may be school, university, industry, organization, company etc. You may access million application in your life while deal with internet.

Internet characteristic

Information provider – internet huge where house information store spread in server of client shape in global village, where many information data web content posted upload for public use with the of internet search engine let you know exact information about your search criteria.

Connectivity – internet provides global social publicly network connectivity, to share feeling understanding exchange data information business material for public use, this network connectivity reaches your access across nation international wide.

Dynamic info – internet information posted in form of web page web site, so they can easily update modify or change or reflect same time online world wide web system, all the information posted in web as hyperlink information system, so authorized person may be edit change old material information with new one easily, unlike newspaper old they unused after reading, but web content is may be dynamic or static depend on web change.

Increase information quantity – internet provide many moderate or un moderate information links for internet user, if you need solution of your need another method solution available posted by someone related your essential need, so you get many information quantities related your search term.

Interesting and important resources – internet provides you commercial non - commercial ordinary entertainment audio video multimedia graphic web catalog and interested topic material related, browse once or many topics belong to different choice and need of user, all information posted as hyperlink you can click and navigate display your topic.

Large free database – internet is combination of small sub network work independently form inside outside world, telecommunication technology connectivity provide facility to use internet resources free database for public use, some internet resources are restricted or block so you need to access use them give special member ship id or password, otherwise most information are free based.

Self-learning material – internet is gallery of multimedia audio video animation 3d 2d object collection now days most of web site provide link of video of any coaching class food class, programming video awareness video child learning material video of any movie tuition class instruction material that help you to understand visualize any topic material that meet your need, site that provide you self-learning material is www.youtube.com/www.google.video.com etc.

Secure and safety (in some case if following rules) – internet technology more secure and safe technology those regular access network resource for many commercial and non – commercial routine purpose, by default while made online transaction, e-transaction, banking transaction, installed malware antivirus and other internet program making secure communication with outer network world through these software facility.

Global advantages – internet provides global benefit to its user while user using or access network usage, features name online communication make easier or simple, task from world any continent, use smart features to know more about search term, commit and share valuable resources, provide and get information easier, quick provide and access text, video, multimedia and other resources material as attachment shape, use voip, video conference, e–transaction, sharing, download, upload and many other features have through internet.

Benefits and losses of internet

No doubt internet is tremendous technology for new or old generation, it makes easier our life work experience knowledge and sharing behavior, but fact is you can't deny internet some time create problem for you your social or personal life, so use it safe or securely.

Benefits of internets

Faster/easier/quick communication – internet is prove it is tremendous technology that use and access by everyone who are directly indirectly connect with information technology, internet provide you everything that are you search through online internet services like google or other popular search engine just type required information in search engine text box and click on search box to find out desire information in it very faster easier or quick way.

Huge collection of www resource (bank of www information) – internet is mass collection of world wide web server or client computer where everyone exchange raw information and data through network connectivity, there are lots of more million billion trillion article web content posted across the world these information access read and post by millions network user, log in system and search required desire content according to need from www services.

E-commerce – electronic commerce replacement of traditional business environment where hawker shop keeper selling their product from fix or movable location, e-commerce completely different from tradition cultural business environment where buyer and seller buy sell product online from online product selling web site, here anybody view product from all side 360 degree angle view with product configuration specification price warranty even 15/30 days replacement policy, place order online pay online through net banking atm master visa card and receive buy product at home through post or courier service.

Online transaction – online transaction include all the buying selling goods product online transaction, do online payment to client company any online buy sell vendor company, it reduce time money increase work efficiency today's bank provide online transaction account holder eligible to do any payment online through www concept.

Online report – view send online government official non-official commercial, noncommercial report, memo, query, letter, document, content, delivery information and other document content easier send or receive even view online through network services.

Fund transfer – transfer online funds online through net banking, neft, rtges, through master card, debit card and other plastic currency, now banking play a role of mediator during product buying or selling bank transfer huge amount of funds between buyer and seller even bank pay online your trade bill amount at requested client, you pay some amount or bank transaction fee from you during using bank services.

E-education – electronic education possible now days now learner study from home, now you have terminal or personal computer include laptop, desktop, tablet, or ipad, learn online–education facility provide by many online companies, institution, even organization, you must have internet connection with microphone/headphone, attain global classes lecture video from any country or continent through net meeting, skype, yahoo messenger, facebook, or we chat, and many group education provider companies, e-education save your time money expenses even record lecture ask live question query and getting immediate answer through online network services, electronic education increase moral student behavior and education standard than traditional education method.

Global access resources – global access resources now possible through internet you can download any textual, graphic, multimedia, informational material through internet, getting online material web content e-resources and other relevant information with worldwide connectivity.

Social connectivity – social connectivity allow you to share your feeling, emotion, affection, live chat do video conference, send receive online material and e – material etc. With connected social client like facebook, skype, we chat, link din, twitter, yahoo messenger, rediff messenger, irc and other social client, in global village now possible to share your idea opinion even feelings with other easier in quick time immediate response.

Chatting – chatting include text, audio, even video communication between two or more connected network user, they share information talk to each other send receive text message quickly with connected messenger user, talk commercial emotional feeling with anyone who you know better, call any one for talking with phone call communication.

Entertainment – internet is huge collection of multimedia entertainment resources anybody connect with internet and getting download upload multimedia resources internet allow you to watch video online listen new movie audio song play animated video, 2 dimensional and 3dimensional object online.

Download www content – very best advantage of internet technology is that now everyone can download their favorite content from online web resource, we can able to download computer software, game, program, graphic, audio, video, multimedia object, animated object, report, fax, query, letter, memo, table, result, statement, even any other type of www electronic document in shape of paper of graphic, now everyone use internet for downloading movie, audio mp3 song, software, specially computer games and other relevant material from internet.

Upload content – upload content on world wide web known web host you can upload company government report, fax, document, video, audio, multimedia object, other textual material if you have web hosting permission, publish web content online for every one read access interested in related information.

Losses of internet

Hacking – hacking term popular in internet network even computer world where everyone know losses of computer, internet hacking perform by computer expert genius who break system security services even know system weak point during hacking processing hacker hack your system copy important material information theft all type of data resource destroy system startup process even modify system setting he can copy your secure password atm bank or other type secure information copy easier, so they can loss you, hacker intentionally damage corporate company industry system, hacker hack your system web site online during hacking period you can't do anything if you don't have latest antivirus definition and protected windows firewall, latest malware software etc. Hacker may be person who criminal mind but genius expertise in field of hacking subject.

Cracking – creaking involve process of creak any system installed protection software security and control system environment and perform desire function destroy system information damage software working function, it also perform by computer expert who get special expertise in field of computer science, creaking include creak of any company software code and sell illegally without manufacturer permission against company copy right law, all these task perform by who actually know about exact them.

Loss of information – loss of information include lost essential computer document file folder while online working, if two or more computer connected through network services like lan (local area network) anybody access your system copy read write even delete file data and information without our permission.

Theft – theft big losses of internet technology where everyone who connect internet through their personal computer, laptop, desktop even other portable gadgets now days' insecure if any body copy theft important non-sharable data and resources from your machine to other machine, computer hacker, cracker, code developer who deep expertise about computer hacking can easier copy theft as well destroy your secure essential data and information if you are connect with internet with low security software services.

Violation of software piracy – violation of software privacy include violation of computer software by unauthorized internet user, crack license software redistributes in cheap rate create multiple copy and sell any one, company got big losses while their product sell in low price by illegal vender in market, now anybody download software from company web site reedit it with crack software and redistributed it with their own name.

Forgery/frauds – internet became easier medium of forgery of any printed document even anybody became easier victim of internet frauds many internet criminal send e – mail and giving them bonus huge lottery amount against deposited amount in their account, a common man easily became victim of any kind fraud operated by internet.

Spamming – spamming big tension for everyone who access online electronic mail services, spamming is a huge collection of unwanted e-mail that send by unknown person companies as purpose of know about you it may be about your confidential e-mail, every spam gives you attractive offer about any product services and theft your credit card/debit card password or other secure information during e-mail communication be secure while dealing unwanted e-mail or installed latest malware protector in your personal computer.

Malware – malware are small design e-mail computer program that are spread while click or open them reading as a common e - mail information, it damage your machine decrease system performance, for protecting system through install latest malware protector software in your computer while online surfing, update malware program definition every day better performance.

Privacy – privacy insecure in internet network while you talk to personal video sharing conference even your system contain your personal visual non- visual content that harm you if any one illegally access or misuse them, so be secure never share personal photos data video and other information between you really you don't know otherwise your privacy share by many one in global village, remember always keep system up to date while perform online communication never share personal information user identification with password with unknown.

Threat – threat include psychical or paper based through electronic mail, anybody send e-mail for ransom against kidnapping or other purpose, threat demand on strong bases while threat demanders know your weakness, threat is an offence/crime and if anybody found guilty send him in prison against indian information technology act.

Virus – virus is computer generated program that are design developed by computer programmer who intentionally damage any company organization file data even program or software each virus design for specific purpose virus designer design virus to destroy or corrupt system software windows utilities and impact system performance, first of all it halt application software than windows bootable file and after damage windows routine operation.

Pornography – pornography are biggest problem for those there children are teen age and routinely access internet services like social sites online game, they view inappropriate porn web content related pornography, even other porn matter that affect their brain mental condition.

Leakage of information – leakage of information meaning while you work in open network environment you can't believe any one, you can't which one is authenticate or reliable network user while you sharing/passing information between multiple computer user there is no guaranty to misuse of resources among many client any authenticate network user misuse their privilege and access for benefiting other network user.

Internet addiction over age – internet addiction now is common problem between teen age and mature internet user, they spend lots of time money potential energy to find out specific topic information, they access internet services unlimited in all days' so they became physically weak, mentally disturbed, became addict of internet uses spend hour and hour on any social sites chat to other make video call even send receive text on desktop, laptop, cell phone, even tablet etc.

Growth of internet

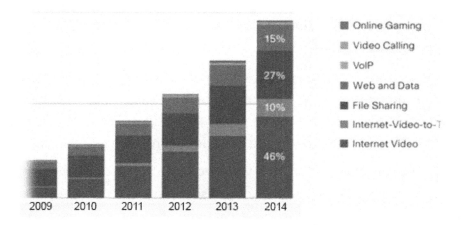

Internet spread across the whole world all world community may literate or ordinary person who belong to attach or connected technology must access internet resources, local and global network create global of information via technology connection every day internet became popular between professional engineer common individual students etc. Now days most of task action work done with help of machine like computer after use of internet it became more popular to ease of access information, internet till then june 2012 internet user is 2336 million 33%.3 of world population and every day it grow in large size according to use its commercial purpose.

Owner of internet

Internet is world largest growing network connect million billion large network in global village, attach computer in internet there no clear conclusion about ownership of internet, because it is not controlled and operated by any particular government organization industry or country, internet is disconnected or segment network combine many small individual network along it, internet really design or created by arpanet us defense services in early 1964, even internet is oversee or govern by some group large agencies or company who sell or buy telecommunication technology in favor of public private or academic use purpose.

Anatomy of internet

Internet anatomy shows internet physical body structure all the elements work use along networking terms, we already internet is world network/spread network, so many services application utilities or web supported facility use in term with internet.

Anatomy of internet elements

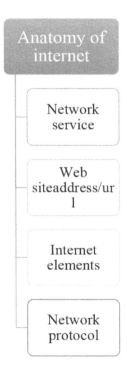

Application of internet

Surfing – internet surfing indicate to explore world wide web content online search online web resources interesting url links online spend lots of more time online or desire interested topic in world wide web, move previous back between interest web topic in internet moving or jump between two or more web site through internet connectivity.

 Downloading – downloading refer to copy web server content from server to client system, download including transfer file or data from server to client or client to server to new location, download indicate term send or receive web content.

Upload – uploading is refer to transmission of file from client computer location to server computer location, in term of network or internet user many time use these world called upload, in basic term while user post some information from his computer to other computer called upload or you post some text, audio, video, multimedia, document, and other information through any ftp server or web server at requested client or server machine it called upload, similar downloading in term of upload your network speed play important role when user ready for upload, if slow network speed then many chance to broken upload data link during session.

 **E-mail** – e - mail is mass mailing facility that allow to send exchange or receive online web content letter, e-mail, fax, biodata, informational content, now days traditional post replace with e-mail, e-mail popular in mid-1995 where company organization industry regular exchange business e-mail or communication information.

Web hosting – web hosting online company that provide space on server for storage world wide web content on 24/hour online service, web server companies available space for new host web site even maintain regularly  update web site.

 **Video conference** – video conference allow you to connect and communicate with audio and video devices include internet services, now days many companies organization industry meeting held online through video conference software like yahoo messenger, skype, google plus, facebook, even windows net meeting software even other popular open source category software available for anyone who are interested in video conference, in past traditional days business or individual attain meeting physically go to meeting location travel long distance, and presence physical appearance, in video conference you need huge terminal lcd screen to listen or watch other online meeting member from worldwide location, in net meeting or video conference you ask question place your query even participate from your home office location directly, video conference reduce time money and increase work efficiency in global village.

Ftp server – ftp stands file transfer protocol internet standard protocol specially used while communicate or transfer file data and online information between client and server, each ftp server dedicated for specific file and data transfer between two individual dedicated server, ftp client software called ftp client ftp client communicate with ftp server finally connection established now client able

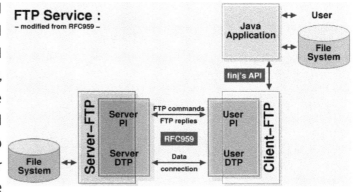

to send and receive file and information, enter user name and password each ftp server allow two mode of file transfer one is ascii and second binary mode common ftp client called quite ftp and ws ftp server.

E-commerce – e – commerce stand electronic commerce it mean you can buy and sell product online through internet, now many online web site offer and dealing product through internet called internet many online company promote their product online with 2d 3d view product specification even get all other document configuration through web site, company allow online currency for buying and selling product, some e-commerce play as a business to business and some play online as a business to customer, some web site play online e-commerce product like ebay, flicker, homeshop18, olx and many other web, some e-commerce service are mobile commerce, fund transfer, online marketing, world wide web etc.

Social connectivity – social connectivity allow you to group together communication, in social connectivity group people share their relationship, understanding, feeling, opportunity, study their relation now day's many web site allow you to connect people with social connectivity website are facebook, linkdln, we chat, twitter, my space, rediff bol, yahoo messenger, skype, google plus and many more other web site allow to connect socially, in modern social connectivity web site offer simple tool to create web site profile easier crate chat attain

conversation call video chatting share file folder image text information video make internet call chat one or more social network at a same time in common or different platform.

TOPIC
06

Internet Technology and Protocol

- Packet switching technology.
- Internet protocols.
- Internet addressing scheme.
- Common e-mail address.

Internet protocol

Packet switching technology – packet switching technology commonly used in networking computer for transmitting computer data packet from source to destination, it divide large message of data into small of packet, when network connection established data sending continuously from source to destination in group of data packet any data packet deliver first from source to location, it may depend on which data packet route fast, small packet of data travel between source to destination host, each data packet contain address of sending source location network hardware switch and router decide which data packet where to go and where stop, x.25 tcp/ip and frame relay are common packet switching based technology.

Internet protocols – internet protocol are some unique rules and standard followed by client and server during network communication, internet protocol define term of secure network communication with reliability accuracy and flexibility, internet protocol define addressing scheme during internet network communication internet protocol allocated to every client separately for individual communication in wide area network or local area network internet protocol substitute large network communication in small sub category network communication, a common manually added ip address on any client machine are 111.112.113.1 these ip address provide individual mechanism of communication, internet protocol collaborate with tcp(transmission control protocol), remember internet protocol possible global communication.

Tcp/ip – tcp abbreviated as (transmission control protocol) protocol work along ip where internet protocol define network source to destination location, but transmission control protocol establish relationship between client and server and start data stream transmission, even tcp reliable for designing successfully of data packet/stream from source to host location without error bug free communication, tcp.

Internet protocol

Tcp protocol – tcp abbreviated as transmission control protocol where tcp used for transmit data packet between client and server, tcp established connection between client and server(host), tcp responsible for deliver successfully data packet from source to destination, tcp protocol commonly used with common ip(internet protocol) tcp control data packet stream data from source to destination.

Ip protocol – ip stands internet protocol set of prctocol addressing system in computer global network each network system contain unique ip address that are not same in common established network, ip commonly similar to home office addressing system where post properly reach between sender and receiver, same as computer internet network world data and packet easier moving or travelling between client and server architecture.

Ssh protocol – ssh protocol use to keep protect network system security while communicating accessing or exchanging some network information, purposely using ssh protocol in network to access remote computer with privileges of a network administrative task for controlling and modifying client role or behavior.

Ftp protocol – in term of network ftp stands file transfer protocol, protocol specially used to sharing and exchanging some useful information and database between client and server computer with tcp/ip protocol and using a network system, ftp protocol used widely while some information upload or download mode, ftp server access client server environment/architecture for transferring some useful data and information.

Smtp protocol – smtp stands simple mail transfer protocol used to sending user created e-mail between source and destination path, smtp widely responsible for sending list of user mail account e-mail, where smtp used to send e-mail protocol similar pop and pop3, imap e-mail receive protocol work with smtp protocol, smtp common e-mail sending protocol work with linux, unix, window and mac based operating system e-mail client application.

Http protocol – http protocol recognize as hypertext transfer protocol, using for accessing and navigating information placed in web page in shape of static or dynamic web pages, while user access world wide web for exploring www resources a first protocol automatically link and connect with open web portals, in simple when user made any request of search web portals and web address server produce client machine requested web page with http protocol connectivity.

Ssl protocol – ssl know as secure socket layer internet authentication security checking protocol work cryptography system, share and exchanges some outside network data packets and information using network in client server environment, using a pair of key to access information which secure with cryptography system public and private key using between sender and receiver when opening and dealing content protected with ssl protocol.

Pop protocol – pop stands post office protocol popular e-mail protocol use for receiving e-mail in client server system, you may have e-mail client or online e-mail program receiving all inbox e-mail through pop protocol, two protocol simultaneously using for accessing or receiving e-mail pop, pop3, and imap specially for laptop system, when user inbox indicating any new mail it receive in user inbox through pop protocol.

Ppp protocol – ppp protocol recognize point to point protocol using in network to connect one to more computer network system, using phone line, cable or internet to connecting and sharing a point to point client server system information, ppp protocol commercially using for sending and receiving a network data packets between connected network.

Imap protocol – imap stand as internet message access protocol using for accessing and receiving e-mail message from client and server environment, imap protocol use for portable smart devices in laptop and gadgets device, imap protocol working similar to pop protocol it's also receive form server side computer.

Tls protocol – tls stands transport layer security protocol used for security of data security and privacy sending between client and server environment, using telephone line and network connection for sharing data information with complete data packet integrity, security, include security.

Udp protocol – udp stand user datagram protocol optional communication protocol for sharing with tcp, using a udp protocol working with other computer with other network, sending small data packets information with udp protocol in network.

Dns protocol – dns abbreviated as domain name system using to conversion domain name and server address into internet protocol equivalent address, each web address show in text format dns system or technique convert these web portals text into a decimal ip address format.

Dhcp protocol – dhcp stands dynamic host configuration protocol, dhcp protocol provide ip address to the network ip address system, in network each client and computer connected in network automatically get receive ip address allowed by dhcp protocol, dhcp server allows every client to connect and receive network address for proper communication between client and server.

Icmp protocol – icmp stands internet control message protocol, used to check network error reporting producing network system, data packets travel in network from source to destination address between client and server, view information about any loss, misplace network data packet information.

Ipv6 protocol – ipv6 stands internet protocol version 6, new generation internet protocol exchange with older ipv4, advantage of using ipv6 protocol to connect one or more network devices and computer at large level for sharing high volume of network data.

Rip protocol – rip stands routing information protocol, network router protocol using to know short best path of searching network information between client and server computer, while user made any search request in network rip protocol communicate with server and locate a path for client to server with router device easier and shortest.

Ospf protocol – ospf indicate open shortest path first, using for to finding a shortest network path in connected network, it using algorithm to filter proper shortest path to quick search and access search information, advantage of using ospf network to connecting a best open short first path between linked network devices.

Egp protocol – egp stand exterior gateway protocol using for sharing information among two connected network same region host computer, use in large organization, industry, government organization, advantage of using egp protocol is getting's information about connected hosts, control and view activities of same region hosts, include provide and sharing latest updates and information.

Bgp protocol – bgp stand border gateway protocol using to pass network information between connected routing device network, important role of these protocol in network for internet services providers users.

Arp protocol – arp stands address resolution protocol using to changing internet protocol ip address, network added internet protocol address define and modify through arp protocol.

Rarp protocol – rarp stand reverse address resolution protocol enable network client computer to making ip request made by server or network computer, using these protocol to converting these ethernet address into physical address.

Imap4 protocol – imap protocol stand internet message access protocol, role of imap4 protocol in group of e-mail protocol it receive user inbox e-mail address information from server location, imap4 more advance and features full e-mail protocol for e-mail account user in network.

Snmp protocol – snmp stand simple network management protocol using to manage and network services, in network information, devices, share, among connected network devices control and implement network privileges.

Telnet protocol – using telnet protocol to connecting computer with telnet services, connect and share telnet protocol services, connecting with telnet and access its services or advantage.

Slip protocol – slip stand serial line internet protocol using slip connection to connecting internet network computer using dial up connection, in year before 2000 all internet user using these protocol using to internet services with dial – up network connection.

Atm protocol – atm stand asynchronous transfer protocol, atm technology capable top sending data in 53 bytes' cell format in connected digital network system, using these protocol to sending data and voice with connected network.

Dhcp protocol – dhcp protocol stand dynamic host configuration protocol protocol used by routers device in network to providing ip address to all connected network device or client machine, when new client added in group network or internet dhcp protocol providing it ip to communicate in network for sharing data and information.

Ldap protocol – ldap protocol stands lightweight directory access protocol, for internet using e-mail program located and searching on network location directory for information locate or access, using these protocol in internet to view and access some kind of program application stored contain directory in network path.

Xmpp protocol – xmpp protocol stands extensible messaging and presence protocol, using in xml (extensible markup language, for sharing and communicate easier using xmpp protocol in connected similar network component location.

Udp protocol – udp stand user datagram protocol, udp using as additional network communication protocol in connected network to find out network error and other services issues.

Sip protocol – sip protocol stands session initiation protocol, using these protocol in multimedia network communication mode, operated multimedia network session behavior, many services online control and manage by sip protocol while user using video conference, voice call, chat program instant messaging for communication.

Routing protocol – routing protocol deign to find quickest path between connected network and provided services, important role of router to pass network made request path easier and faster, include control behavior of connected client session.

Internet addressing scheme – internet addressing scheme control global network while we communicate in global world many client communicate same time from many workstation or terminal they all follow different internet protocol and unique ip address that separate and provide secure network communication, ip address just like name of the computer machine used in network we just compare it with human name house name or label of any product that can't assign one or more in single domain or group, we take example of small local area network in lan number of assign client workstation have unique internet protocol address separated allocated by each and every client now you decide which client have how much right in network what type service he consume, commercial role of internet addressing scheme provide secure separate and reliable communication in design local area network or global area network, internet addressing scheme avoid network communication collision.

E-mail addresses – e-mail address are address similar to your bank account number while you open any bank account and when you need to withdraw some amount from account you need account number for processing, similar that e-mail address are e-mail account used on internet for creating send receive e-mail message worldwide, e-mail is mass mailing facility that allow you compose and deliver message across the world, e-mail address is your online communication account which enable you to exchange e-mail, you see different server provide mechanism for e-mail format, remember two e-mail are never same each user have unique e-mail address and password.

Username@domainname.com

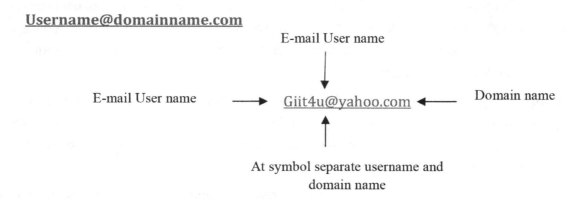

E-mail User name

E-mail User name ⟶ Giit4u@yahoo.com ⟵ Domain name

At symbol separate username and
domain name

TOPIC

07

Internet Connectivity

- 🖥 Dial up internet access.
- 🖥 Isdn.
- 🖥 Dsl.
- 🖥 Adsl.
- 🖥 Broadband connection.
- 🖥 Wireless network connection.
- 🖥 Leased line.
- 🖥 Internet over satellite.
- 🖥 Internet setup dialup.
- 🖥 Modem.
- 🖥 Firewall.

Internet connectivity.

Connectivity types

➲ **Dial up internet access.**

➲ **Isdn.**

➲ **Dsl.**

➲ **Adsl.**

➲ **Broadband connection.**

➲ **Wireless network connection.**

➲ **Leased line.**

➲ **Internet over satellite.**

Dial up internet access – dial up internet connection analog telephone line based internet connection, normally each dial up connection are slow in speed before using dial up internet connection configure installed modem, fill isp (internet service provider)company user name and password in dialup internet connection dialog now click on connect to make connection  with internet service now wait till network connection established open modem device convert receive analog signal into broad band connection, normally 56 kbps dialup internet connection are more popular in earlier time, now open web browser type web site name and starting surfing web content.

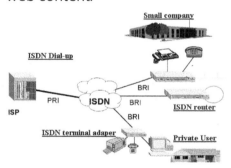

Isdn – isdn abbreviated as integrated service digital network advance than pstn(public switched telephone network)which enable us to send voice, data video, over digital telephone line, common isdn speed range between 64 kbs to 128 kbps, todays video conference video chatting cellphone calling data sending easier possible after invention isdn technology.

Dsl – dsl abbreviated as digital subscriber line telephone line, dsl cable using telephone copper wire telephone service, it setup connection with analog dial up connection service, common dsl connection speed between 128 kbps to 9 mbps.

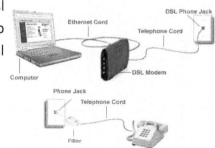

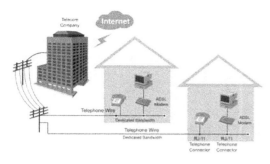

Adsl – adsl stands (asymmetric digital subscriber line) adsl subscriber line provide data rates between 1.5 to 9 mbps in copper telephone line cable, using these cable for faster dsl communication data and information with connected network device, sending huge volume of data over adsl cable wire simultaneously in both size single session, using adsl for better bandwidth then dial up network connectivity, connected all adsl device and compute able to share information while request made by connected user in connectivity.

Broadband connection – broadband internet connection using on the basis of install cable modem, broad band internet connection provide higher data transfer rate from 512 mbps to 20 mbps, surfing web resources at high speed broad network response, modern internet service provider high speed broadband internet commercial or home plan.

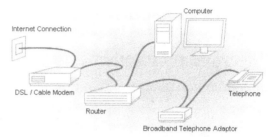

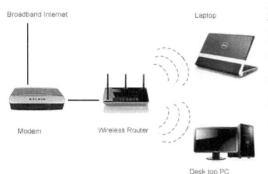

Wireless network connection – wireless broadband internet connection high speed broadband connection, wireless broadband connection established on the basis of wireless router wireless/radio frequency spread in specific range sender or receiver receive wireless broad connection.

Leased line – leased line broadband option available for commercial user, sometime lease line permanent connection between source point to destination point, government organization, business corporate industry use these kind of network to connect and share network services.

Internet over satellite – internet over satellite facility allow user to access internet over satellite, anywhere where satellite access across the globe use device capable to access and receive satellite signal for accessing internet signal, signal receive on earth placed earth station direct satellite internet user easily to access and use these signal to connect services of internet surfing and accessing while interacting network service and application, biggest advantage of internet over satellite allows its user to access these service anywhere everywhere where network reach or access.

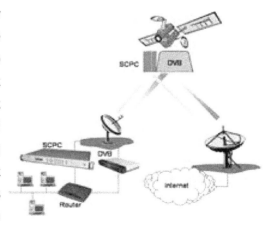

Setting up internet dialup connection

- ➲ Open cmd type control.

- ➲ Open network and sharing center.

- ➲ Click on setup new connection or network.

- ➲ Select or choose internet connection option choose from connect to internet, set up new network, connect to work place, set up a dial up connection.

- ➲ We select set up dial up connection enter dial up phone number, user name, password finally apply create connection.

- ➲ Now open dial up connection and make internet connection.

Hardware requirements for network and dial-up connections

Depending on your configuration, you may need some or all of the following hardware:

One or more network adapters with a network driver interface specification (ndis) driver for lan connectivity

- ➲ One or more compatible modems and an available com port nic card.

- ➲ Isdn adapter (if you are using an isdn line).

- ➲ Dsl adapter.

- ➲ X.25 adapter or pad (if you are using x.25).

- ➲ Analog telephone line, isdn line, x.25 line, or dsl line.

- ➲ Smart card reader.

- ➲ Wireless adapter.

Selection of a modem – modem device used for network internet communication, modem device convert analog telephone signal into digital computer form, modem selection for internet connectivity, depend your network need what type you work how long you surfing on network, generally two basic type of modem available in computer network there are internal and external modem, select one of them according to need.

Internal modem – internal modem fix on computer pci (peripheral computer interconnect) slot, internal modem available at low cost, advantage of internal modem it works similar external modem but it available easier on low price, but remember now days all modern computer hardware motherboard manufacturer build or design mother board onboard modem/ethernet port, but in the time of earlier internal modem manually installed on pci slot and configure or installed on motherboard, proper installed modem, installed

modem software driver, now plug rj45 lan connector to connect machine with modem device for accessing internet services on installed computer, while modem proper install and work proper it indicate lime color light, or modem failure it indicate red color light during working mode, even other cause may be red light modem color display.

External modem – external modem fix external outside from computer case, advantage of using external modem is service of external modem so high, secure, and heavy duty then internal modem, externally connected modem provide more network bandwidth, data transfer rate, less communication error, better network transmission frequency, even use long duration session internal modem, these modem available in shape of small router, that play role of small router, switch, or modem, it mean connect share and access information between connected number of network client user.

Software requirement

- ➲ Windows/unix/linux mac os.

- ➲ Web browser (internet explorer, firefox, safari).

Modem – modem are peripheral device that essentially used to connect networking resources, modem convert digital data over telephone line modem modulate to demodulate telephone signal, some modem are built in on board modem and some modem type externally purchase from computer vendor finally installed them on motherboard pci(peripheral computer interconnect) slot.

Installation modem in computer (internal)

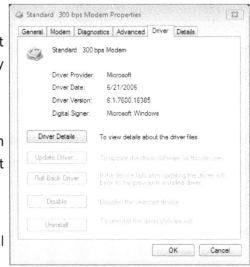

- ➲ Buy new modem from modem seller company, first decide which type of modem your requirement is may be internal or external.

- ➲ Always login as administrator user.

- ➲ If internal modem purchase, that installed it on motherboard pci slot, if external modem connect externally with usb or com port.

- ➲ Open windows control panel window.

- ➲ Select modem and phone option in windows 10 control panel windows.

- Select modem tab, click on add it detect and add newly install modem configuration, if automatically not done apply manually attach installed modem manufacturing and modem detail click next choose port finally click on setup.

- Now days modern all platform operating system contain plug & play device facility which automatically detect and install attach hardware related driver software sometime need manually configure it.

- Create internet dial up connection for network connectivity.

Installation modem in computer (external)

- Buy new external modem from modem seller company, if you decide type of external modem.

- Always login as administrator user, administrator account contain full pc right.

- If external modem purchase, that installed it on motherboard usb or com port .

- Wait till than attach modem automatically configure, modern microsoft operating system contain plug and play facility which automatically detect configure or install required hardware driver.

- If not automatically occur open windows control panel window and manually install modem.

- First properly all configure modem related installation complete now run cd/dvd come along with new buy modem now plug cd into dvd rom install manually modem vendor driver configuration according to install operating system apply default setting finally modem will be manually install.

- Create dial up or broad band internet connection.

- Enjoy network connectivity and share & access internet resources globally.

Modem configuration – modem configuration belong to existing installed modem, sometime preinstalled modem couldn't work properly than we need manually configure it modem setting from windows control panel open windows control panel select modem and phone choose properties configure modem different setting according to need, view modem general setting modem diagnostics advance driver and remaining detail through phone and modem setting.

Internet accounts by isp – isp abbreviated as internet service provider company that located nearest your region, provide internet services broadband modem account user name and user password for personal or commercial use at monthly rental plan, isp company offer dial-up, wired, or dsl(digital subscriber line) fiber optic you get bill according to selection internet pal every month, for accessing internet services you have wired or wireless telephone services include landline number, at large level service provider isp are at&t worldnet, ibm global network, mci, netcom, uunet, and spinet, in indian internet service provider company listed below bsnl, vsnl, idea, reliance, tata docomo, mts and more other companies in stand row, these all above listed company are large level telecommunication service provider.

Isdn – isdn abbreviated as (integrated service digital network) upgradation of old pstn(public switched network) isdn is international standard communication provide facility of voice, video, data communication, isdn service invented for voice and video communication it is digital communication, isdn based on circuit switching telephone network which also enable packet switched network with facility of voice data and video communication with telephone line, for accessing isdn service you must install isdn capable modem adapter.

Type of isdn

B channel – b channel abbreviated as basic rate interface using till 64 kbps for voice and data signal in isdn network communication.

D channel – isdn d channel using to manage and operate isdn producing signal information in communication mode.

Slip – slip abbreviated as (serial line internet protocol) used of slip protocol to connect pc with dial – up internet connection, commercially slip used in unix system in late 1980 now days slip protocol replaced with ppp (point to point) protocol widely used in windows operating system for network connecting, slip communicate between client and server one is responder and other one is request made for communication,

Ppp – ppp protocol abbreviated as point to point protocol we already discuss ppp is replacement of slip protocol used in unix operating system, point to point protocol communicate with telephone line in server it established link between two network node it follow term of encryption, compression, authentication, and transmission, point to point protocol more reliable secure and error free even stable version previous slip protocol, point to point protocol define standard of dial up connection it collaborate with install modem and decide how device exchange information with other modem during communication.

Service options

E-mail – e-mail abbreviated as electronic mail mechanism of sending and receiving electronic mail online over computer network two or more computer, toddy's internet environment e-mail services widely used and access by many corporate, business houses, industry, organization, government offices, even ordinary user can able access e-mail services, e-mail completely replace old paper based post messaging services.

Www – www called as world wide web global based information system, in general language world wide web is huge collection of http hypertext pages, web page, web site, ftp server, e-mail service, new server and many more www allow internet user to access internet resources like download information upload information surfing, web browsing web hosting and many more, www is a collection of server local network along global network, software specially design for accessing www resources called web browser.

Types of news server

News – news posted on internet from many regional national and international server broad caster, usenet article generally news group an online discussion forum online information message news post by new broadcaster.

Firewall – firewall is computer program that protect your personal business computer from hacker, viruses, network infection, and outsider access in network, firewall design for security measure prevent unauthorized access in computer through online internet network system, firewall check all incoming packet reach from outside network location, it block all sensitive malicious data packet from outside world, secure firewall may be collection of hardware and software program that detect malware infection and stop it block it, firewall protect local network as well as global network.

Type of firewall

- ➲ **Packet filtering.**
- ➲ **Application gateway.**
- ➲ **Circuit level gateway.**
- ➲ **Proxy server.**

TOPIC
08

Internet Network

Internet network

Network definition – network interconnect group of online offline network system or combination of client server network hardware software that combine network features even setup of network equipment like hub, switch, repeater, router, cable and more network combine two different word first net it belong to internet second work belong to work from home office computer network are basic fundamental that combine multiple different network, generally network combine all type of local or global network like local area network, campus area network, metropolitan area network, wide area network, virtual private network or may be small han(home area network), pan(personal area network).

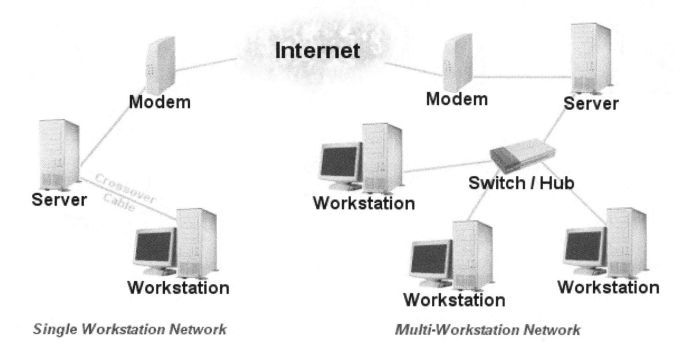

Single Workstation Network   *Multi-Workstation Network*

Common terminologies

Types of network

- ➲ **Lan** – local area network.
- ➲ **Can** – campus area network.
- ➲ **Wlan** – wireless local area network.
- ➲ **Wan** – wide area network.
- ➲ **Man** – metro politian area network.
- ➲ **San** – storage area network.
- ➲ **Pan** – personal area network.
- ➲ **Dan** – desk area network.

Local area networking (lans) – lan abbreviated as local area network, spread in small geographical area, lan cover at least 2 km area, in 2 km area you connect office, building, home, and other location, generally land design in specially in offices for sharing valuable resources between office client, share files, folder, document, audio, video, and other document at 10 mbps, 100 mbps, or more 1 gbps resources sharing bandwidth, share printer, scanner, storage device, control group policy manage user and many other task perform like lan e-mailing, chatting, remote desktop, connection facility integrate all client as single user environment, for design lan you need windows terminal, lan cable, switch, hub, network operating system, lan is a may be commercially or non-commercially setup you don't have permission to setup permission for lan any authority.

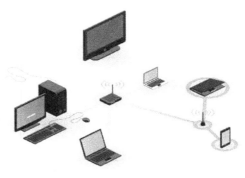

Lan configuration for client

- Pentium 4 i3, i5, i7 intel microprocessor.
- Ram 1 gb or more.
- Lan/ethernet card.
- Ip address.
- Operating system for client (windows 7, windows 10).
- Lan cable.
- Graphic card.
- Web browser (internet explorer, mozilla firefox, google chrome).

Advantage of lan

- Network control.
- Share hardware devices.
- Share software devices.
- Speed.
- Cost.
- Easier setup.

Disadvantage of lan

- Higher hardware cost.
- Expensive software cost.
- Expensive network devices.
- Setup cots.

Metropolitan area network, (man) – man stand as metropolitan area network extend version of lan where lan cover 2km but man cover 5-kilometer to 50-kilometer geographical area, generally man cover small lan at large level for making man, lan connected with high speed backbone fiber optic link for information sharing, man setup by government agencies, organization at large level for covering huge geographical area in your city or town, man bigger in size from lan but smaller from size wan.

Advantage of man

- ➲ Share data and information through high speed network system in man network.
- ➲ Build up large area to cover or creating desire network connections.
- ➲ Easier to connect other nodes connect and operate large volume of network database easier through man network system.

Disadvantage of man

- ➲ Complexity during designing large level network.
- ➲ More hardware cost cable and connector, software cost, critical to operate its subsystem network.
- ➲ Complicated to protect secure sharing information changes of leak data packets in networks.

Wide area network (wan) – small constructed lan, man, can create wan, wan abbreviated as wide area network spread in globe, wide area network cover large country or continent, public network create wan network at large level, internet is an best example of wide area network, which connect small network it may be lan(local area network), can(campus area network), man(metropolitan area network), pan(personal area network), han(home area network)or san(storage area network) network, wan connect nationwide/continent country as a client server architecture and offer service like web page, web site, hypertext information worldwide.

Characteristic of wan

- ➲ Connect computer all over the world, share, access and control connected device and component.
- ➲ Connect country, continent, small geographic and more large area through wan network.
- ➲ Wan combine small network in shape of lans, man, and other kind of local network system.
- ➲ Wan generally complex network which is provide lower bandwidth connectivity during connection.

Advantage of wan

- ⟳ Connecting large area of network for sharing, accessing and connecting network resource and information.
- ⟳ Connect with all word continent and network system to access all kind of network query.
- ⟳ Easier to access wan services on any network system in connected network device.

Disadvantage of wan

- ⟳ Large network difficult to handle & manage.
- ⟳ Slow network, more error, difficult to access or reach search elements, sometime don't access desire and get other unnecessary information.
- ⟳ No one claim to publicly to ownership on wide area network system.
- ⟳ Large network of system so sometime to access, locate, and client and server elements.

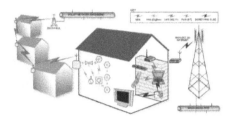 **Home area network (han)** – home area network design on the base of user home, connect home electronic device with digital gadgets, computer, networking equipment, home security system, cellphone, video game, television, wi-fi device and other all peripheral device use by home user can come in category of home area network.

Advantage of han

- ⟳ Create home group network of user for sharing and accessing at cheap rate network database and information.
- ⟳ Connect and share files, folder, movie, audio, video, projects, data and information at high speed network.
- ⟳ Connect wired & wireless network devices for connecting each other system or network.
- ⟳ Share han network internet and sharing connectivity information.

Disadvantage of han

- ⟳ In large home network became problematic during controlling, sharing and apply administrative task.
- ⟳ Cost of hardware peripheral, network equipment, cables & connector so high for build network.
- ⟳ Complicated to connect and troubleshoot connected network node and hardware device.
- ⟳ Disturb whole network due to broken cable and network wires, difficult to handle large network.

Personal area network (pan) – pan stand (personal area network) created between personal, relative individual share common thing for mutual purpose, connect home devices include cellphone, headphone, laptop, desktop, printer, fax, wireless stereo phone, bluetooth device, wi-fi device, etc. In personal area network.

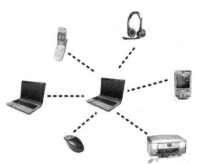

Advantage of pan

- ➲ Sharing some essential information and data between smartphone, cellphone, pda, digital camera & other electronic gadgets.

- ➲ Advantage of using pan complete wireless network it mean no need to wired at fix position, use able to share wireless data and signal at specific range or meters.

- ➲ Secure network using wireless communication, only authenticate user access and control these network.

Disadvantage of pan

- ➲ Buying of expensive wireless network device and its component it more costly then wired network.

- ➲ More chances to handover some important information between some illegal user and network client while communicating and sharing network services.

- ➲ Remember pan complete wireless device or network connection control and operated by human or computer user sometime long duration network user fill some health-related issues and complexity while working with radio signals or wireless frequency.

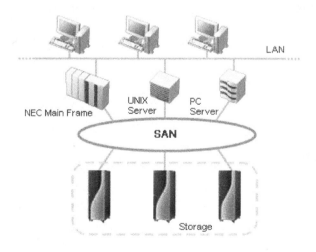

Storage area network (san) – storage are network design for storage resources and data for dedicated client server, storage area network may be local or global it depend on its storage data nature type, san moving data and information between dedicated network, storage area specially for user those always need to secure reliable and high speed network data and information sharing, storage network setup by industry, large organization, company or firm they dedicate own customize server for their network user in small storage network user access hardware resources local storage media and optical device etc.

Advantage of san

- ➲ Share and store high confidential data and information with connected client.

➲ Improves data connectivity, data integrity, data security and data communication between connected clients.

➲ Easier to taking backup and restore, control connected client with administrative privileges in network system.

➲ Share high speed data cable for long distance with using a fiber cables in communication.

Disadvantage of san

➲ Installation of hardware component, price of fiber optic cables, skill to operate these network components.

➲ Operating, controlling, and managing these large networks so complex.

➲ Large network to optimize, manage and control services, application and its features.

Wireless network – wireless network mean digital communication between electronic network and gadgets without any physical wire, wireless network communication is replacement of older wired network communication, generally wireless network spread radio wave that communicate between wireless device and exchange information with resource in secure manner, wireless communication held between cellphone/smart phone, wi-fi, infrared, bluetooth device microwave and terrestrial wireless  network, wireless network is combination of wpan (wireless personal area network) wlan(wireless local area network) wman(wireless metropolitan area network)cellular network (cellphone mobile network), exactly two wireless device on wireless services between both them such as wireless laptop and wireless cellphone on their wireless service include wi-fi, bluetooth service for information exchange, radioactive wave communicate wirelessly along other wireless device.

Advantage of wireless network

➲ Easier to connect wireless network or device in specific range or meters, using password or other authentication services to access and use wireless network.

➲ Reliable, accurate, flexible and faster information exchange network between connected client and its user.

➲ Generally wireless device name smart cellphone, wireless laptop, notebook, bluetooth device, pda, digital camera, and other handy network device.

➲ Connecting one or more network node and device easier to connect and disconnect after providing and accessing search information.

➲ Plug and play device no need to install additional hardware, use infrared, bluetooth and wi-fi to access or connect wireless network component.

Disadvantage of wireless network

- ⮞ Sometime wireless network unsecure, lack of information access, control and integrity issues.
- ⮞ More expensive of buying expensive wireless device name pda, notebook, smart cellphone, digital camera and other electronic gadgets in network system.
- ⮞ Cost of wireless device, work in limited range or area, limited user connectivity and authentication, low speed, and security issues held in wireless network.

Node – in reference of networking node may be network computer network printer and may be other device according to internet protocol node may be ip address or dlc(data link control)or mac (media access control) address location, according to networking node connect two terminal or network device, node play important role for connecting networking device.

Host – host computer play role to provide service to the remote login terminal, host may be local or global host may be computer that are connected globally with tcp/ip network and provide network services, host computer give services to the connected local global computer world widely host offer services world wide web resources control connected client host established as network administrator, web hosting part of hosting many companies and web server provide hosting services for client they upload customer web site web pages online for required consumer online, web hosting company take monthly charges for hosting.

Workstation – workstation is common place for all user who done specific work for any company or industry client server is best example of workstation, workstation are individual personal computer for development, software processing, computer designing workstation contain all capabilities of processing managing controlling desire information in reference of computer networking or internet a workstation special type of computer that established for getting resources from web server and store data on main server, even workstation may be client terminal that process server www resources data and information, basic workstation hade more hardware ram, graphic, microprocessor grater hardware and software capability .

Bandwidth – bandwidth measure maximum and minimum data transfer rate of your internet connection working online bandwidth check how much data transfer send or receive at certain time in active internet connection, bandwidth check data transfer moving rate from source to destination in specific moment in limited period, if you have dialup connection than low bandwidth of data rate if you are using broadband internet connection that data transfer bandwidth would be more, bandwidth speed depend on installed modem hardware software support.

Network administrator – network administrator person who represent for control, manage, provide network service, allot network resource, protect and modify network connection and other auditing related network policies control network maintenance, monitor network and network data flow by network administrator, network administrator responsible for installing network software hardware network services take routine backup and protect network security and more network services fulfill all client network goal.

Network security – network security protect network environment while user share upload download web surfing hypertext information processing every time while you connect with computer in network world network security include protect your personal computer from virus, hacking, worm, trojan horse, network attack, unauthorized access, spyware, denial of service attack, network theft from outside world.

Network – network is group of computer or large network is combination of world popular network database warehouses where data and information linked in shape of local area network, metropolitan area network, wide area network, include small sub network be a part of these network, using network for sharing, accessing, providing electronic document and content in shape of http document, these small network design structure of world wide area network information system which is a large network for communicating and sharing resources.

Components – network component are essential network hardware component that necessary to access and control network services and network roles, various kind of network component you will see and found in a large network where each network hardware component setup for particular purpose, where network interface card, router, hub, switches, modem, network cables and connector and other category of component be a part of network component.

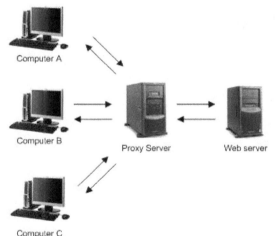

Servers – server is collection of hardware software network resources provide network services and resources for their client, network server or server design or manage network service for client in simple server is powerful machine combination of computer hardware software more higher specification than client computer, network server design for offering network service world widely server may be network file server, web server, print server, proxy server, ftp server, mail server, database server, game server and other type of server in this category.

Clients – client are network service/resource consumer he consume online internet service from internet in connected network environment, client run client application on their terminal workstation for getting online www resource in client server architecture client always made request for resources and server service responder.

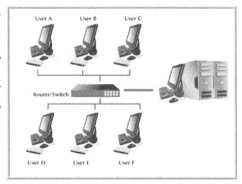

Communication media

➲ **Twisted pair.**

➲ **Coaxial cable.**

➲ **Fiber optic cable.**

Twisted pair – twisted pair cable commonly used in telephone wire for connection dialup network connection, twisted pair cable combine two insulated cooper wire together as twisted manner benefit of twisting two wire it reduce communication error and faster transmission telephone signal, twisted pair used in traditional pstn (public switched telephone service) service, twisted pair divide in general two category called stp (shielded twisted pair) or utp (unshielded twisted pair) we describe briefly them in next section.

Advantage of twisted pair cable

➲ Cheaper than other transmission cable, easier to maintain or implement.

➲ Less communication interference.

➲ Reduce transmission noise.

➲ Some twisted cable version faster data accessing rate.

➲ Twisted pair transmit both analog and digital signal.

➲ If some part of cable damage it doesn't affect entire network.

Disadvantage of twisted pair

➲ Slow performance weaker signal carry transmission rate.

➲ Attenuation ratio more.

➲ Lower signal data transmission bandwidth comparison with another cabling media.

➲ Provide lower security level.

➲ Easier to break damage affect part of network.

➲ Complexity of designing.

Type of twisted pair – you see below combine picture demonstrate type of twisted pair cable, these cables used in ethernet or connecting local area network between company home industry or organization, each cable design to full fill purpose network industries, shielded twisted pair or unshielded twisted pair two common network cable categories used at different places for many purposes.

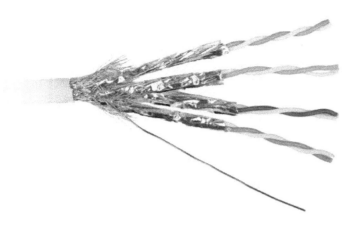

Shielded twisted pair – stp stands shielded twisted pair cable stp contain two cooper wire that are shielded together as helical manner two copper wire coated with insulation material shielded insulated material protect shielded cooper wire reduce electromagnetic interference, or provide higher pstn data transfer rate than unshielded twisted pair cable, each cooper wire shielded together with shielded material.

Advantage of shielded twisted pair cable

- ➲ Shielded twisted pair grater bandwidth.
- ➲ Less rational of noise.
- ➲ Reduce cross talk.
- ➲ Reduce communication interference.

Unshielded twisted pair – utp stands unshielded twisted pair cable utp cable contain two unshielded cooper wire twisted together around from beginning to end, unshielded twisted pair cable cover with plastic wire cap or cover open each wire for connection local area network component for sharing resources between connected network device, unshielded cable bandwidth normal transmission slow but cheaper in price or older transmission technology slow data transfer.

Advantage of unshielded twisted pair cable

- ➲ Higher bandwidth.
- ➲ More protective.
- ➲ Reduce error.
- ➲ Improve device transmission speed.

Coaxial cable – coaxial cable another solid network using cable used to transmit video audio communication the bandwidth of coaxial cable higher than traditional used twisted pair cable, commercially coaxial cable connect your satellite receiver antenna direct from your television sets, your tata sky, dish tv or may be any one company setup box wire come from your home

terrace known as a best example of coaxial cable, another use of coaxial cable in network industry for connection cable modem with broadband network service, coaxial cable surrounded with plastic sheath inside cover with wire mesh same as inner side cover with round white plastic circle and finally cooper wire located within surrounded white plastic cover,

Advantage of coaxial cable

- ➲ Coaxial cable is a common medium of multimedia transmission.
- ➲ Cover more distance with higher data bandwidth transmission.
- ➲ Easier to implement modify.
- ➲ Less noise interference.
- ➲ Low error rate in broadband connection.
- ➲ Support multiple channel greater frequency.

Disadvantage of coaxial cable

- ➲ Coaxial cable is more expensive.
- ➲ Installation procedure different then twisted pair.
- ➲ Easier to break damage whole network.

Fiber optic cable – fiber optic cable high speed network data transmission technique, small threads of fiber in group of one or more thread collection reliably sending and receiving electronic data, fiber replacement of old cable, twisted and coaxial cable wires, using optical fiber cable to sending large volume of high speed data packet in dedicated network at greater speed on high light frequency, modem network adopt fiber optic cable for data accuracy, reliability, and flexible data transmission in connected network.

Advantage of fiber optic

- ➲ Improve system performance.
- ➲ Increase bandwidth.
- ➲ Immune from electronic noise.
- ➲ Fewer amount of signal attenuation.
- ➲ Cover long distance at lower price.
- ➲ Faster transmission data bandwidth.

Disadvantage of fiber optic

- ➲ Costly, skill to manage, control and update fiber optic connection.

- ➲ More chances to breakage of small thin fiber galas plastic wires cause of network down.

- ➲ Best advance technology difficult to find error, troubleshoot, issue solving process.

- ➲ Expensive hardware equipment, can't afford by small organization and firm for setup fiber cable network.

Types of network

Peer to peer network – peer to peer network is type of internet network connect with common network line, easier network communication for sharing resources and network service between connected client without server, in peer to peer network all client access resources data and information with center computer even each p2p client have capability of administrator computer.

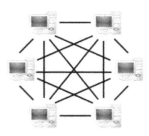

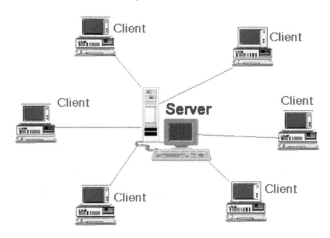

Client server network – in client server network server is service responder where client is service requester where client and server may be connected through lan(local area network) or wan (wide area network) commercially reason of design client server network is sharing business commercial non- commercial data and resources between server to client, server is a powerful machine that contain heavier hardware software list, like dbms program is a suitable program there information stored by client on server machine, server establish as network administrator who responsible for managing service of all connected client and server, client pc operated as working workstation terminal control by network user.

Dns – dns abbreviated as domain name system online internet service convert dns into ip address because computer easier to read or find any link ip address, domain name system provide any web site domain alphabetic name but internet can't process it in same manner network switch router and other network device convert it into internet protocol format, while url enter in web browser address bar it convert url into ip address.

Network topologies

Bus topology – bus topology popular in large organization company industry, where all sequence of computer connected in same row continuously known as bus or backbone one by one all connected computer share common line for data information sharing.

Benefit of bus topology

- ⊃ Easier to implement bus topology.
- ⊃ Minimum cable requirement in bus topology.
- ⊃ Minimum cost of set up bus topology.
- ⊃ Bus topology can be used in small as well as large network.

Disadvantage of bus topology

- ⊃ Connect limited client for better network speed, if more client and node connected network will be slow and down.
- ⊃ More chances to down all network sudden when a main cable damage or corrupt in network.
- ⊃ Upgradation, maintenance, and troubleshooting became more critical in network communication.
- ⊃ Less security network, leakage of information, controlling and managing service difficult in large bus network.
- ⊃ More computer connected in bus network more changes to network data traffic collision and network breakdown.

<u>**Start topology**</u> – start topology can be easily implemented in small office building and company, in star topology all connected client cable connect with central hub/switch/server or computer, most of computer network designer implement common network with star topology, reason each network workstation share individual cable medium network sharing.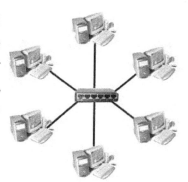

Benefit of star topology

- ⊃ Easier to implement than bus, ring, graph, or mesh topology.
- ⊃ Better device network performance.
- ⊃ Fast transmission reliable network.
- ⊃ Accuracy reliability and better communication between workstation.
- ⊃ If any client fail network continue run.
- ⊃ Control all client behavior with central computer.
- ⊃ Easier to maintain add remove new or existing node.

Loss of star topology

- ⊃ Heavier network transmission load on center computer.
- ⊃ If central computer fail all network down.

➲ If adding more than client computer network go fail, low transmission data rate.

➲ Leak of security.

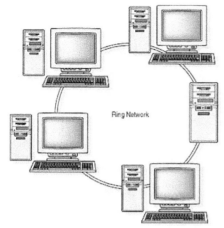

Ring Network

Ring topology – in ring topology each computer connected with two nodes called previous and next node, shape or ring topology look like as circle ring, two node moving or share data in ring network, ring topology specially implemented where computer setup in circle or ring order.

Benefit of ring topology

➲ Data and information faster quicker in ring network a central network system control all network component environment.

➲ Network data packet moving in previous or next computer from ring network server to all ring network client computer.

➲ If adding many more client then ring network limit it will cause of network slow data transmission, and lack of information security issues.

➲ No network data traffic, collision of network data and information transmission information in world wide web system.

Loss of ring topology

➲ Difficult to manage every node and link of ring network, troubleshooting error, and other issues generated when operating ring topology network.

➲ When ring network connected any node disturb, or broken it affect remaining network services when collision generated.

➲ A single cable using from start to endpoint in ring network holding network data traffic information when sharing its resources.

➲ When central ring network server down it will automatically shut communication between all connected network device and services.

Ethernet – ethernet term used in network for connecting local area network connection and connectivity, ethernet developed by xerox corporation share high speed network data and information between connected network client at 10 mbps to 1000 mbps speed during sharing and receiving information with connected node/client.

Fddi – fddi stands fiber distributes data interface for sending digital over fiber optic cable fddi token passing networking and support data rates of up to 100 mbps per second it is used for supportive backbone wide area network, fddi enable local area network connectivity with 100 or 200 mbps.

Atm – stand asynchronous transfer mode high speed networking technology that allow to share data and voice at 53 bytes, it work in long distance data network with osi second layer called data link layer atm control and manage high speed data and voice network.

Intranet – intranet is prototype of internet where internet is global network where everyone participate from different world corner location, but intranet limited in single organization where authenticate organization company member access particular intranet web site resources similar local area network intranet operated in local small geographical are with limited user for common purpose sharing, internet share common goal of common use company member but it is based on common tcp/ip internet network method.

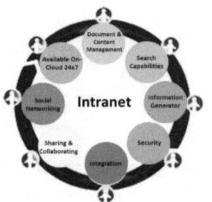

TOPIC

09

Service of Internet

- 🖥 E-mail.
- 🖥 Www.
- 🖥 Telnet.
- 🖥 Ftp.
- 🖥 Common ftp software.
- 🖥 Irc.
- 🖥 Rediff messenger.
- 🖥 Yahoo messenger.
- 🖥 Window liver messenger.
- 🖥 Pidgin.
- 🖥 Skype.
- 🖥 VoIP.
- 🖥 We chat.
- 🖥 Lime.
- 🖥 Facebook.
- 🖥 Twitter.
- 🖥 LinkedIn.
- 🖥 Search engine.
- 🖥 Type of search engine.

Services on internet (definition and functions)

E-mail – e-mail standing as electronic mail using e-mail for mail document between e-mail account sender and receiver user, you must have at least e-mail account of any e-mail service provider company name, yahoo, rediffmail, gmail and other, using e-mail for exchanging electronic messages include attach document, worksheet, presentation, audio, video, multimedia object and other electronic content and information through e-mail technology easier at long distance and network communication.

Www – www stand worldwide network system, world biggest largest network for hypertext information exchange and resources sharing, all world online server be part or world wide web system, internet servers, data server, large corporate network, and other lan, can, man, & wan web based electronic hypertext document in shape of world wide web server storage content, world wide web linked information created in html, javascript, vb script, and other kind of web programming web pages linked in web portals, websites to easier quick navigate information and data access.

Telnet – telnet stands terminal emulation program designing for tcp/ip network in client server structure just like internet, telnet program run in client machine and provide network connectivity between client and server control client operation from server for log in in telnet session you must have authenticate user name and password for telnet access, accessing and control remote computer through telnet program you became administrator computer right for control other run telnet client computer online you had command line experience to better deal with telnet command line statement.

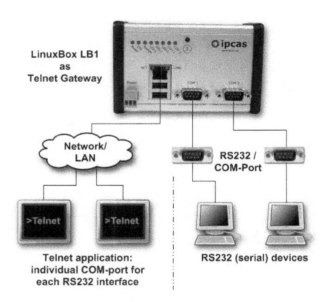

LinuxBox LB1 as Telnet Gateway

Network/ LAN

RS232 / COM-Port

>Telnet   >Telnet

Telnet application: individual COM-port for each RS232 interface

RS232 (serial) devices

Turn on telnet features in window

- ➲ Click on start menu – control panel.
- ➲ Open – program and features.
- ➲ Select or click turn on window features for on/off mode.
- ➲ Select in window features dialog, turn on telnet client check box features.
- ➲ Click ok to manually install all system telnet related features and services.
- ➲ Now telnet services loaded in installed, manually follow start telnet session procedure.

Start telnet session in window

⮑ Click on start menu.

⮑ Click on run – type – cmd.

⮑ In cmd type – telnet.

Telnet command – telnet command used to start and end telnet session when user communicate with telnet services in established telnet session.

Telnet – telnet command connect computer run telnet protocol services, apply these command in cmd at telnet prompt.

Open – open command connects client computer to remote telnet session window, it open or start telnet session for working.

Quit – quit and terminate client role in connected telnet session type quit or q command to quit form telnet session window.

Close – close command close or disconnect client computer from remote telnet session window, type command on front of telnet prompt screen.

Time – show current system time with time command in telnet session, time display in system define time format preview mode.

Tree – Tree command display system tree structure in detail, show drive file structure, drive each files contain information detail and other information preview.

Ftp – ftp stands file transfer protocol internet standard protocol specially used while communicate or transfer file data and online information between client and server, each ftp server dedicated for specific file and data transfer between two individual dedicated server, ftp client software called ftp client ftp client communicate with ftp server finally connection established now client able to send and receive file and information, enter user name and password each ftp server allow two mode of file transfer one is ascii and second binary mode common ftp client called quite ftp and ws ftp server.

Connect vista and windows7

1. Click 'start'

2. In the search bar, type 'cmd' and press enter

Step 2: connecting to a ftp server

1. In the cmd window type 'ftp domainname.com' and press enter.

2. After opening ftp server enter your username and press enter.

3. Now enter your password, enter it and press enter.

Finally windows open below like this

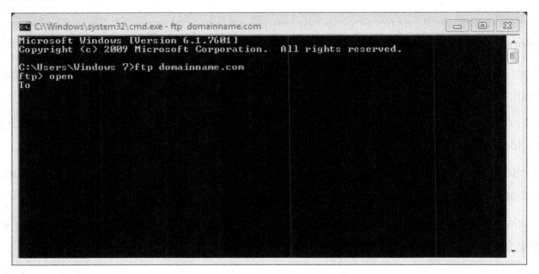

Common ftp software

- ➲ Ws ftp.
- ➲ Complete ftp server.
- ➲ Filezilla server.
- ➲ Microsoft internet information server.
- ➲ Zftp server.
- ➲ Smart ftp.
- ➲ Cute ftp.
- ➲ Wing ftp.

Ws ftp – ws ftp is web client developed by american company name Ipswitch, for windows plat form operating system, ws ftp shareware software anybody can download it, ws ftp stand win sock file transfer protocol, upload client file data information audio video animation content document easily upload at define server location with ws ftp client, while you trying to upload information browse the location of stored file web resources stored in secondary hard drive location.

Windows of ws ftp server

Complete ftp server – complete ftp server allows its user to transfer files and network database at ftp server location, using your computer installed wsftp server to transmit server files between connected clients and network user, using graphical dialog or windows of wsftp server that guide its user to transmit network data and information between network computer and internet services, transmit data with wsftp server more secure, with control and privileges, easier and convenient way to information exchange when user need.

Filezilla server – fileszila another free and cross platform ftp client or server software, that permit its user to sharing and transmit files and data between user computer to server/remote computer, it depend what kind of filezila ftp version you use for transmitting files and data, using file zila ftp software in your installed machine linux, unix, mac, and other open source program, follow step of filezilla ftp client software to transmit files and data on server or client computer.

Microsoft internet information server – iis stands microsoft internet information server manager ftp application software created and supported by microsoft company developer team, complete license ftp software that allows its user to share or transmit data and information, used iis in microsoft windows nt or windows 2000 operating system, iis internet management file server where manage internet files and data with ftp server.

Zftp server – zftp server allows its user to transmit user data and files over internet services from local computer to remote computer user connection, using zftp server like other ftp server using it wizard to downloading and uploading ftp server data and information at define server location, maintain web portals link, updates, image, text, audio, video, and other content through zftp server application.

Smart ftp – using smart ftp server to share files and network data and information between your network computer to define host/server/remote computer location using internet service, follow step of dialog to transmit smart ftp manager files and data, published web portal content and information on server, using for downloading, sending, receiving and uploading web content and information.

Cute ftp – using cuteftp application to upload and download web portals web sites information from user local computer to defined network/internet remote/server computer, upload hypertext web static and dynamic pages, text, multimedia, video, audio, visual, and more web content easier to post at remote computer using cuteftp and other tools.

Irc – irc abbreviated as internet relay chat, chat system developed by jarkko oikarinen in finland in year 1980 -1988, it became popular in field of computer networking while any one need to communicate with each other with text conversation used irc client for sending and receiving text based message through irc client software between irc server or client, for these you must download irc client software from irc client software web site even find on google google will track you actual position of irc web site and configure required setting than start text based conversation live across the world, irc company design irc for all platform it available for mac, windows, unix, linux or androids operating system now days, while irc client send text based conversation message irc server responsible to deliver message between right or requested participated client, bot sender and irc message receiver client must be connected with irc server at a same time during textual conversation, send text message between one or more irc client at same time but all message receiver client must should in same room.

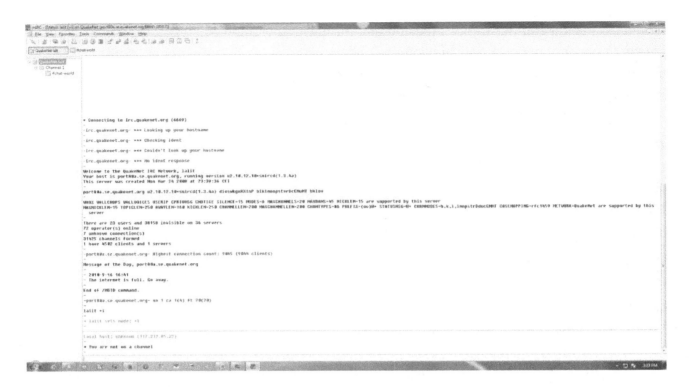

Yahoo messenger – yahoo messenger popular across the world among yahoo user, yahoo messenger created by yahoo company in year 1998, in short it called(ym) yahoo would be soon popular between internet user because yahoo contain capability of text communication, phone call with video conference internet radio even file transfer facility enable, it show all new inbox mail from receiver, keep instant message in track list while you are offline, in yahoo messenger available various category of chat room according to culture, environment, interest, choose desire room and enter with given yahoo key, yahoo messenger available for download at yahoo messenger web site after downloading you need yahoo account user id and password for log in in yahoo messenger services, yahoo messenger provide sending phone call, making video call, phone between pc to cell phone now day's yahoo messenger 11 popular.

Rediff messenger – rediff bol messenger developed and publish by rediffmail organization, rediff bol similar to other social chatting client software, rediff bol messenger allow you to chat with rediffmail user in same room but at the same both use rediffmail account id and password even may be available in same during text conversation.

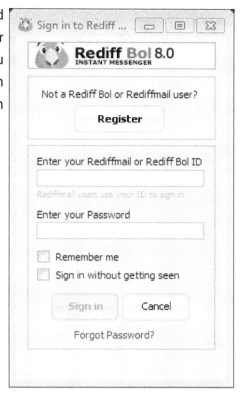

Windows live messenger – windows messenger created and supported by microsoft organization even we say that windows messenger replacement of microsoft windows msn messenger, short abbreviates as (wlm) windows live messenger similar other instant messaging services provide windows live messenger automatically loaded in windows 7 & 8 even windows phone system, manage graphic create chatting with windows user send receive message between one or more client at same time, wlm interoperability between yahoo, facebook windows sky drive.

Pidgin – open source application that permit its user to communicate online with many user in various language and text communication technique, be part of pidgin group member and talk with each other user, using various kind of language tool to communicate and sharing text information when using a pidgin messenger, for configure pidgin you must have online user id to log in, access list of buddies to became part of pidgin user network.

Skype – skype instant messaging, voice call, video call software free internet call application software easier to download from skype web site, make voice video text instant message file transfer easier with skype software across the world its free of charge anybody can download it from skype web site or use it available for download for windows mac linux mac even android operating system, than register on skype web site get user name and password for making low cost free skype call on any cell phone number, you can download it for your desktop, laptop, note book, tablet, ultra-book, even cell phone remember during skype communication you must need high speed internet connection for sharing communication resources otherwise it display transmission delay.

VoIP Diagram

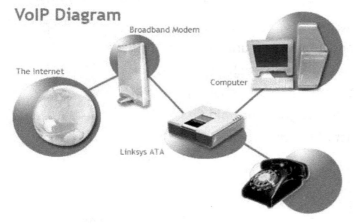

Voip – stands voice over internet protocol new technology that allow people to communicate together through, communication between two user using internet technology for transmit text information into voice signal or data form using voip technique on base of old pstn(public switched telephone network) for transmitting data into computer digital form, using voip application to create talk and communication in long distance or area, advantage of using voip technique to talk on low price change across the world, normal call rate higher and using voip user just need to have internet technology to access its services and controls.

We chat – we chat software design by chinese company specially for smart cell phone, we chat contain instant messaging, voice, video call, file transfer services, photo/audio/video sharing capability, like yahoo, rediff, skype, irc and other messaging application software, you can download it from its web site cell phone capable to handle internet services run we chat in androids, nokia, samsung, spice, windows phone, apple iphone, black berry based smart phone, you need user account and password for making we chat call and instant messaging at free voice call communication, keep in regular touch of social networking client talk share text while walk.

Line – line became popular smart cellphone instant messaging system, developed by line corporation line messenger are available free of cost for smart phone after proper installing of line messenger you can able to exchange text, message, picture even make voice with video call, voip call, manage video conference at same time with other line client in online internet system, advantage of using line messaging system is to exchange free text, audio, video, graphic message with friend, relative, colleague whenever wherever between one or more individual user it provides you line striker and emotion that represent your communication behavior during online messaging system, anybody can download it from its web site and access its features.

Facebook – facebook is popular social network web site which keep you in touch with your friends, relative, colleague, partner, business associative, staff, employee, and other individual that in your group share text message make call create video conference share file folder image audio video and other object group client post new article read existing article share feeling create social understanding between connected client.

Twitter – twitter is also another popular social media connectivity web site where people work together communicate share text information message it is similar to we chat, line, facebook, and other popular category text based chatting software in twitter you tweet any one for answer for asking question, send and receive twitter user message till than 140 character per message limit, you need twitter connection id and password for accessing twitter service.

Linkedin – linkedin is specially design or develop for those who professionally communicate online with each other, it allow business professional to share their comment text message and business activity only linkedin register member can access services of linkedin online services, you must should be registered member of linkedin services before using it, update and keep professionally contact easier in linkedin services at linkedin platform you share your professionalism opinion idea and opportunity among business partner professional or associate.

Search engine – search engine work online on internet for searching some specific document, graphic, web content, online resources, web link, even other all type searching elements, common search engine are system software and strict predefine algorithms that work according to system input, there are many popular list of search engine available in market for searching online web resources some are google, bing, yahoo, rediffmail, and other popular are available, each search engine search keyword type in blank search address bar while clicking on search button it will search required content and elements online of million connected web server and manage them as a directory or index view now you can pick your desire links from given choice, generally world wide web is a wide collection/bank/ocean of www resources, any popular search engine search information with the help of robot and spider search program that search html, xml, asp, java, php and other web site linked database a beginner internet user used search engine to getting online resources now modern search engine allow

you to search web, images, news, videos, maps, books, application, people, news group, and other common search elements are listed in this category .now internet became collection of huge ocean of worldwide connected web server, each server contain required information or database for serve sufficient purpose or need.

What to do by a common search engines

- ➲ Search specific web resources online with help of search engine.
- ➲ Play a role of online guide in internet.
- ➲ It collect vast index of search information online.
- ➲ Promote product register online product so any one can access it easier.

Disadvantage of search engine

- ➲ Produce huge collection or irrelevant web index.
- ➲ Critical and complex process of searching during search desire element.
- ➲ If searching element not find at specific moment it frustrates for searcher.

Which search engine is best – google is the best smart search engine, because database, web links, result, information provide more accurate, reliable, and exact then other search engine in search engine category, include service provide by google not provided by other search engine name, default search of google create google account for e-mail, search web, text and other information online on world large database, locate google maps location, explore google acquire you tube videos, access google play store on smart phone, view latest news articles, use online google drive storage, view calendar online, access google plus services, translate source text into various language text, share and view photos, crete google online document, view book category, maintain google blogger, list number of google contact, use google hangouts services and more other information provides by google search engine.

Popular search engine

Www.google.com	Www.yahoo.com	Www.bing.com
Www.rediffmail.com	Www.justdial.com	Www.ask.com
Www.yippy.com	Www.dogpile.com	Www.altavista.com
Www.alibaba.com	Www.wow.com	Www.infospace.com
Www.info.com	Www.webopedia.com	Www.msn.com
Www.excite.com	Www.aolsearch.com	

Google search engine – now everyone know about google while they interact with information technology google is a first web site where many user access its services for accessing or creating web searching resources strategy, google became popular search engine in the world in short for its services and facility provide mechanism let's move on google history google was developed by larry page and sergey brin while they were ph.d. Students at stanford university in year 1998.

Google offer services

Web search – web search special google service which exclusively access by everyone who are internet user, while we access internet that we don't know actually what to do search and where it will be find than web search features of google search engine help us to find out our required data and information on google and www server according to given address bar search key google search algorithms search find object on global server finally it index all search information as a link from top to bottom view or open them according to need, just click and jump on desire web link use and or not boolean operator for efficient searching google robot and spider search information according to given criteria.

Toolbar – google toolbar contain some shortcut tools to control and operate google events and task during work with google search engine services, advantage of using these toolbars it provides quick mechanism to connect required tools and control during communication.

Search for mobile – search for mobile google services launces for smart cell phone that are capable to view or navigate www information worldwide, it depend on cellphone make may be android, black berry, or symbian cell phone operating system you get pre-installed google web site with search engine similar search all information and data on www server, google listed or index all information that meet your requirement.

You tube – you tube service launces by google where you view see or play upload and download latest and old video post host video if you are getting e-mail account of gmail, you tube allow to watch movie, technology, education, serial, food making, industry, organization, medical, mechanical, engineering, motivate, cultural, music, sports, gaming, tv shows, spot light environmental and many other category video search desire video in this category even download them for offline watching reading load you educational personal video same as web hosting free of charge on you tube, some you tube are prohibit for accessing them or log in with you tube password.

Image search – image search are brilliant features of google that allow you to search different kind of picture, wallpaper, image, cartoon, sceneries, animation, logo, snap and other jpg, gif, png, tiff, even other popular image extension easier search with google image search features, you can download, edit or store it for future.

Picasa – picasa is google based image view application software that allow online view picture edit photo apply effect through option, after downloading picasa it automatically search all graphic picture audio video multimedia object even animated object, customize image, video with given image editor effect.

Maps – maps known as google maps popular google online web based earth route navigation facility, google map display you map of any city continent different transportation route from source to destination places, get direction of any city to another city view miles number of hour taking number of city village and town come between source to destination from source to destination during travelling print satellite map view weather, photos, web cam terrain etc. Google map downloaded on smart cell phone download them from google play store, if you want more than turn google earth service that show you geographically view of any country and continent.

Blog search – blog search feature provided by google to search and locate desire blog information search at google blog search features, read blog, comment blog, and print blog essential information.

Gmail – google offer online web based e-mail services name (google mail), gmail offer you to create gmail e-mail account online getting user name and password now compose e-mail read e-mail send e-mail view calendar write note text store inbox e-mail store draft e-mail keep e-mail recipient user contact list, gmail e-mail account enable you to access and download you tube video for permanent secondary storage.

Calendar – google calendar is free online calendar service that display current month calendar along current date maintain schedule, create appointment, store contact and more lesser than microsoft outlook but online available so you can access it anywhere according to need.

Google cloud point – using google cloud point services to access its features and control in working google search engine while user need.

Blogger – using google blogger google features to create google blog, view, modify, share audio, video, text, photos and other electronic information in shape of blogger tool.

Google chrome – google chrome developed by goggle now google chrome became very popular web browser between many internet user access google chrome for surfing, navigation www resources online, it's free and easier to download from google web site, goggle chrome design for windows, mac, linux, androids, and ios platform operating.

Books – search online collection of books from google store, google books collection provide you set of books you can view read even download them, even google provides you many global online books collection choice you can download them even view or read them online.

News – google new broadcaster updates you with latest online collection of worldwide news according to you country region you get here local regional, national, international, business, entertainment, sports, and other news, click and view copy read news.

Translate – google translate online web based multi-language translator or called huge collection of multiple language dictionary, type desire word sentence from current language to another language like you can change english dictionary vocabulary spelling meaning words from english to hindi or other regional national even international language, it's like a wikipedia that immediate response to you about related your search terms, it facilitate you to listen show example of usage word read phonetically even rate selected translation object, it provide collection of many language like french, russian, spinach, japanese, thai, hebrew, urdu, swedish and more collection of almost world language.

Groups – google groups are online google provided services that allow to everyone to topic on interested subject, title, and related information share information blog posted article create question and find many solution query it is common similar to online bulletin news broadcaster many google user access these service and get advantage of it many people share common understanding feeling and opportunity create meeting, organize meeting, conference, create social meeting with group people, google group available you to various category of groups pick from arts and entertainment and arts, news, society, business and features, people, computer, health, science and technology, choose or select region online discussion group from international country choice.

Orkut – orkut service launches by google participate role in field of social networking, orkut very common to other social web site where user people share their text blog message share information comment each other, you connect with orkut user share understanding feeling before using you must be create orkut profile sign with e-mail id and password now you access orkut features according to need.

Yahoo search engine – yahoo search engine part of yahoo web site it is leading search engine before invention of google search engine, yahoo search engine similar to other popular search engine where you search desire criteria search element on world wide web yahoo provide online search database yahoo search engine search or index them according to user search need pick desire search elements and open link that meet your requirement yahoo search offer you search online yahoo web, images, video, news, game, travel, messenger, e-mail, shopping, finance and more search category available according to need.

Yahoo services offer

Web – yahoo web provide useful indexing arrange links according to searching condition, search desire searching text in yahoo address bar.

Image – yahoo image option allow you to search specific image, type name of image graphic clip art picture wallpaper background greeting and other type of graphic easier search through image option.

Video – search yahoo video option allow you to search online search keyword information type in address bar, pick desire category and play with supported media player.

New – view latest posted news article in yahoo news option, pick any subject topic whatever you want to read open or copy, news always update you what happening in the world.

More – yahoo more option through more yahoo search option category like, local, answer, celebrity, and related information.

Bing search engine – bing is replacement of microsoft previous launch msn/hotmail search engine, microsoft re launch msn with new features ability with efficient searching in new technique in bing search engine, bing allow you to efficient search web, image, video, news, maps, search history, and more category offer.

Bing offer services

Web – searching web url information with microsoft bing search engine, web features search user enter web url term information on specific server, search tools automatic provide moderate and unmoderated search link at below screen display in web browser.

Image – search particular images of any picture, graphic, background, scenarios, photo, book, map, and other kind of pictures search and found in category of bing image search category.

Video – search world popular video links at bing video gallery collection, type name of find search video and wait till the popular video links appear or preview in result window, open play and view multimedia video content in working web browser supported application.

News – searching current news affairs or active news related to regional, national, and international news from in news category, explore news view news link, include learn news article in various world popular language.

Maps – view and explore world popular map of any country, continent, region, just go on bing maps option type name of search location move on any geographic location, find route of any location, view world any country map, map elements, other information.

Search history – search history option enable you to view microsoft bing search history from start to end, use search history features to know more about search related in bing search engine.

More – search a more bing category web information and links in working web browser through bing search engine in working web browser.

Msn – move on microsoft msn web site to explore updates everyday links and web information on microsoft msn website, view all updates dynamic web information, link, news, updates, and category of web information on microsoft msn website.

Outlook.com – move on microsoft outlook.com website to view microsoft outlook e-mail, or other features to use microsoft outlook features called calendar, task, journal, contact, and other outlook features in outlook.com.

Rediffmail search engine – rediffmail popular search engine include popular web url where everyone access their required information, like access rediffmail e-mail to send and receive mail online, view livestock shares and prices online, view online video, shopping online product on its web sites, view rediff news and article, search global information as rediff search engine, get latest updates and all kind of category of information, and other kind of category electronic information easier to access on rediffmail web site.

Rediff offer services

Real-time news – rediff real time news option enable rediffmail user to searching and navigating real time news article display and broadcast news of rediffmail server, use these page to getting new always updates online national and international news access from rediff real – time news web page links.

Images – searching online rediffmail images just type name of search image, background, graphic, sceneries and other kind of electronic background or graphic images at search location in web browser websites.

Books – search online rediffmail collection of book buy categories of rediff collection books here, view category of book, select view book specification and other detail through rediffmail book option.

More – explore rediffmail more option to access redifffmail online services and control to know more other subject and information at working rediffmail web search engine when user need.

Just dial search engine – just dial also knows as jd local indian search engine that search local indian community portal information include movie, restaurant, hotel, travel, finance, automobile, electronic, computer, doctor, education, entertainment, food, furniture, jobs, mobile phone, real estate, shopping and local, regional, even national level information easier search easily through just dial search engine, type desire search category information in just dial search engine dialog box it provide you various links of information searches, the web address of just dial search engine are www.justdial.com.

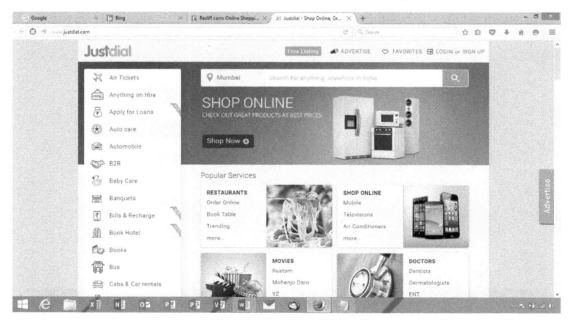

Ask search engine – ask search engine is old search engine, and popular in previous year, these kind of search engine provide a small amount of database server to show and display search engine information, now days ask search engine stand behind some popular search engine and it not to completely outdated but a technique of searching include search database small in size, so it less popular between internet user, but you can access ask search engine to access star gazing, yoga, sea creatures, gardening, legends, birds and more categories of elements according to user input search term.

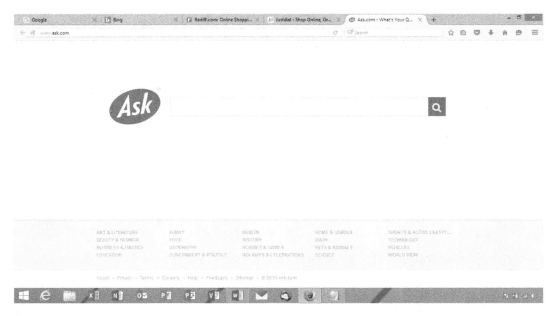

Yippy search engine – yippy search engine less popular engine reason is search technique and small amount of search data and information include services provided by yippy search engine, you able to search news, weather, audio, video, pc information, tablet, or mobile information on which hardware device or platform you use to access yippy search engine, using yippy with small search database sources and limited content of information.

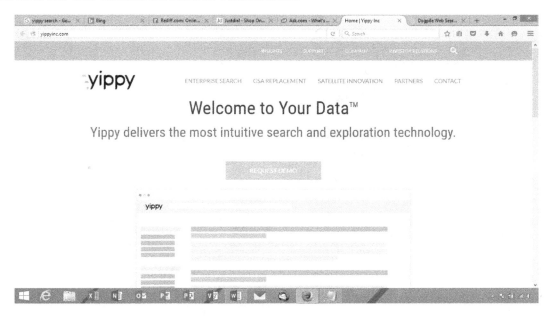

Dog pile search engine – dogpile search engine looking some graphical attractive operating system, and provides various links for searching web, images, video, news, shopping, and white pages, you see down empty search box in dogpile search page, type whatever you want to search and access with dogpile search engine, advantage of dogpile search engine is it connected with various search engine while user search anything or something on internet, dogpile produce search similar page link from many sources, configure and customize dogpile according to your need.

Altavista search engine – altavista search engine kind of internet search engine that allows it user to search and access to help various kind of online information through its connected source and network links, now all the rights of altavista purchase by google, when user starting and searching some required information on alta vista search engine it will moves you on a yahoo web search engine and you know about yahoo services, type search and access some online information on yahoo server with altavista search engine.

Alibaba search engine – alibaba search engine specially operated and use by those you made online payment, making online buying and selling consumer business product include web search tools and technique, type name of www.alibaba.com to access its search features, alibaba search engine provides you facility to access e-commerce, e - transition, e-fund transfer, portable gadgets commerce, shopping and more services.

Wow search engine – wow search engine is another kind of search engine where user making search technique for searching, entertainment, health, tech, food, lifestyle, family, sports, money, & more kinds of services search and access easier through using a wow search engine online, just type those information you want to access or find with wow search engine and access them online, type www.wow.com to access wow search engine online.

Info space search engine – info space search engine provide search with less search technique, search brands, network, web, image, news, portals and many other link easier online with info space search engine, default its searching technique not to provide so much link and information, but you using its database to search some essential kind of information online.

Info search engine – search web, shop, jobs, images, news, video, yellow pages, text, and other information at working web related information search term, like other search engine you have option to use info search engine to search some desire information, type the name, content of search elements, and click to find command to search or find information as a link in shape of result.

Webopedia search engine – webopedia search engine looking some graphical and more colorful search engine that allows its user to search some specific find keyword elements in working web location, juts type information and content that one you like to search their information in shape of search engine, e circular empty text box get search information from user side and starting to search and locate those information online in current web location.

Msn search engine – msn search engine created operated and dynamically updated by microsoft company web developer, advantage of using microsoft search engine to get latest updates news, sports, microsoft company program and software review, updates easier to access through it, search desire web, text, multimedia, web portal elements, include access outlook.com, microsoft office, one note, one drive, maps, face book, twitter, skype and more services, get link of fresh updates dynamic web link, news, and other national include international news events through msn web search engine, previously user more msn but now use moves on microsoft bing search engine.

Excite search engine – excite search stand in line of search engine category you can access excite search engine to get search query and result about search information in working web browser application, search desire text, audio, video, movie, multimedia and other information in working web browser location through excite search engine.

Aol search engine – aol search engine know as american online search engine use type online internet web site www.aol.com to find some web portal text, music, multimedia, check mail, search information, sign in online account, view entertainment content, view finance, life styles, explore online dynamic news, locate category of sports, shop online web portals information and many more with connected network.

TOPIC
10

Electronic Mail

Electronic mail

Email – e-mail short as electronic mail popular or widely used services on internet today, using e-mail need to register or create e-mail account on any e-mail facility provide web site like google, yahoo, rediff, msn and other line up companies, in ancient time they used traditional medium for sending message, letter, or any parcel at receiver location they used pigeon, horse rider, ambassador, postman, radio, television, and other that time popular transmission technology, but e-mail are completely different from above discuss transmission  media in e-mail we can send later, matter, document, report, fax, query, attach audio, video, graphic, animation, software, catalog, and other computer data or resources easier in quick time send across the world with quick response, low cost, and immediate upgradation, remember you must should be create e-mail account before using e-mail services create new e-mail account on any web site and login in account now you can read inbox receive e-mail, send compose e-mail, view spam mail and display colander, use notepad connect with social web site, and apply many other operation it depends on your e-mail service provide company.

Characteristic of e-mail

- ⮞ Medium of communication.
- ⮞ Verbal communication.
- ⮞ Abstract communication.
- ⮞ Fast reliable & flexible.
- ⮞ Cheap.
- ⮞ Quick response.
- ⮞ Other benefit.

Advantage of e-mail

- ⮞ E-mail are easier to use.
- ⮞ Cheap/lower cost medium of communication.
- ⮞ Fast response.
- ⮞ Global advantage.
- ⮞ Efficient.
- ⮞ Versatile.
- ⮞ Secure and reliable.

- ➲ Getting update.
- ➲ Touch in communication.

Disadvantage of e-mail

- ➲ E-mail content virus.
- ➲ Can't express emotion.
- ➲ Misunderstand.
- ➲ Spam.
- ➲ Very long.
- ➲ E – mail hacking.
- ➲ Inappropriate content.
- ➲ No guaranty of reaching.

Email protocols

Smtp – smtp stands simple mail transfer protocol work with tcp/ip (transmission control protocol/internet protocol) smtp responsible for sending and receiving e-mail message between client and server, smtp check e-mail message source destination and reliably deliver at recipient client machine, while compose/create electronic mail started process of sending smtp play role of delivery compose message from current source to recipient destination.

Pop3 – pop3 stands (post office protocol) version 3 popular e-mail protocol specially design for receiving e-mail from server in client mail box, each pop3 client e-mail protocol check server mail box in every few second finally download them at client inbox, while user configure their microsoft outlook, netscape, thunderbirds in linux, mail in mac os x e-mail client, or other e-mail client software check periodically e-mail message in server filter each message and send at appropriate client mail box.

Imap4 – imap abbreviated as internet message access protocol similar to pop3 e-mail protocol, standard e-mail protocol that are designed for laptop notebook or other portable device, imap receive e-mail message from your server mail box imap specially work on portable media where pop3 have less capability to perform than imap get additional e-mail client features, it was developed by stanford university in 1986, imap check online e-mail message on server while client connect with internet broadband services.

Mime6 – mime abbreviated as multipurpose internet mail extension it allow electronic mail internet user send ascii(american standard code for information interchange) text along audio, video, graphic, animation, even other electronic information in computer format, it grater capability than imap or pop3 e-mail protocol, mime available in various version.

Structure of an email

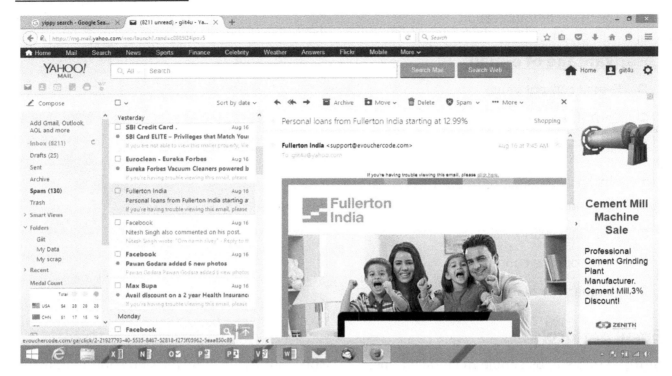

Email address

Username@server/domainname.com

Yahoo! E-mail services

Home – home moves you in yahoo e-mail home windows where you access other yahoo mail, news, sports, finance, weather, games, groups, answer, and other popular yahoo services.

Mail – yahoo mail are popular yahoo services where you access yahoo e-mail services like read e-mail compose e-mail send e-mail view other e-mail related services. Check e-mail view draft, folder, sent, trash, calendar, contact.

News – view updated current day's year news from yahoo web site and other news web site posted article like us, india and other local national international region get world, politics, tech, science, odd news, opinion, comics, and other popular new category easier access from yahoo news.

Sports – yahoo sports popular in sport lover they can access latest tournament news like tennis, golf, cricket, football, soccer, hockey, olympic, baseball, basketball, collage & high school, even other more popular category sport news information can be easier access from yahoo sports services.

Finance – yahoo finance brings you latest stock market watch information you can see company stock national international stock price view portfolio, market data, business & finance, personal finance, watch latest stock market video and related information from yahoo finance.

Weather – view latest weather information of any city national international weather in centigrade, click and save your city weather visibility, humidity, see weather forecast todays, tomorrow, weather detail.

Games – play latest yahoo online game, yahoo provides you list of arcade & action, board & card, casino, puzzle, strategy & rpg, word & daily, news & features, even download new yahoo games, play or download desire yahoo game.

Groups – yahoo groups are very common to google and other groups provide services, yahoo offer your business & finance, computer & internet, culture & community, entertainment and arts, family & home, game, government & politics, health and wellness, hobbies and craft, music, regional, romance or relationship, science and education, if you want to open or explore yahoo groups click and explore according to need.

Answers – yahoo answer online yahoo collection of helpful article posted by million yahoo or other user according to asking question, get answer about art and humilities, beauty and style, business and finance, cars and transformation, computer and internet, consumer electronic, education and reference, education and reference, entertainment and music related answer service.

Flicker – flicker link in your yahoo e-mail id, when user click on flicker it will moves user on yahoo acquire flicker website contain picture collection, web hosting contain video, photos and text, connect and using these services in working e-mail account.

Mobile – yahoo mobile available you for using and download latest yahoo mobile apps you can access yahoo mobile service on your smart cell phone access yahoo mobile mail, weather, search, finance, sports, fantasy, screen, news digest, flicker services.

More – yahoo more mail option available for you other yahoo popular services like celebrity, shine, movies, music, tv, health, shopping, travel, autos, homes services.

Yahoo search mail – yahoo search mail are popular yahoo services which possible you to search inbox electronic mail according to need, search desire electronic mail type recipients e - mail address and click on search yahoo mail, it listed all mail come from search yahoo recipients address.

Compose e-mail – compose mail option enable you to compose blank e-mail write recipient's address e-mail subject matter, attach file folder information along current mail, edit e-mail body text with given yahoo mail toolbar finally doing everything deliver current e-mail on clicking send button for final message delivery.

Email header – e-mail header contain e-mail related query, generally you can send one or more e-mail recipient's at a same time, send first user in to second recipient's in cc, third recipient's in bcc subject describe current written e-mail nature or e-mail subject type, then click on send e-mail for proper e-mail delivery.

Body and attachments – e-mail body contain the e-mail matter detail send along current e-mail, type desire information text information written in active message body, attachment allow you to add or attach document, letter, file, folder, audio, video, and related data online even send at defined e-mail recipient's, some e-mail services allow you to add data till 20 megabytes even some new e-mail service provider allow you to send more data greater than 20 megabyte at a same time.

Compose mail toolbar

Send – send e-mail option allow you to send current e-mail, after making desire changes, if current electronic are completely ok than remember while click on send e-mail button it will deliver your e-mail at define unique e-mail recipient's address.

Attach file – attach file option allow you to attach file along send electronic mail address, attach file, folder, image, audio, video, and other visual non- visual computer component, attachment enable you to store additional content information with sending e-mail material.

Font – font are style of representing text information in various format modify compose electronic message format appearance during sending at recipient's address, each font look like difference between them even font allow you to decorate and appreciated you text.

Bold – make bold appearance of compose message style format, bold effect make wide appearance of created electronic message.

Italic – italic convert active electronic message in some vertical down order view, italic effect are common effect added during highlight some specific text during sending.

Text color – text color option allow you to change compose message text background and foreground color from given color category choice.

Bullets – add bullets front of compose electronic message bullets option align compose text in specific order by order even you easier understand or read them better.

Increase indent – increase text position from current position to continue in right direction slowly till than we click on increase indent position.

Decrease indent – it work reverse of increase indent option it move compose message text from right to left direction till than we move it in continue click on decrease indent position.

Insert link – insert any web page, web site, even ftp link along sending electronic message, while you click on insert link option its allow you to insert desire http, ftp link along deliver e-mail.

Emotions – emotion are small smiles that represent your behavior during sending and receiving electronic message, each emotion smiles show verbal communication.

Check spelling – check spelling in compose message correct grammatical vocabulary error in current written electronic message.

Yahoo e-mail option

Compose – compose option allow to compose and write electronic message, after composing message you can edit it customize it add additional attributes and effect on it finally deliver or send it at define e-mail recipient's address.

Inbox – yahoo inbox contain all recipients' incoming/receive electronic message in yahoo inbox, you can read, download forward, delete, copy of current view electronic message, if you want to find any one message type e-mail address in search yahoo inbox filter you search message from inbox.

Draft – draft contain all message send by you now and earlier with send message and store in draft copy, while you need to check any draft store message click on draft view message and read desire information in it.

Sent – sent option allow you to view all sent electronic message item in sent folder, even you memorize all sent electronic mail information from sent folder.

Spam – spam folder contain some unwanted e-mail collection and information posted by user in using e-mail services, view all e-mail account storage spam collection in spam e-mail account folder location.

Trash – trash keep all deleted electronic message in trash folder, you can view move even delete it permanent from trash folder, it just like dust bin you recover any item before till than it completely clean it.

Folder – create one or more individual folder in folder inbox item arrange all folder sequentially according to their creation method, now store individually item in desire created folder.

Recent – view all information access in recently form yahoo e-mail services it show step by step all activities perform by you from the time when yahoo electronic mail services access.

Messenger – connect with yahoo messenger services and send or receive live yahoo connected client message in yahoo mail services windows.

Calendar – view calendar of current month year maintain your schedule, business meetings appointment and more with yahoo calendar features.

Contacts – contact yahoo option allow you to create import e-mail contact used during send receive electronic mail, each contact define any mail user identity.

Notepad – notepad is small yahoo mail provide text editor windows, that enable you to write or edit some specific information in yahoo electronic mail.

Yahoo mail for mobile – yahoo for mobile service launch for smart cell phone you can access same yahoo web features on cell phone.

Send feedback – send feedback to yahoo if you are satisfies services provided by yahoo, each feedback send by company user increase company potential in market.

What is a e-mail client – e-mail client are application software provided by the company who developed e-mail client application software for personal computer, e-mail client called e-mail agent, e-mail reader, or mail user agent, you configure you web based e-mail account in e-mail agent software, now you read and download new messages, if you installed personal e-mail client software on your pc you can able to read access send receive compose e-mail message offline but send them online your e-mail account must should be configure before apply these setting, e-mail services design on the basis of client server architectures.

Benefit using e-mail client

- Time money saver.
- Quick response.
- Download print read forward e-mail message.
- Offline message storage.
- Check receive configure online mail account e-mail messages.
- Avoid process of login web based e-mail account.
- Create task schedule maintain notes store address of recipients with chatting program inbuilt.
- Make offline editing reading and similar task.

Popular email clients application software

- Netscape mail clients.
- Mozilla thunderbird.
- Evolution linux/windows.
- Windows live mail.
- Dream mail.
- Postbox express.
- Em client.
- Opera mail.
- Ibm lotus notes.
- Kmail.

Web based e-mail service provider – web based e - mail client software allow e-mail user to check manually e-mail account with unique provide e-mail identification and login password, create online e-mail account any one web based e-mail service provide company like yahoo, gmail, rediffmail and other after creation online e-mail account login enter id and password, now create compose send receive forward delete modify e-mail account web based e-mail services provides you some additional facility like create notes, manage schedule meeting, and many more other facilitate.

Below bulleted web site provide web/browser based e-mail service

- Yahoo.
- Rediffmail.
- Gmail.
- Lycos.
- Facebook.
- Skype.

Netscape mail clients – netscape mail client recognize as netscape mail program developed and design by netscape communication netscape communication create bundle software packages include netscape web browser, netscape messenger, news group, e-mail client, html editor, chat program, address book, web server, proxy server and many more netscape communication provide suite facility, netscape mail client permit us to create compose send receive edit print e-mail messages direct from your windows terminal, netscape mail client available for download microsoft windows, apple mac os x, linux and related operating system, it similar to web based e-mail client services but major difference is that it work offline even operated from client terminal.

Mozilla thunderbird – mozilla thunderbird free open source offline/online personal computer based e-mail client developed by mozilla foundation/organization, its available for microsoft windows, linux, apple mac os and other platform, in mozilla thunderbirds create e-mail message send receive e-mail message create online chatting with online participate, store client, relative, friend, business associate contact e-mail web address and other offline, first of after installation of mozilla thunderbird e-mail client in your machine you manually configure your web based e-mail account id and password, finally account creation process terminate, now you able to download read upload message create offline message and send online message no need to logging online in web based e-mail service account.

Advantage of using thunderbird

➲ Free of charge.

➲ Open source.

➲ Multi-platform for windows, linux, mac, unix.

➲ Rss management.

➲ Inbuilt web browser.

➲ Chatting client.

➲ Address book and directory.

➲ E-mail filtering facility.

➲ Junk mail removal.

➲ Mail security provider.

➲ Create and manage multiple e-mail account.

➲ Configure easier e-mail send or receive e-mail message.

File menu

New – create new option enable us to design new mozilla thunderbird messages, folder, chat, feed account, address book contact, chat contact, than fill desire information in it, each describe above option enable you to record specific information related fields.

Message – create new e-mail messages fill recipient's e-mail id in to, cc or bcc, attach any object in it format compose message add e-mail subject than final click on send button to deliver e-mail message from source to destination.

Folder – create new folder whatever names you given now you placed your selected e-mail, contact, schedule, and related information, new folder allowing you to manage you electronic document carefully and securely.

Saved search – saved search related specific e-mail searching criteria, save search element locate at inbox element in mozilla thunderbird e-mail client.

Get a new mail account – get new e-mail account option enable you to getting's new e-mail features in working e-mail application.

Existing mail account – configure you existing web based e-mail account in mozilla thunder bird e-mail client software package, even add up web based e-mail account installed in opera mail client software.

Chat account – configure new chatting client configuration with available link in mozilla thunderbird e-mail software, you configure chatting account with facebook, google talk, irc, twitter, and xmpp services, choose any one from these and installed chatting program configuration.

Feed account – configure blog and feed account fill required setting in given empty text box, and create new e-mail, chat, news group, or news feed related account configuration.

Other account – create online news group account now view read edit print online broadcast new related information, fill all information correct with given news server detail finally you receive newsgroup news broadcast information your mozilla thunderbird.

Address book contact – address book enable you to store digital contact information about your friends, relative, colleague, business associate, online offline user detail, store their contact, private, work, other, chat, photo related deep information while you need some specific information in contact you will check address book contact detail information.

Chat contact – create new chat contact it work only in condition while you setup chat account related configuration properly, chat contact keep the information about all of them regularly communicate with us.

Open save message – open save e-mail message in your local hard drive partition or a my document folder, or it may be other storage location manually set by e-mail store person remember if e-mail saved it can be retrieve or access any time while we working as offline user.

Close – close option immediate close mozilla thunderbird e-mail client application software.

Save as – save as option save current view e-mail, message as file or template, after saving format you can access or retrieve it in same format shape .

File – save current electronic document as a file format.

Template – save current electronic document as template format.

Get new message for – get new message from all configure mozilla thunderbird e-mail client messages even manually download new receive message from individual e-mail account.

All account – all account option configures or receives all e-mail account to receive new messages from e-mail account services provide.

Current account – current account regularly function to check new e-mail messages and download periodically new receive e-mail message.

Send unsent message – send unsent e-mail message that are don't send properly to the recipient's address user click on unsent message and wait till all unsent message will be properly deliver at proper e-mail address.

Subscribe – subscribe option enable you to subscribe or unsubscribe selected folder list display in mozilla thunderbird electronic mail client, click any one form given choice that one you don't need to unsubscribe.

Delete folder – delete folder option allow you to delete current folder where it located in configure e-mail account, remember apply only while sure to delete selected folder.

Rename folder – rename selected previously created folder in mozilla thunderbird e-mail client, rename allow to replace existing folder with new one given name.

Compact folder – create compact folder view store and control compact folder created item and information in working e-mail client program.

Empty trash – empty trash option enable us to remove unwanted electronic document e-mail messages from trash folder we can't receiver back it after apply empty trash option.

Offline – offline option disconnect current network profile, configure manually download and sync e-mail message and news group, configure offline mozilla thunder setting, configure get started or gest selected messages setting according to need.

Page setup – change current page format customize default page orientation from portrait to landscape changes page scale, enable print background color edit information of page margin from left, right, top, bottom, customize header footer and related configuration according to printed page.

Print preview – configure print preview of printed mozilla thunderbird e-mail account electronic messages or document, modify page setup, view page one by one in previous or next order customize page orientation scale to fit printed page according to need.

Print – print current view electronic document with attach installed printed if two or more printer installed configure which one default print even customize print copy number of pages than finally apply print to done it.

Exit – immediate terminate open mozilla thunderbird e-mail client application software.

Edit menu

Undo – undo all last apply action in current electronic document e-mail message or related information, undo option enable us to re get undo work again.

Redo – redo option work opposite of undo option it reverse all undo action apply in current electronic document.

Cut – cut unnecessary selection of electronic document or electronic message remember cut text of portion can be paste at new location.

Copy – copy some repeated similar portion of electronic mail or document now paste it with paste command at new desire selected location.

Paste – paste option work after copy option copy command keep copy of copy text in buffer (temporary area of memory) finally apply paste it.

Delete message – delete message option allow you to delete selected unwanted message from inbox message category.

Select – select option enable you to select all message in your e-mail account message category even you share thread or shared messages from e-mail inbox.

Find – find dialog box allow multiple find strategies control by the information finder find in this message, find again, search message or search address, in mozilla thunderbird e-mail client software.

Find in this message – these option find only these message related information in current view mozilla thunderbird e-mail client.

Find again – find again option research previous continuously search elements in current electronic mail.

Search message – search specific message according to search category.

Search address – search a specific category address in mozilla thunderbird e-mail client software.

Favorite folder – mark your favorite folder in category of given inbox manually created mail folder.

Folder properties – view folder properties, related information name general information, retention policy, synchronization, sharing, and quota related tab settings and configuration easily get through folder properties.

Calendar properties – view mozilla thunderbird use calendar detail properties in working calendar elements, view properly all settings and information related used calendar properties.

View menu

Toolbar – toolbar option enable us to enable or disable appear or disappear toolbar in mozilla thunderbird e-mail client, you can on off mail toolbar, menu bar, status bar, quick filter bar even manually customize default created toolbar and menu bar in mozilla thunderbird mail client software.

Layout – layout option enable you to customize default layout of your mozilla thunderbird e-mail client, change default layout with classis view, wide view and vertical view, even show and hide folder pane or message pane from layout windows.

Folder – view mozilla thunderbird created folder view unified folder, unread, favorite, and recent folder item from folder category given choice.

Sort by – sort by option allowing you to arrange number of inbox receive e-mail in specific order like arrange inbox e-mail as, date, receive, star, from, recipient's, size, status, subject, tag, attachment, organize e-mail as ascending or descending threaded and group by sorted order select one of them that meet your requirement.

Threads – view thunderbird e-mail client received thread in multiple category you can view read unread even expand all thread or collapse number of appear thread in category.

Header – view current watch read electronic document header or all document portion from header option view, here it you can show or hide specific header option view setting.

Message body as – view current electronic message body in original html format which display message in default format plain text convert html text in unformatted text and simple html option remove original html font attributes and apply editing.

Display attachment inline – display attachment inline option show all attachment received with inbox e-mail, attachment may be graphic, document, presentation, or program and other attachment detail.

Zoom – zoom in and zoom out two option work opposite order where zoom in function continuously increase size of selected electronic document but zoom out option reduce continuously size of zoom in text, reset zoom category or set zoom text only option default.

Character encoding – change default character encoding format of view mozilla thunderbird e-mail client messages, select message format western, unicode, or default auto detect character encoding format.

Message source – view message source written in default language may be html, java script, php, asp.net or other, message source contain raw message related information.

Message security info – view received message related security issue like view message contain digital signature message is encrypted or not encrypted, these security standard protect electronic messaged during long distance travel from source to distance between sender or receiver.

Go menu

Next – next option allow you to view next inbox messages continuously, view unread message next by next, view started messages and unread thread messages from next menu .

Previous – view one by one previous messages, unread messages or started messages from mozilla thunderbird e-mail client application software.

Forward – forward option allow to send someone received inbox messages to new e-mail address, open existing e-mail messages type new recipient's e-mail address and click on send button to finally deliver messages at proper address .

Back – move one by one e-mail messages in back order.

Chat – go to on features of chat option configure chatting option with facebook, google talk, irc, twister, xmpp, enter user id and password for chat with finally join chat room make chatting with available client.

Folder – go to or jump at configure e-mail account online folder location, include moves on local folder list and location through these options.

Recently closed tab – view recently closed tab page information in detail, all the tab you access and use to working with previous in working thunderbird application.

Mail start page – mail start page option moves mozilla thunderbird user to move on thunderbird configure e-mail account main page view information about installed thunderbird support, features, tips, contributes, help and other product information.

Message menu

New message – new message option enable us to create or compose new message for recipients, in message header add recipient's address in message body write message for recipient's at footer add remaining information related to compose message, format compose message with available font color bullets add similes picture and other information.

Reply – reply receive recipient's electronic message to someone else e-mail address, even you can reply existing as well fresh e-mail message to your recipient's list user .

Reply to all – reply to all option enable you to send or replay current e-mail message one or more recipient's at same time, one or more.

Reply to list – reply to list option enable you to reply current selected e-mail messages on or more list e-mail recipients user at a same time, click and send to the list of user.

Forward – forward current selected mozilla thunderbird inbox e-mail message from your side to another user e-mail recipients user address, just click on forward messages now type the name of forwarded user mail address finally click on send message from completion.

Forward as – forward as option allow you to send or forward existing received or current e-mail message as inline or attachment file format, type name of mail recipients and click to send finally delivery.

Edit message as new – these option enable you to send current e-mail message with enable editing messages facility, finally edit messages and click to delivery at destination address.

Open message – open selected current mozilla thunderbird inbox e-mail message in separate windows for reading easier apply thunderbird menu related operation easily, on another windows appear in thunderbird existing windows .

Open in conversation – open selected e-mail message in conversation mode, where you made conversation with other e-mail recipients.

Attachment – view list of attachment include document, graphic, text, video, audio, animated object along current received e-mail message in thunderbird client software, you can open save delete or detach attachment come along current message.

Tag – add tag on current or existing received e-mail received messages, tag indicate the nature of received current e-mail messages, you tag with your messages with important, work, personal, to do, later even add own customize tag on selected e-mail messages, now you can add your desire tag on individual e-mail messages at a time.

Mark – mark current e-mail message as read, unread, thread as read, add start, add junk, related effect on desire mozilla thunderbird e-mail message, after marking you will be easier know about mark electronic mail.

Archive – add archive attributes message on selected e-mail message.

Move to – move to option allow you to move you selected e-mail message from e-mail account folder to local folder, select the location where to you really moves your messages than starting process of messing moving.

Copy to – copy to option allow you to copy current configure e-mail message account content from current location to another location on clicking to select right copy location.

Move again – move again option enable you to move again another inbox item from current location to another location easier.

Create filter from message – create filter enable us to filter specific category of e-mail message in group of hundred or thousand message. Filter e-mail messages easier to read of identify in various category of received message.

Ignore thread – ignore any thread display along current received e-mail message, thread comes along any received e-mail message.

Ignore sub thread – ignore sub thread identify in current or existing e-mail mail category list.

Watch thread – watch thread find in current e-mail message, you can watch even identify the nature of received threads in selected e-mail messages.

Tools menu

Address book – address book application automatically install during mozilla thunderbird e-mail client load in use personal computer, create new contact store contact related information like first name last name, contact, e-mail, web address, home, work, office contact detail, store address city state country web page, chatting detail, add photo of user.

Save files – view information of saved files in mozilla thunderbird e-mail client, save dialog display the list of all download material include multimedia object, text, picture, and other information.

Add – ons – add – ons are collection of additional mozilla thunderbird application features, it enable you to add or get add-ons, extension, appearance, plug in.

Activity manager – activity manager windows show you all activity happened in background of mozilla thunderbird e-mail client, view current activity perform in activity manager.

Chat status – chat status option allow you to view current chat software status in available, unavailable, or offline mode, even show current configure chat account also.

Join chat – join chat option allow you to join pre-configure chat room account, now chat with chart room client share chat text messages and other information quickly with connected network.

Message filter – message filter option allow you to filter inbox message according to given category wise, filtering group specific category of messages in same location.

Run filter on folder – run filter message option on particular created or existing inbox folder, it categorized you message according to filter category.

Run filter on message – run filter on particular message category, it arrange same category e-mail message in a particular location.

Run junk mail control on folder – run junk mail control on folder these option automatically scan all junk mail or spam mail it add junk mail category on it.

Delete mail marked as junk folder – delete marked as junk mail folder e-mail message in junk mail folder category, these option remove all junk mail category inbox e-mail message.

Import – import option allow you to import address book, mail, feed subscription, setting, even filters category according to need, importing other category of item from different location or source.

Error console – error console windows show you all errors, warning, message, generate during communication with current mozilla thunderbird e-mail client.

Allow remote debugging – allow remote debugging mode enable you edit or debug mozilla thunderbird e-mail client for remote location.

Clear recent history – clear recent history generated in current mozilla thunderbird session, recent history is collection of visited information located in current e-mail client session.

Account setting – view configuration related configure mozilla thunderbird e-mail client, view server setting, incoming, outgoing e-mail message even everything detail related configure account.

Options – configure option setting related menu command or appear many bar toolbar related features in mozilla thunderbird e-mail client software, pick any desire category of option choice in option windows now configure or modify it according to need.

Help – help option display you everything about using application product, you know about mozilla thunderbird version info, license information, user agreement, privacy policy, and other detail describe clearly in help menu.

Evolution e-mail client – evolution e-mail client by default e-mail client program in linux operating system like ubuntu, kubuntu, debian and other linux distribution it is very similar to microsoft windows outlook program, linux gnome desktop environment always consist evolution personal information manager, evolution e-mail client supported to windows linux and mac operating system, evolution permit us to create new messages, mail folder, appointment, assigned task, contact, contact list, meeting, memo, task, address book, calendar, memo and task list, create and manage other evolution services, you can access use or download evolution personal information manager under the act gnu(general public license).

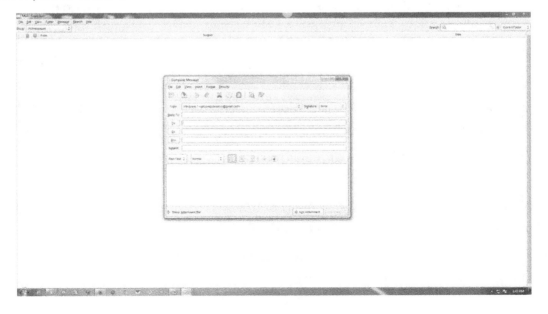

Windows live mail – windows live messenger previously recognize msn messenger, developed and supported by microsoft organization, windows live mail client by default loaded in windows 7 and windows 8, windows live mail working as online web based e-mail client services known as hotmail, windows live messenger provide instant messaging, pc to pc calling, offline notification view print edit modify existing web server messages, you can buy or use trial windows live messenger for your smart cellphone or personal computer, wlm(windows live messenger)support hotmail, gmail, yahoo, mail plus web based e-mail service, wlm provide service e-mail client, news client, feed reader, electronic calendar.

Dream mail – dream mail e-mail client download on your machine configure registered e-mail test e-mail account detail and information, create or configure existing e-mail account to send and receive e-mail in user inbox folder location, advantage of using dream mail e-mail client you able to direct send and receive server e-mail, create new e-mail, use address book to store contact, search new e-mail, use webmail features, explores rss and more category of dream mail service in these group, download server message and information direct in installed or configure dream mail e-mail account location.

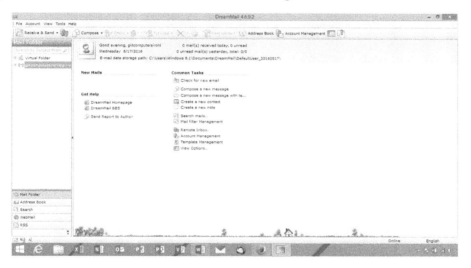

Postbox express – postbox express freeware based e-mail client software that provide include rss feed, or news client features it is great e-mail client software packages that based on mozilla thunderbird software, create two or more e-mail account profile in postbox express manually download e-mail from your server based account, the download link of postbox express are.

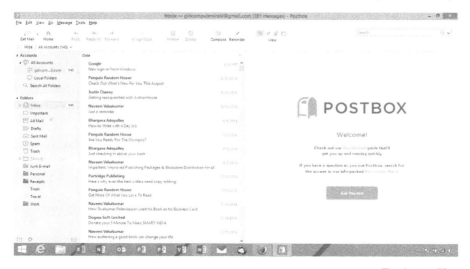

Em client – em client client based e - mail agent that enable us to read write edit print modify existing e-mail along access services of calendar, contact, task, schedule, distribution list, some em client available as free and commercial download, it available for all platform operating system.

Opera mail – opera web browser another popular web browser that group of software suite it add opera web browser, opera mail, irc chat program, news client facility provider, create e-mail, read mail, send receive mail edit print e-mail and perform other e-mail related task, opera mail work on desktop smart cellphone or other platform operating system, the download link of opera mail are - http://www.opera.com/computer/mail.

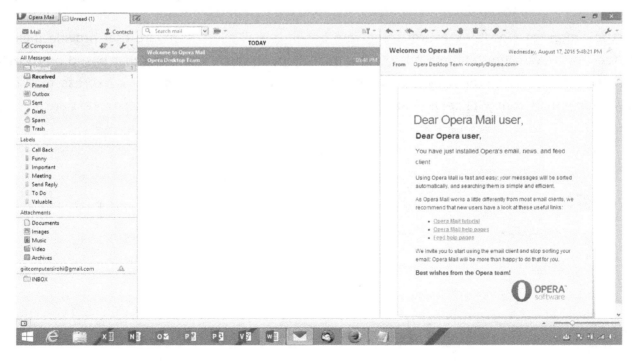

TOPIC
11

Introduction to Microsoft Office 2016

Office 2016 application interface.   Definition of office menu, tab, & dialog.

Topic will be discussing in microsoft office 2016

About microsoft – microsoft company world no 1 famous company about creating legacy of microsoft application product, microsoft work on windows operating system, office suites, skype for business, microsoft smart phone operating system and visual studio include many other products created and supported by microsoft company, now days microsoft became world leading company for creating license software package, these company started by mr. Bill gates and his friends 30 year ago, todays microsoft company create software application for computer hardware, electronics, smart phones, virtual xbox game, office, and other application.

What is a microsoft office suite – microsoft office suite popular office suite worldwide in different world continent, everyone know about microsoft office suites, microsoft company build and bundle microsoft office product as complete need package for their client need fulfill, we work on various legacy version of microsoft version suites name microsoft office 1997, microsoft office 2000, microsoft office xp, microsoft office 2003, microsoft office 2007, microsoft office 2010, microsoft office 2013, and now microsoft office 2016, each release microsoft office suite some application continue adding or update with microsoft office suite these are microsoft word, microsoft excel, microsoft power point, outlook express, microsoft access, and some added with time duration name microsoft groove, one note, share point, visio, project, skype, one drive, some office application added or some removed or upgrade with time and year and year changes.

New features of microsoft office 2016

- ➲ New graphic, theme, modern application interface.
- ➲ Added new control and application features.
- ➲ Instant boot, more - easier and graphical then previous release.
- ➲ Available in various kind of version and application format.
- ➲ Added new formula, improve application interface, working behavior and more control.

Version of microsoft office suites 2016.

Legacy of microsoft office version from start to today's date

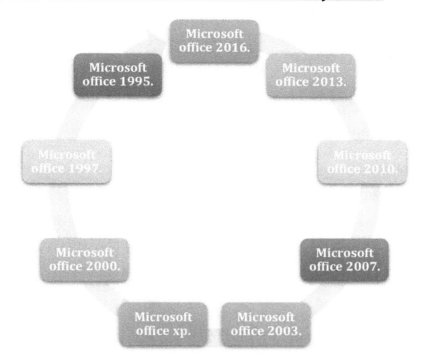

How microsoft office help in organization/office/industry/home – every industry, organization, company, or home user be a part of electronic world and know how to save time and money with computing technology, using microsoft office product suites to make work easier and faster, microsoft office suite provide all kind of creating, sharing, printing, publishing, calculating, and drawings facility application provided, you must have skill or experience to how to work and deal with microsoft office suite product, while user using microsoft product then he able to create document, worksheet, presentation, drawings, publishing, database, one note digital document, check send and receive e-mail, appointments, task, schedule, notes, and calendar, use skype to online communication with audio and video chat along instant messaging facility, with one drive for business enable microsoft any user or category to save and store roaming cloud document with portability across the world, so simply we say that microsoft being a part of human life in many sector to work easier, better, faster, reliable, and versatile communication.

Craze about microsoft office suite – worldwide people crazy about using new features and version of microsoft office suite package application, because company launch new features, control, menu, tools, integrate modern environment need object every time company bundled with new launch office suite product, reason of versatility and so much famous thing about microsoft office is from earlier time microsoft office suite product became successful complete need of industry, organization, company, or individual along that time open source suite not so much invented and famous, but major impact of microsoft office on information technology it introduce earlier with all kind of user need tools and function that not provides and launch that office suite provides company, but we don't discuss comparison of microsoft product, the question is remain as well as so the answer is microsoft cover world 90% market of information technology globe wise, or company service product feedback tremendous include provide policy, ligancy, customer feedback, environment need related services provided with accuracy.

Reason to use microsoft office

- ➲ Multiplatform.
- ➲ Sleek design/user interface.
- ➲ Always updates.
- ➲ Fulfill all kind of need.
- ➲ Great online feedback.
- ➲ File conversion format.
- ➲ Globally famous.
- ➲ Portability.
- ➲ Online used and recognize.
- ➲ Continuously upgrade and full fill customer need.
- ➲ All tools, menu, control, function, features contain that may be need of any user of computer while working with microsoft office.

Microsoft office 2016 application sites product.

What's new in microsoft office 2016

➲ New function formulas added or improved with excel.

➲ New theme, document style, search features, dialog and window improvement.

➲ Adding more digital notes, control online offline one note digital information.

➲ New theme, custom animation along slide transition effect, slides, windows and control effect.

➲ Upgrade lync with microsoft skype for business.

➲ Updating share point, sky drive, online folder with one drive for business.

➲ New visio stencils, control, design control and plan.

➲ Create project, plans, and overview with project application.

➲ Handle e-mail, contact, task calendar, journal, and other outlook item easier than previous version.

➲ Modified option, customize, macros, and other default tools windows and working behavior.

Popular world license and free open source office suites

Where to buy microsoft office – allover world and continent microsoft open their regional center or headquarter, they offer microsoft product service for retail/online/offline buy or selling microsoft company software product, if you live in any metro city then you easier to find microsoft store or company link organization that help you to buying or using microsoft software package, even if you have high speed broadband internet connection then you got to microsoft website name www.microsoft.com website for online buying company product, here you know more about using or buy product information along online/chat conversation while buying microsoft product, if you have internet banking or online money transfer service then you buy microsoft any software package form your home town, and in time bound period you get microsoft office and other application package get at your home address.

Download microsoft office 2016 trial – microsoft launch new office suites product name office 2016, it contain all most microsoft legacy office suites product and new release along it, the default application installed in microsoft office name microsoft word 2016, microsoft excel 2016, one note, publisher, access, skype for business, one drive for business, some website provide alpha and beta version to windows user to download and use these product for limited period of time session, include you have to buy license product form microsoft web site, after download or buying original microsoft office 2016 iso, extract or install in current operating system, and starting using or exploring microsoft office suites product, in trial you have limited functionality of office suites, some features function restrict microsoft user to avoid accessing, but in license microsoft office suites you able to access and get all micrcosoft product features, function and control according to need.

Minimum hardware specification for office 2016

- ➲ Windows win 7, windows 8, 8.1, include windows 10 operating system.
- ➲ Buy or download microsoft office 32-bit/64-bit version of office 2016.
- ➲ Ram – 1 gigabytes or more recommender 2 gigabytes.
- ➲ Had 20 gigabytes recommended 50 gigabytes or 1 terabyte.
- ➲ Intel or amd based microprocessor.
- ➲ Directx installed.
- ➲ Include update existing version of microsoft office 2013 with microsoft 2016.

Install microsoft office 2016 in windows 10 – first of buy license microsoft office 2016 iso or setup source from microsoft website, now start process of installing these setups into your laptop, desktop, notebook, computer, please read above hardware specification before installing microsoft office suites product, now follow step by step instruction to install microsoft office 2016 application.

Installation of other software packages such as microsoft office 2016

Step first – when first click on microsoft office 2016 setup shortcut key, it will immediate preview dialog that contain setting related to installed office 2016 settings, these dialog contain two default tab name main windows and about tab, in main windows you have choice of installing microsoft office 2016 version and about tab show information about microsoft office 2016 installation, again we move on main windows in these dialog you have choice to install microsoft office version between 32 – bit and 64 – bit include select language of installation hardware, if user manually need to customize office 2016 setup, like you want to uncheck some application of default office, remember by default microsoft office 2016 install all check mark application, at least 12 application

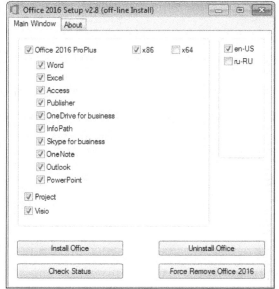

name microsoft word, excel, powerpoint, access, publisher, infopath, skype for business, one note, one drive for business, microsoft project and visio application, at office 2016 bottom windows you have choice of button name install office these option installing microsoft office on local machine, check status option checking microsoft office installation status, uninstall office button uninstall previous install microsoft office 2016, or force remove office 2016 application immediate start process of removing microsoft office 2016, but you install fresh copy of microsoft office so just click on install microsoft office and wait till next dialog and windows appear in windows.

Step second – step second indicate startup of microsoft office 2016 installation process, these screen continue moving small dots or point of line from left to right direction till then next dialog or screen appear, these dialog show office 2016 setup in progress wait till next dialog or window appear.

Step third – when above step complete next office 2016 dialog appear below during microsoft office 2016 installation process, in below dialog you see logo of microsoft office at front of it you see close button to close office 2016 installation, include view number of office application icon or picture display as thumbnail view in office setup dialog window, see red line progress indicator moving from start point to end point showing a microsoft office 2016 installation in progress mode or showing message we'll be done in just a moment message, always remember if you have broadband network connection always on during installation microsoft office 2016 software, wait till next dialog or screen appear in step of microsoft office 2016 setup dialog.

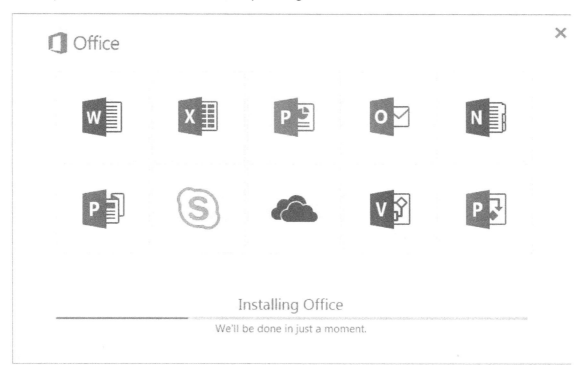

Step four – step for show at windows taskbar notification area and indicating microsoft office 2016 in installation progress, these dialog show percent amount of installing microsoft in taskbar, remember don't go offline during installing microsoft office system will automatically restart and proper setup microsoft office 2016 application files.

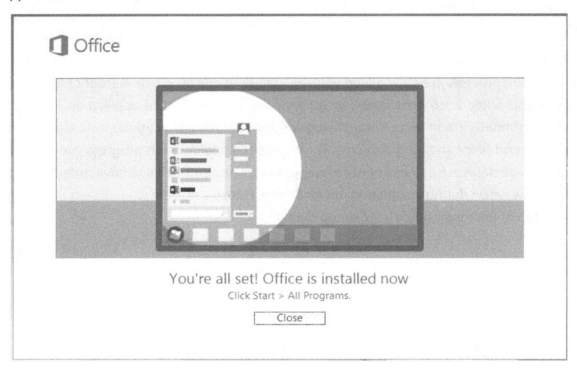

Office is installing in the background (90%) ✕
You can use your programs now, but please don't go offline or restart your computer.

Step five – step five indicating microsoft office 2016 properly installed in your computer, and showing dialog of how open launch or working with microsoft office 2016 application in you machine, now you able to close these window or dialog to move on real installed microsoft office 2016 application.

You're all set! Office is installed now
Click Start > All Programs.
Close

Where to buy

⮑ Buy microsoft office 2013.

⮑ Buy online license microsoft office 2013.

⮑ Download 365 microsoft office 2013 trial from microsoft official web site.

Minimum requirement for office 2016 installation

Sl. no	Component	Requirement	Recommended
1	**Microprocessor**	1 gigahertz (ghz) or faster x86- or x64-bit processor	3.0 ghz intel amd processor
2	**Memory (ram)**	1 gigabyte (gb) ram (32-bit); 2 gigabytes (gb) ram (64-bit)	2 gigabytes or more for faster performance

Sl. no	Component	Requirement	Recommended
3	**Hard disk**	3.0 gigabytes (gb) available	500 gigabytes or more available
4	**Operating system**	Windows 7 (32-bit or 64-bit) Windows 8 (32-bit or 64-bit) Windows 8.1 (32-bit or 64-bit) Windows server 2008 r2 (64-bit) Windows server 2012 (64-bit)	Any new version release by microsoft company like windows future release windows 9
5	**Browser**	Internet explorer 8, 9, 10, or 11; mozilla firefox 10.x or a later version; apple safari 5; or google chrome 17. X.	New version of ie 11 firefox 41 safari 5.0 and above newly version
6	**.net version**	3.5, 4.0, or 4.5	

How to set up

- ➲ Open microsoft office 2013 source folder.
- ➲ Double click on setup or right click on setup click on run as administrator.
- ➲ Follow number of setup dialog during microsoft office 2013 setup.

Steps involved during legacy microsoft office suite version 2013 or previous version

Click on below given microsoft office 2013 setup icon

Collection information – microsoft office 2013 installation began wait till microsoft office 2013 get essential hardware software information about required office installation.

License term – read carefully microsoft office 2013 office installation setup procedure agreement, move down vertical scrollbar continuously till end of line, finally click on i accept the terms of this agreement check box on, generally this agreement telling you about using microsoft product policy you follow microsoft eula (end user license agreement), click continue to step in installation of microsoft office 2013 software.

Choose the installation you want – microsoft office 2013 setup dialog provide you two default option for office installation, first one is install second one is customize if you choose install now option during microsoft office 2013 setup you install microsoft office with 2013 minimum installation configuration, and if you choose customize option now let's choose microsoft with desire microsoft office component if you want add some additional component or even install microsoft office 2013 with desire install features click select and enable disable office 2013 customize installation function.

Installation option – installation option allows you to customize default microsoft installation type, many default office 2013 function already selected and if you want to add or remove other microsite group menu then click on category select or deselect make it according to need.

File location – change default microsoft office 2013 installation location default location is c:\program files \microsoft office, if you want changing location of install microsoft office 2013 default location, click on browse command button select desire location of microsoft storage location, then click on install now if all desire changes made.

User information – add installation user information, like user full name, initials, organization name and other essential information in given text box, if all information fill click on install now option to permanent microsoft office reside in your computer.

Install now – finally all tab configures properly like installation option, file location, user information now click on install now option to start remaining installation procedure.

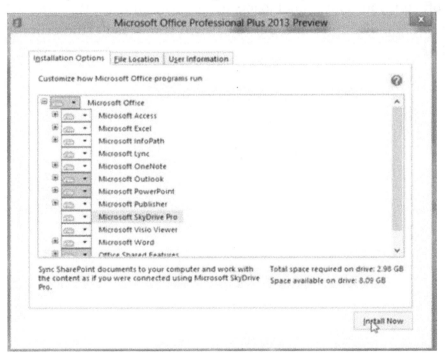

Installation progress bar – installation start from 0 to 100 it indicates your microsoft office 2013 installation begin and wait till progress bar automatically finish from start point to end point, remember during progress bar microsoft office 2013 set storage location of office files and folder.

Complete installation – while microsoft office 2013 setup complete it show you dialog which moves you on microsoft office 2013 installation website now you check newly microsoft upgrade features install new update function features on existing microsoft office 2013 installation.

Brief introduction about microsoft office

Microsoft word – microsoft word popular application of microsoft office suite worldwide user in offices, company, industry, organization, stores, mall, and other application of electronic document format default you able to create, modify, edit, print, and customize any shape kind of electronic document format in document format include create professional document, letter, e-mail, fax, receipt, memorandum, mail merge, greeting, report, form, query, tabular database and any other information that can be used and implemented in shape of document format while user need, new version of microsoft word application support .docx file format and other popular document format in list.

Default opening window of microsoft word 2016

Microsoft excel – microsoft office excel another application used for calculate and count some numeric calculation on worksheet placed electronic information and content, commercially used microsoft excel used to create workbook, sales report, agenda, budget, billing statement, expense report, purchase, sales, balance sheet, profit and loss statement, easier to create and manage in microsoft excel worksheet, important role of excel application for any user is it helpful for student, company, organization, industry user to create a numeric calculation statement apply built list of microsoft excel formula more 300 hundred include other control through microsoft excel application, new version of microsoft excel worksheet support .xlsx file extension, apply microsoft excel worksheet various tools control function and menu control from provided application various menu and tab.

Default opening window of microsoft excel 2016

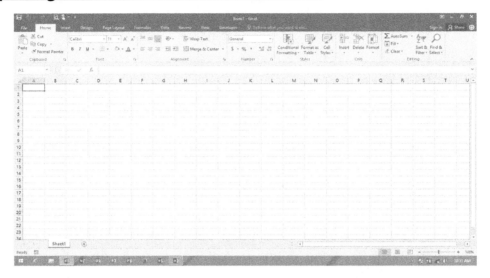

Microsoft power point – microsoft power point software used to for creating group of multimedia application, slide of group, create animated, multimedia, presentation slides, add presentation slides, prepare office meetings, agenda presentation slide, add graphic, video, audio, multimedia, sound, animation, 2d and 3d effect high resolution graphic effect and pixel resolution to support large scale size of image preview of projector or multimedia device, after creation these high resolution presentation slides just preview on projector screen.

Default opening window of microsoft power point 2016

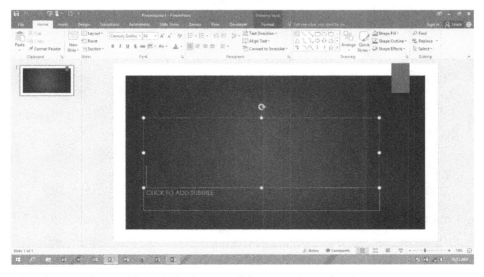

Microsoft access – microsoft access bundled along microsoft office suite, these application mostly used for creating database, table, form, report, query, label, and other kind of database tools and information, access is best tool for database management tools for managing database, query, table, form, report, include create database relationship, created mail merge database, import and export database, print, edit, modify, fill database records information and other query, through access application, even created macros code, events for database control with other facilities provided by microsoft office suite.

Default opening window of microsoft access 2016

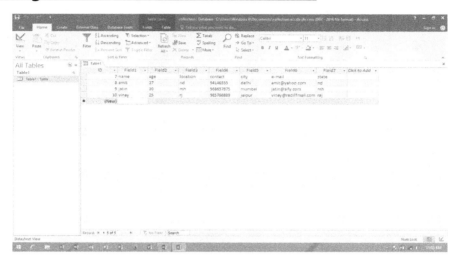

Microsoft one note – microsoft one note introduce in microsoft office 2007 suites till dated it added by microsoft developer in each and every release of microsoft office suite package, commercially microsoft one note use of creating electronic notes, digital notes, or any kind of electronic that can contain text, graphic, multimedia, animation, video, graphic, shapes, word art text, table, chart, draw pen control sketch design, template, equation, symbol and other content in shape of digital book, using one note as a digital notebook where you created and store your digital notes, school, universities notes, subject notes store, edit, modify and print with microsoft one note application, even you use one note as electronic notebook information container.

Default opening window of microsoft one note 2016

Microsoft publisher – microsoft publisher using for design graphic, pamphlet, broacher, advertisement, logo, business card, e-mail, envelope, flyers, labels, letter, letterhead, menu, postcards, timesheet, official advertisement, book publication design/cover, news, biodata, resume, get new theme, template, and design from microsoft website, certificate, award or other kind of sample get from microsoft software generally we slightly compare microsoft publisher with libre office draw or some function like photoshop or corel draw application, in version of publisher 2016 you have new function tools, graphic, theme and control for designing publisher document and information.

Default opening window of microsoft publisher 2016

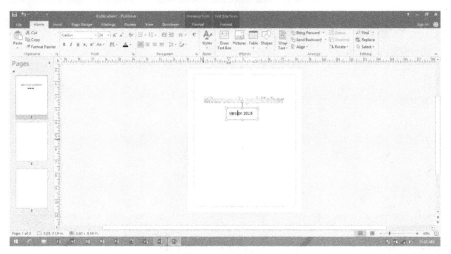

Microsoft visio – microsoft visio using for creating large volume of scale compute graphics, shape, design of any object, building material, plan, overview, drawings, design, plan and overview of any network, schedule, floor plans, design, database, engineering, business, directional map, basic diagram, and blank diagram, flowchart and many other kind of shape stencils small reserve for drawing and design desire shape or control for making graphical diagram or map through visio application, microsoft visio similar to auto cad and other graphic design software, where you can create some pre-graphic of any object and control before make it finally.

Default opening window of microsoft visio 2016

Microsoft share point – microsoft office share point server know as microsoft share point server, using microsoft share point for sharing, using, downloading and uploading some essential data and information among connected share point user, using microsoft share point server as a server where you can get or access some useful or meaning full required data locate, advantage of microsoft share point server is it allow collaborative computing with many users, create or design own website portals for share and post required information on it, using business smart technique to get instant search quick information, using like internet, extranet, or communicating work technique, if some information needed to share among many user using share point server for access or post these kind of information simultaneously share or suing one or more client at a time with microsoft share point server.

Microsoft outlook – microsoft outlook application used for online and offline communication, we called microsoft outlook with personal information manager, that allow its user to view send receive e-mail, create contact, group of contact, task, task schedule, calendar, calendar schedule, calendar appointment, meetings, conversation, notes, group of notes, journal entry and shortcut outlook item in microsoft outlook application, these application like you secretary, that maintain all information about your business meetings, business schedule, conference detail, appointment calendar, routine task, journal, send and receive business e-mail, business people contact and other information will store and retrieves easier through installed microsoft outlook application software.

Default opening window of microsoft outlook 2016

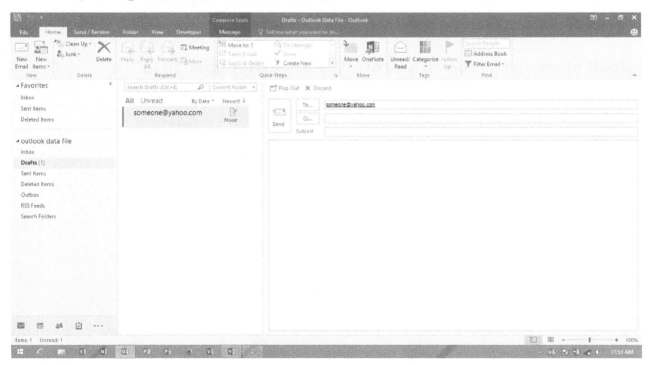

Microsoft project – microsoft project application automatically bundled with microsoft office 2016 application, advantage of microsoft project 2016 application is to create project plan of any agenda, allocate project resources, divide task of layer, manage or create project plan schedule, create a project about any industry, company, organization, construction company to manage their work, allocate or allotted resources, create plans, making schedule, arrange money/finance, man work, resource allocation, task management and other schedule and task easier to create and manage in microsoft project application.

Microsoft groove – microsoft groove replaced and redesign with name of microsoft share point workspace, advantage of microsoft groove application is it allow collaborative computing it mean simultaneously many user working on same project form different location or place, microsoft groove allows facility to its user to store, share, edit, and modify created electronic document from groove connecting location,

Microsoft equation – microsoft equation software group or installed with microsoft office suite, these option appear while user work with microsoft equation application, insert and control math equation logic, formula expression and similar mathematics elements insert and deal with installed application while user need.

Microsoft infopath designer – microsoft office infopath specially used to create format of various kind of form, insert various kind of form tools and control specially three category tool name input, objects, and containers, all infopath designer tools divide in these category, user just drag and drop these control at working infopath design window for making some meaning full form and control for accepting information contain in it, some common form control is label, checkbox, textbox, list box, combo box, date and time, picture, button, attachment, containers, section, choice group or selection, etc. Include use many add-ins control for making desire kind of infopath designer form, include you code or program source for inserting form control during operating these controls in working mode.

Default opening window of microsoft infopath designer 2013

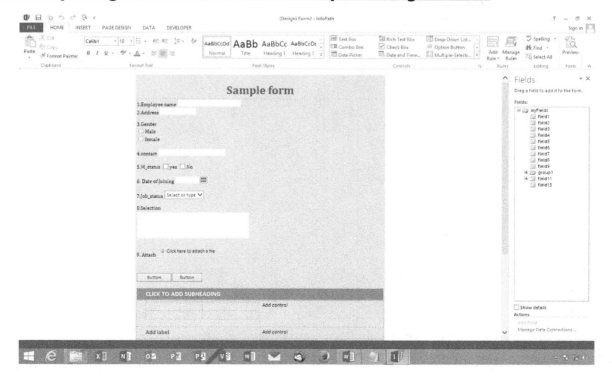

Microsoft filler – microsoft infopath filler application helping microsoft infopath designer user to preview and fill placed form control information value and information record at particular placed form control in filler preview mode, include apply home and insert control on working filler form control while user need, we must to understand here filler just used to preview and filling information crated by microsoft infopath designer application.

Default opening window of microsoft infopath filler 2013

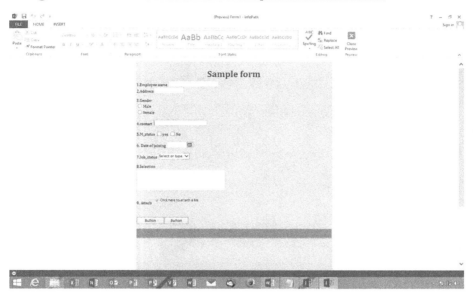

Microsoft lync – microsoft lync default bundled with microsoft office suite version 2013, lync used to create or making online video, audio, call, net conference, voip communication, instant messaging application, data and file sharing, through installed lync software, but in microsoft office 2016 it completely replaced with microsoft skype for business only name change but you see working environment, application interface, and communication order similar to skype for business, use microsoft lync for online communication, sharing, import and export system resources.

Default opening window of microsoft lync 2013

Microsoft skype drives for business 2016 – microsoft skype for business application newly launch and rename function of microsoft lync, but microsoft skype for busies provide more control better environment for instant messaging, voice call, video call, online conference tool, voip communication, file and data transfer service, worldwide connected and sign in as skype user, these application integrate features or function of microsoft lync along skype application collaboration, you work in same like work in lync, but more useful then lync because skype famous glob wise across the nation or continent, you need to download it additionally default it group part of microsoft office 2016 suite, just create microsoft skype account, gmail account, msn/hotmail account to log in skype for business application, and use its all function and control according to your need.

Default opening window of microsoft skype for business 2016

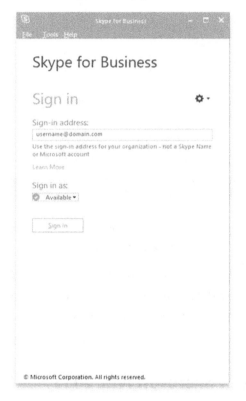

Microsoft one drive for business 2016 – microsoft one drive popular services of microsoft office suite with one drive microsoft user able to roaming create, open, edit or print electronic document, presentation slide, e-mail, and other kind of company service, but you have microsoft account for logging as one drive user at microsoft one drive user able to store, retrieves, files, document, advantage of one drive these application provide its user versatility for using resources from anywhere or everywhere, but just you have internet network connectivity then you able to store and retrieves one drive storage document and electronic information world – wide, just login as one drive use and access 15 gb free space for storage but you want more then buy online space from microsoft company for storage document and information at one drive storage location.

Discuss microsoft application menu control and windows display

Menu of microsoft word application

Menu name	Description about menu/tab
File tab/menu	File menu used to create, open, save, save as, print, export, customize, option share and export word document related option.
Home tab	Home tab provide control for cut, copy, paste, formatting's, font, paragraph, styles and editing tools apply on selected word document.
Insert tab	Insert pages, tables, illustration object, add – ins, media, links, comments, header & footer, text or symbols object in working document.
Design tab	Design word document or add theme, document formatting's, colors, fonts, watermark, page color and border.
Layout tab	Configure layout of word document page setup, paragraph indent and spacing, arrange paragraph object, wrap text, position, align, selection pane or rotate.
Reference tab	Use or insert document reference table of content, footnotes, citation & bibliography, captions, index, and control table of authorities control.
Mailing tab	Create envelope, labels, start mail merge wizard, writer or insert mail merge fields, preview mail merge result, finish mail merge with option.
Review tab	Review document proofing, insight, change language, add comments, track document, accept track changes, compare document, protect document with password.
View tab	View current document in various views, show control, set zoom and window position, switch among window, operate macros default function.
Developer tab	Use and insert developer control name macros code, insert or control add – ins, drag and drop control, protect and restrict document.

Additional menu when object select in microsoft word application

Additional menu appears while certain object select in microsoft word	
Toolbar name	Description about describe toolbar function
Add – ins	Add – ins tab contain some add – ins tools to adding or greater ability of current application.
Blog - post	Using blog post tools to publish and post word blog, add blog clipboard control, using basic text font effect on blog, apply blog styles, adding proofing tools.

(Contd.)

Additional menu appears while certain object select in microsoft word	
Toolbar name	**Description about describe toolbar function**
Outlining tab	Using and inserting a outlining tools in word document outline view, adding master document outline effect, and close outline tab
Background removal	Remove background removal tab contain some important tools to crop, resize and adjust current insert word document image.
Smart art tools	Smart art tools appear while microsoft word user inserted smart art from insert menu.
Design tab	Design tab allow tools to design graphic smart art object, change smart layout shape, change or add color combination form choice, get smart art styles, and finally move back with reset graphic option.
Format tab	Format smart art object shape change shape, shape styles, fill shape color, outline, add shape effect, add word art text add text fill, text outline, text effect, position, wrap text, include arrange shape and object.
Chart tools	Chart tools appear while user ready for working and editing tools control of insert chart.
Design tab	Add chart elements, add quick layout, change chart colors, modify chart styles, move chart switch row/column, select chart data, edit data, include change chart type.
Format tab	Format inserted chart elements current selection, insert chart shape, change shape styles, fill shape, shape outline, shape effect or color, add word art styles, fill text color, text outline, and text effect, arrange object in front, back, align, group, and rotate chart object.
Drawings tools	Drawings tools appear while user drag and drop some object, shape, and other content.
Format tab	Insert shape, edit shape, draw text box, change shape styles, add shape fill, shape outline, shape effect, word art styles, change text, outline, text effect, change text direction, align text, change position, wrap text, arrange or align object, group and rotate drawings object.
Picture tools	Picture tools appear while user insert a any kind of picture, image, wallpaper, etc.
Format tab	Format word document inserted pictures remove background, change correction, color, add artistic effect, compress, change picture, add picture styles, change picture border, add picture effect, picture layouts, change picture position, wrap text, arrange, align, group, rotate object.
Table tools	Table tools appear when microsoft word document user insert a table and modify control.

Additional menu appears while certain object select in microsoft word	
Toolbar name	**Description about describe toolbar function**
Design tab	Design inserted word document table design control, on/off table style options, change or add table styles, add shading styles, customize table border styles, line, width, pen color, border, border painter.
Layout tab	Add or configure layout of inserted table and structure, select table, properties, draw table, erase table, delete table, row, column, insert row & columns, merge, split, cells, table, auto fit, cell size, add alignment, sort table, add formula and other content.
Header& footer	While user click on top and bottom of document header and footer tab appear, include click on insert menu to insert header into document.
Design tab	Add document header & footer information, insert header footer date & time, document info, quick parts, pictures, online pictures, navigate among header and footer, on/off options, change position of object, finally close header and footer tab in document.
Equation tools	Equation tools appear when user click on insert equation in microsoft word document.
Design tab	Insert equation, ink equation, professional, liner, normal, add symbols, insert fraction, script, integral, large operator, bracket, function, accent, limit and log, operator, matrix in document.
Ink tools	Ink tools appear while user selecting or inserting a ink for creating object or shape.
Pens tab	Pens tab provides some list of control or tools that helpful to creating some object and shape line and control.

Menu of microsoft excel application

Menu name	Detail description about menu/tab
File men/ tab	Create new worksheet, open, save, print share, export, excel worksheet, include customize configure excel option and customize settings.
Home tab	Add home tab effect on worksheet name clipboard, fonts, alignment, number, styles, cells, and editing tools, click and select desire tools category for apply on working sheet content.
Insert tab	Insert excel worksheet tables, illustration object, add – ins, charts, spark inline, filters, links, text, and symbol inserting as a working sheet object.
Page layout tab	Configure worksheet themes, set page setup, arrange worksheet scale to fit, on/off sheet option, include arrange placed object and control.

(Contd.)

Menu name	Detail description about menu/tab
Formulas tab	Insert and apply worksheet formulas, function category, defined names, control formula auditing, and calculation option settings easier to configure or applying.
Data tab	Apply data tools on worksheet name get external data, get & transform, sort & filter, data tools, forecast, and outline option add in working worksheet.
Review tab	Adding review control on worksheet name proofing tools, insight, language, comments, protect sheet, and workbook, track changes, and other control.
View tab	View worksheet or workbook view, show worksheet toolbar, zoom, arrange window, switch window, and control or create macros events.
Developer tab	Insert and develop developer worksheet control name macro code, add – ins, control insert, and operate xml events on current worksheet.

Additional menu when object select in microsoft excel application

Additional menu appear while certain object select in microsoft excel	
Toolbar name	**Description about describe toolbar function**
Add – ins	Insert some additional add – ins tools and control in working excel worksheet, these tools helping you to manage and work with some application add – ins.
Background removal	Background removal to mark area select some desire picture portion and make it to complete background removal process.
Smart art tools	Smart art tools appear when user click on insert button to represent object with smart tools object.
Design tab	Use design tab to add smart shape, bullets, text pane, move up, down, change smart art layouts, change smart art shape colors, smart art styles, reset or convert to shape smart art object.
Format tab	Format smart art shape in 2d and 3d, change smart shape, make larger, smaller, modify shape styles, add shape fill, shape outline, add shape effect, insert work art text fill, outline, text effect, arrange, align, group, and rotate smart art object.
Chart tools	Insert chart tools to describe chart in excel worksheet with database sheet.
Design tab	Design tab display some chart design elements like, add chart elements, change quick layout, change colors, add chart styles, switch row/column, select chart data, change current chart with choice of chart, move chart.
Format tab	Select chart elements for formatting's, insert shapes, change shape, add chart shape styles, change shape fill, shape outline, shape effect, word art styles, change word art text, arrange object, align object, group chart, and rotating chart shape.

Additional menu appear while certain object select in microsoft excel	
Toolbar name	**Description about describe toolbar function**
Drawings tools	Drawings tools appear while excel user insert any kind of shape and object.
Format tab	Format inserted sheet drawings tools object, insert new drawings shapes, edit, change shape, add shape styles, fill shape color, outline color, add shape effect, insert word art styles, fill word art text, outline, text effect color, arrange, align, group, rotate shape.
Picture tools	Picture tools display when excel user manually insert picture in worksheet.
Format tab	Remove picture background, add corrections, color, add artistic effect, compress, change reset picture, add picture styles, modify picture border, picture effect, picture layout, arrange, align, group, or rotate, crops image, change height width of picture.
Pivot table tools	Select worksheet numeric data and values to create pivot table data information.
Analyze tab	Analyze tab display some analysis tools to analyze pivot table values, view pivot table name, active field, group/ungroup pivot table data, filter, refresh, change data, ass pivot action, control calculation, create pivot chart, show pivot table elements.
Design tab	Design tab provides some designing pivot table data and information, change layout of created pivot table, turn on/off pivot table styles options, add or modify created pivot table styles colorful background effect on it.
Header& footer	Header & footer appear when user need to add sheet header and footer information.
Design tab	Add sheet header, footer elements, manually add header or footer elements name page number, number of pages, current date & time, file path, name, picture, move with header or footer, turn on/off default header footer options check box settings.
Table tools	Select sheet area click on insert and get table tools for making some attractive tables.
Design tab	View table properties, use table tools, insert slicer, export, refresh, get properties of table data, manually on/off table style options check box settings, include add color full table styles effect with multiple attributes in current table sheet data.
Pivot chart tools	Pivot chart tools appear when user create pivot table with chart features.
Analyze tab	Analyze tab allows some control to analyze pivot table chart elements, display chart name, active field information, expand or collapse field, control filter, insert slicer, timeline, refresh change data, clear or move chart, control calculation, or show/hide.

(Contd.)

Additional menu appear while certain object select in microsoft excel	
Toolbar name	**Description about describe toolbar function**
Design tab	Add pivot chart design features on it, add chart elements, change chart quick layout, change chart color, modify default chart styles, on pivot chart object, switch pivot chart row to column, select chart data, change chart type, or move chart location.
Format tab	Add formatting effect or attribute son current design chart, select chart elements, insert chart shape, change chart shape, add chart shape styles color, fill shape, outline and add effect attributes, insert word art fill text, outline color, arrange, group, rotate.
Ink tools	Insert ink tools to draw and design some ink created shape and object in sheet.
Pens tab	Insert pens for create draw text, display highlighter, erase pens text, shape, select object, change pens, pens color, and pens thickness, and close pens tab or control,
Sparkline tools	Sparkline tools appear when user working or excel chart data information.
Design tab	Adding working chart sparkline editing information, select chart sparkline type, show and hide sparkline elements, apply chart style, create group or ungroup sparkline chart elements, clear sparkline chart elements.
Time line tools	Use time line tools on created pivot table data and chart elements in worksheet.
Options tab	Adding timeline captions, report connections, apply timeline styles, arrange timeline tools in back or front location, set size of time line elements, show time line header, selection, scrollbar, and time level and more information.
Slicer tools	Using slicer tools effect on working worksheet data and selection range information.
Options tab	Select change or apply slicer caption, make slicer settings, report connections, apply quick slicer styles, moving, arrange, group, rotate, chart elements, turn on slicer buttons effect, configure default height & width size & properties of slicer tools.
Search tools	When spreadsheet information search in worksheet it appear for searching information.
Search tab	Find name, description, from, data source, this week, certified elements in worksheet, apply recent searches information at working spreadsheet, finally close search tab.

Additional menu appear while certain object select in microsoft excel	
Toolbar name	**Description about describe toolbar function**
Query tools	When query use or selected operated in working excel worksheet query tools appear.
Query tab	Edit worksheet query, view query properties, delete existing query, load, refresh query, reuse use query, combine & merge query create send to query catalog information.
Equation tools	Equation tools display when user insert equation in current worksheet.
Design tab	Insert equation tools, equation, ink equation, add equation basic math symbol, manually insert or deal with fraction, script, radical, integral, large operator, bracket, function, accent, limit & log, operator, matrix for adding or solving equation.

Menu of microsoft power point application

Menu name	Detail description about menu/tab
File menu/tab	Create, open, save, save as, protect, share, export, power point presentation slides, get account info, configure and customize option settings.
Home tab	Add clipboard controls, insert or change slide, add fonts, paragraph control, insert and operate drawings control, find, replace, and select presentation effect.
Insert tab	Insert new slide, tables, images, illustration object, add – ins, links, comments, text control symbols, and multimedia object at working presentation slide.
Design tab	Add design themes and theme variations, customize presentation slides and format background.
Transition tab	Adding slide placed object and control transition effect, or transition on slide, preview, set timing slide control.
Animation tab	Adding slide placed object and slide animation, configure effect, control advanced animation, set animation timing control.
Slide show tab	Add or configure start slide show effect, setup slide show, display monitor preview slide view.
Review tab	Adding slide proofing tools, insight, language, comments, compare, ink, and one note.
View tab	View presentation slides on different view, view master slide view, show hide bar, zoom, color/grayscale, control window, and macros event and task.
Developer tab	Insert or code macros control, insert add – ins, drag and drop activex control in working presentation slides.

Additional menu when object select in microsoft power point application

Additional menu appear while certain object select in microsoft power point	
Toolbar name	**Description about describe toolbar function**
Add – ins tab	Insert add – ins some additional application features and control to increase capability of working application with add new add- ins features in current presentation slide, in general you add – ins menu commands, toolbar commands, or custom toolbars.
Merge tab	Merge tab provide some control to merge resolution made change accept, reject, move previous changes, next changes, show hide changes in reviewing pane, finally control or close merge tab preview in microsoft power points presentation slide.
Grayscale tab	Grayscale tab appear when user adding image color effect in grayscale, black and white or other color attributes in slide picture or object, change default picture object in b & w, grayscale, light grayscale, inverse grayscale, black and white and more effect.
Black and white tab	Black and white tab provides some picture black and white conversion color choice among b & w automatic, b & w grayscale, inverse grayscale, black and white, and similar choice to making picture graphic in black and white shape order.
Slide master tab	Slide master tab appear when slide master inserted in current presentation slides, insert slide master, insert slide layout, delete, rename, or preserve slide, change slide master layout, insert place holders, add theme, change colors, fonts, effect, background, or close.
Handouts master tab	Handouts master tab appear when user insert handouts in presentation slides, set page setup of slide handout master view, turn on/off handout placeholder, edit theme, add slide master background effect, finally close master view in presentation.
Notes master tab	Notes master tab appear when user insert a notes master in presentation slides, change handouts orientation, slide size, slides per page, turn on/off placeholders, edit slide themes, change colors, fonts, add effect, background, hide background and close master.
Background removal	Insert picture and select background removal option to remove some unnecessary part of picture, mark picture deletion area and location and keep change after background removal.
Home(master view)	Home tab display for master view in working presentation slides, insert and control home master clipboard, slides, font, paragraph, drawings, editing control on master view presentation slides and its display preview.

Additional menu appear while certain object select in microsoft power point	
Toolbar name	**Description about describe toolbar function**
Smart art tools	Smart art tools display when presentation slide user insert smart art shape tools.
Design tab	Add design tab smart art tools effect or attributes on working presentation slide, add smart art tools shape, bullets, view text pane, move up/down, promote, demote smart art tools, change smart art layouts, change colors, add smart art 2d, 3d effect, reset or close.
Format tab	Add some format effect or attributes on smart art tools object, change smart art from 2d to 3d change shape, make larger or smaller shape, add or change shape styles, change shape fill, outline and add effect, modify word art styles, arrange, align, rotate, smart art.
Chart tools	Chart tools preview when presentation slide user insert chart with data in slide.
Design tab	Add slide chart elements, quick change chart layouts, change chart colors, modify chart styles, move chart among row to column, select or modify chart data, refresh chart data, finally change chart with available choice of chart elements in working chart layouts.
Format tab	Add formatting's on inserting chart and its elements, add chart format selection, insert chart shape, change chart shape, fill chart shape, outline, effect, insert chart word art styles, fill word art text, outline, add effect, arrange, align, group, rotate, other control.
Drawings tools	Drawings tools display when presentation user manually insert any drawings shape.
Format tab	Format slide inserted drawings shape, insert new shape, edit shape, insert text box, modify inserted shape styles, fill shape, outline, add shape effect, insert word art styles add color, outline and effect, arrange, group, rotate, change height and width of shape.
Picture tools	Picture tools appear when user insert pictures in working presentation slides.
Format tab	Format current picture with remove background, add correction, color, artistic effects, compress, change, reset, pictures, add 2d, 3d picture styles, apply picture border, outline, change picture layout, arrange, align, group, rotate, crop, change height, width.
Table tools	Insert table in current slide you will see a table tools display with it default tabs.

(Contd.)

Additional menu appear while certain object select in microsoft power point	
Toolbar name	**Description about describe toolbar function**
Design tab	Turn on/off table tools table style options, apply some attractive table styles, add table shading, borders, effect, add table quick styles, add text fill, outline, effect, change pen style pen weight, draw table, erase table some unwanted portion.
Layout tab	Insert and configure table layout structure, select table elements, view gridlines, delete table, insert row and column, merge cells, split table, change table cells size, height, width, arrange cell text, change direction, arrange, align, group, rotate slides object.
Audio tools	Insert audio and get audio tools and its control in current presentation slides.
Format tab	Remove audio background, add correction, color, artistic effect, compress, change, reset pictures, add or apply 2d, 3d, audio pictures styles, add audio tools border, outline, and shape effect, arrange, align, group, rotate audio tools, increase/decrease shape.
Playback tab	Control some playback features on working audio tools control name play, add bookmarks, trim audio, edit audio, configure audio options, turn on/off audio options, apply audio styles, select play in background current audio.
Video tools	Insert video in active presentation slide you see video tools and its sub tab along it.
Format tab	Format tab show formatting's features related to video tools, play video, add correction, color, poster frame, reset design effect, change video styles with 2d and 3d video, change video shape, add border, effect, arrange, align, group, rotate, crop, video object.
Playback tab	Control video playback control name play video, add/remove video bookmarks, trim video, edit fade duration, configure turn on/off video options, and other check box settings remain for enable or disable.
Cd tools	Cd tools appear when cd tools inserted in working presentation slides.
Options tab	Control cd tools play options, setup cd tools, slide show volume, set time track, check box option to manually make turn on/off, arrange cd tools object, align, group and rotate placed cd tools object, configure and modify default size of cd tools object.
Ink tools	Insert ink tools to draw and design pens design shape, object, text, information in slide.

Additional menu appear while certain object select in microsoft power point	
Toolbar name	**Description about describe toolbar function**
Pens tab	Pens tab provide some control and function to create pens graphic, use pen, show pen highlighter, use eraser, get lasso tools, select object, get pens style, change pen color, pen line thickness, convert to shape ink object and finally close ink tools.
Equation tools	Equation tools appear in working presentation slide when user manually insert equation.
Design tab	Insert equation tools, equation, ink equation, add equation basic math symbol, manually insert or deal with fraction, script, radical, integral, large operator, bracket, function, accent, limit & log, operator, matrix for adding or solving equation.

Menu of microsoft access application

Menu name	Detail description about menu/tab
File menu/tab	Control database, table, form, query, report, label, macros operation name, new, open, save, print, access database, include configure and customize option settings.
Home tab	Add home menu control on working database form, report, table, labels, query, view control, clipboard, sort & filter, records, find, and text formatting's effect.
Create tab	Create tab allows access user to create application template, tables, queries, forms, reports, macros & code all these created on base of table database.
External tab	Get external database into working database import & link object, export database, and web linked lists database information.
Database tools tab	Control access database tools name tools, macro, relationship, analyze, move data, and add – ins in current access database.

Additional menu when object select in microsoft access application

Additional menu appear while certain object select in microsoft access	
Toolbar name	**Description about describe toolbar function**
Source control	Source control tab display some database source control function, menu and control, click and open source control, manage source control in reference of database.

(Contd.)

Additional menu appear while certain object select in microsoft access	
Toolbar name	**Description about describe toolbar function**
Add – ins	Insert access database add – ins feature to grow capability of microsoft access application, adding some menu command add – ins, toolbar commands add – ins, similar insert some custom toolbars, in active access database software.
View	View tab option display some view settings of display access control and object.
Design tab	Change view of access object, font, font size, control formatting's, datasheet properties, insert and control, manage view tools and properties in working access database.
Form layout tools	Form layout tools appear when access table based form create it show all form layout tools.
Design tab	Design tab provides control for view form layout, add form theme, colors, change fonts, add form layout controls, insert image, add form logo, add form title, insert form date & time, add table form existing field, view property form sheet.
Arrange tab	Arrange form create placed information, view gridline in form, change form in stacked, tabular preview, insert row and column, select form layout, select, row and column, merge, split horizontally, vertically, move up/down, control margin, control padding, anchoring.
Format tab	Format form layout placed control and text structure, select form object, add bold, italic, underline, font effect, apply number of other format, insert background image, add alternate row color, set conditional formatting's, fill shape, outline fill, add shape effect on form.
Form design tools	Form design tools appear when form created with design mode, get all form design tools.
Design tab	Form design tools provides all control, function, view form, change form theme, change color, fonts, add or insert ford design control, insert image, add design form logo, title, date & time, add existing field, property sheet, tab order, view code, change with macros.
Arrange tab	Arrange design form in gridline, stacked, tabular view, remove layout, insert design form row & column, select form layout, row & column, merge table, split horizontally, vertically, move up/down, display control margins, paddings, set size/space, align, front and back.
Format tab	Add formatting's effect attributes on design form and its elements select form elements, add formatting's effect, change form number format, add background image, row alternate color, add quick styles, change shape, conditional formatting's, fill shape, outline, effect.

Additional menu appear while certain object select in microsoft access	
Toolbar name	**Description about describe toolbar function**
Report layout tools	Report layouts tools appear when user create report on the base of access table database, you just open table and click on create menu to create report.
Design tab	Change report layout view, theme, add colors, fonts on report, group & sort report tools, add totals effect on it, hide report detail, insert set of report control in report window, insert report image, add report page number, logo, title, date & time, add existing fields, view property sheet.
Arrange tab	Arrange created report placed control and function, view report gridline, stacked, tabular, insert report row & column, select report layout, row and column, merge report row column, split report horizontally, vertically, move up/down, add control margin and control padding.
Format tab	Format created report and its elements select report object, apply formatting's, number format change, dollar, percent, comma, increase/decrease decimal, insert background image, add alternate row color, fill shape style, change shape, conditional formatting, fill shape fill, outline and shape effect from provides choice.
Page setup tab	Set page setup with page setup tools and control in working design report layout controls, change or modify report size, report margins, on/off page size check box option, change report page layout with portrait, landscape, column, modify report page setup.
Report design tools	Report design tools appear when access user create report with design mode, here you manually need to draw/design placed insert report design control in it.
Design tab	Change report layout view, theme, add colors, fonts on report, group & sort report tools, add totals effect on it, hide report detail, insert set of report control in report window, insert report image, add report page number, logo, title, date & time, add existing fields, view property sheet, view report tab order, view report code, convert report to macros visual basic.
Arrange tab	Arrange created report placed control and function, view report gridline, stacked, tabular, insert report row & column, select report layout, row and column, merge report row column, split report horizontally, vertically, move up/down, add control margin and control padding, set size/space, align report, move back or front report object.
Format tab	Format created report and its elements select report object, apply formatting's, number format change, dollar, percent, comma, increase/decrease decimal, insert background image, add alternate row color, fill shape style, change shape, conditional formatting, fill shape fill, outline and shape effect from provides choice.

(Contd.)

Additional menu appear while certain object select in microsoft access	
Toolbar name	**Description about describe toolbar function**
Page setup tab	Set page setup with page setup tools and control in working design report layout controls, change or modify report size, report margins, on/off page size check box option, change report page layout with portrait, landscape, column, modify report page setup.
Relationship tools	Relationship tools appear when create or manage relationship in working access database.
Design tab	Edit relationship, clear layout, view relationship report, show table, hide table, direct relationship, all relationship and other control to manage and work in relationship tools.
Query tools	Query tools appear when access user create query with query design tools and control.
Design tab	Change query views, run query, select, make query, append, update, add crosstab query effect, union, pass - through, data – definition, insert rows, delete rows, insert column, delete query column, add query total, set query parameters, display table, property sheet of query.
Macro tools	Macros tools appear when macro created from macro in create tab from microsoft access.
Design tab	Design tab provides some control for design report macros control and elements, run macros, convert macros into visual basic, expand/collapse macro action, expand all, collapse all, show and hide action catalog, show all actions in created macros elements.
Table tools	Table tools appear when access user manually create table form create tables choice options.
Fields tab	Change table view, add table field in sort text, number, currency, date & time, yes/no, insert more fields, delete, view properties, name & captions, modify lookups, memo settings, change field type, add number format, turn on/off, check box, set some validation rules.
Table tab	Table tab display create table properties, configure table events before changes, before delete, after insert, after update, delete, view named macros, set table relationship, get object dependencies and other related settings.
Table tools	Table tools appear when table manually created and field set in table design mode.
Design tab	Change table view, set design table fields tools name primary key, use builder, test validation rules, insert row, delete row, modify lookup, show hide property sheet, indexes, create data macros, rename/delete macros, set relationship, view object dependencies.

Additional menu appear while certain object select in microsoft access	
Toolbar name	**Description about describe toolbar function**
Form tools	Form tools appear when working or different elements of form in access software.
Datasheet tab	Change form view mode, add form theme, colors, fonts, adding form tools add existing fields,, view for property sheet, add formatting's form background color, alternate row color, conditional formatting and many more.

Menu of microsoft publisher application

Menu name	Detail description about menu/tab
File menu/tab	Create new, open, save, save as, print, share, protect publication, view user account info, configure option settings of publisher menu and control.
Home tab	Add clipboard, font, paragraph, styles, objects, arrange publication object shape & pictures, include adding editing effect on publication design.
Insert tab	Insert publication design pages, illustration, building blocks, text, links, and header & footer elements at design publication as object.
Page design tab	Design or add publication design template, page setup effect, layout, pages, schemes, fonts, apply image, background and master pages.
Mailing tab	Create mailing tab mail merge wizard, write and insert mail merge fields, preview mail merge fields, terminate and finish mail merge publication.
Review tab	Adding review tab control effect on current publication control name spellings, research thesaurus, translate selected text, and language features.
View tab	Use different view for publication, show publication bars and hide, zoom publication, and control window operation.
Developer tab	Insert and control developer control in reference of design publication name visual basic, macros, macros security, and com add – ins.

Additional menu when object select in microsoft publisher application

Additional menu appear while certain object select in microsoft publisher	
Toolbar name	**Description about describe toolbar function**
Add – ins	Add some add – ins microsoft publisher control and features in shape of menu commands, toolbars command, custom toolbar, these increase publisher capability and ability while user work on.
Web tab	Web tab display when publisher user working on web control and elements in publication.

(Contd.)

Additional menu appear while certain object select in microsoft publisher	
Toolbar name	**Description about describe toolbar function**
Master tab	Master tab display when user working on master page, add master page, two page master, duplicate master, rename, delete master page, show master page header and footer information, insert page number, date, time, finally close master page tab.
Catalog tools	Catalog tools appear in microsoft publisher when publisher user insert catalog pages.
Format tab	Format publisher design with catalog tools, insert or add list of catalog user, edit list of catalog user, change layout of catalog, change layout of catalog in row and column, fill order, insert text field, picture fields, preview result, preview page, merge to new, add or print.
Drawings tools	Drawings tools preview when publisher user insert some drawings shape and object.
Format tab	Insert drawings shape, edit existing shape, change shape, edit text, add drawings shape styles, fill shape, outline, color, shape effect, wrap drawings object text, bring to front to back drawing object, align, group, rotate, increase height/width of drawings shape object.
Text box tools	Text box tools preview when publisher user insert or draw text box at publisher.
Format tab	Format inserted text box text, fit text, change text direction, add font, effect, increase, decrease size, set space, add background color, align text box text, convert text into column, set margin, insert word art styles fill text, outline, text effect, add drop cap, number styles, and other effect.
Word art tools	Word art tools appear in publisher when user manually insert o select word art text.
Format tab	Format tab allows some controls to edit text, set spacing, make upper case, vertical text, change word art styles, change shape of word art text, add shape outline, shape, effect, wrap text, move back or front, text, align, group, rotate, word art text, make size grow and shrink.
Picture tools	Picture tools appear in microsoft publisher when user insert or work on picture in publication.
Format tab	Format publication picture, insert picture, add picture corrections, recolor, compress, change, reset picture, add 2d, 3d picture styles, add picture border, picture effect, caption, arrange picture as thumbnails, align, crop, group, rotate pictures, fit, fill, grow/shrink height width.

Additional menu appear while certain object select in microsoft publisher	
Toolbar name	**Description about describe toolbar function**
Table tools	Insert table tools appear when publisher user manually insert table in shape or row & column.
Design tab	Design tab provides control to design publisher table, change default table format, fill table colors, change table line, line color, add table borders, insert table word art text, fill word art text color, outline, text effect, insert drop cap, number styles, ligatures, stylistic sets and other.
Layout tab	Configure layout of inserted publisher table with select table elements, view table gridline, delete table elements, insert row & column, merge table, split table, align table, text direction, set cell margin, wrap text, move back front, group, rotate, change height, width, of table cells.

Menu of microsoft outlook application

Menu name	Detail description about menu/tab
File menu/tab	Create, save, print, export, microsoft outlook e-mail, calendar, journal, task, notes, people contact, outlook elements, along view user account info with configure option settings.
Home tab	Microsoft outlook play many role with individual outlook tab like create e-mail, calendar, notes, task, people contact, each time home menu will be change, but common effect you add through home menu new, delete, respond, quick step, move, tags, and find, with home tab.
Send/receive tab	Send receive option similar work different in various outlook object, but you send or receive new e-mail, calendar, people contact, journal, task, notes, and other outlook object.
Folder tab	Create new folder for e-mail, calendar, task, journal, notes, and people contact storage and apply folder option effect name new, actions, clean up, favorites, include properties.
View tab	View e-mail message, calendar, task, notes, journal, notes, current view, message, arrangement object, view layout, people pane, and control windows.
Developer tab	Insert and insert control of developer for e-mail, calendar, people, task, notes, insert and code macros events, insert add – ins, custom forms control at design outlook object location.

Additional menu when object select in microsoft outlook application

Additional menu appear while certain object select in microsoft outlook	
Toolbar name	Description about describe toolbar function
Home (mail)	Home e-mail tab display some important control related to getting's, view,, print and manage e-mails in outlook, create new mail & new item, delete e-mail, reply, forward, meeting, setup quick step of e-mail move e-mail at other location or one note, view unread e-mail, set e-mail category, search, view address book, and filter e-mail.
Home(calendar table view)	Use calendar table view control to create new calendar, set calendar created item action, share calendar elements, share calendar, apply option on calendar, include add tag, and set find strategies on working calendar view elements.
Home (calendar)	Home calendar tab display some outlook calendar creation related tools and control, new appointment, meetings, new item, new skype meetings, go to, arrange calendar in many views, manage calendars, share calendars, search people, address book.
Home (contacts)	Create a new contact, new contact group, new item, delete, communicate contact, change current contact view, move contact, create mail merge, one note, forward, share, open shared contact, add tag on contact, create people search, view address book.
Home (tasks)	Create or manage new task, new email, new item, delete, respond, manage task mark complete, remove from list, set task follow up, change current view of created task, set action, search people, and manage address book.
Home (notes)	Crete and manage microsoft outlook notes, create new notes, make selection notes item, delete notes, change current view of created notes in view, manage notes task, categories, search people, manage address book.
Home (journals)	Home journal display when outlook user create a journals, create new journals item, delete journals, arrange number of created journals, change current view of journals, set action, tag, and set find condition on created journals.
Home (group)	Control home group elements control, like create new conversation, new item, delete elements, set respond elements, configure or control group assets membership, members, edit group, calendar, files, notebook, set find control, change or view layout.
Add – ins	Add some additional add – ins features in working microsoft outlook application through add – ins control, add menu command, toolbar command, custom toolbar and other add – ins to enhance ability of current application.

Additional menu appear while certain object select in microsoft outlook	
Toolbar name	**Description about describe toolbar function**
Calendar tools	Calendar tools display when microsoft user create calendar appointments.
Appointments tab	Create appointment, open, delete appointment, cancel meetings, forward, join skype meetings, manage one note meeting notes, control and configure attendees, set respond behavior, configure options, set tag and other priority control on it.
Calendar tools	Calendar tools display when outlook user create recurring appointment in outlook.
Recurring appointment tab	Set recurring appointment action open, delete, appointment, cancel meetings, forward, join skype meetings, manage meeting one note notes, set attendees behavior, configure respond behavior, show and hide options elements, add tag and related activities.
Task tools	Task tools appear when user create a new task in microsoft outlook with task tab.
Task list tab	Open task item, set respond task behavior, manage multiple task, set follow up behavior on various task, set or arrange task, add or display task tag elements.
Daily task list tools	Daily task list tools appear when outlook user create a daily task list elements in outlook.
Daily task list tab	Open daily task list, post reply, reply to all, meeting, instant messaging, manage or mark complete task, remove task from list, set follow up on daily created task, arrange created task, set task action, add tags on created daily task list category.
Search tools	Search tools appear when user starting searching e-mail in microsoft outlook.
Search tab	Set search e-mail scope, view older search result, refine search with to, subject, attachment, categories, sent to, unread, view recent searches, manage search tools, and close search mail tab.
Attachment tools	Attachment tools appear in microsoft outlook application user attach something in outlook.
Attachments tab	Set attachment action, open, quick print, sent to, save as, save all attachment, remove attachment, select all or copy attachment, select chinese conversion translation mode, show and hide message attachment.
Compose tools	Compose tools display when outlook user create some new e-mail in message tab

(Contd.)

Additional menu appear while certain object select in microsoft outlook	
Toolbar name	**Description about describe toolbar function**
Message tab	Message tab provides control to create/compose e-mail message, apply message clipboard, add basic text effect, names, include, tags, show fields, and manage or create add – ins in working application.
Group tools	Group tools appear in microsoft outlook application while outlook user create a group.
Group tab	Control group operation name, set new group conversation, manage group assets elements name, membership, members, edit group, conversation, files, notebook, set or edit multi – group conversation, and related control in microsoft outlook.

Menu of microsoft one note application

Menu name	Detail description about menu/tab
File menu/ tab	File menu contain menu control to manage one note created digital notebook information, like create new note book, open, save, edit, share, export, send notebook, get account detail view and configure one note option settings.
Home tab	Home tab provides control for edit one note digital information, with clipboard control, basic text, change style, add one note tag, e-mail one note page, meeting details.
Insert tab	Insert tab allows you to insert one digital elements name insert space, table, file printout, file attachment, spreadsheet, diagram, images, create links, record audio/ video, date, time, date & time, page templates, equation, symbol.
Draw tab	Draw one note digital information ink pens tools, select ink pens object, add pens tools, change pen color and thickness, shapes, insert space, delete, arrange, rotate, ink to text, ink to math.
History tab	View one note digital notes history, next unread, mark as read, recent edit, find by author, page version, clear notebook recycle bin.
Review tab	Apply review tab control on working one note digital information, spellings, research, thesaurus, translate, language, add one note digital password, created linked notes.
View tab	Change view of one note digital document, normal view, full page view, manage page setup, add page color, rule lines, hide page title, zoom out, zoom in, set 100%, page width, new window, new quick note, always on top.
Pages	Set page on one note digital document, move on previous, next page, search one note page, delete page, and move on digital one note document.

Additional menu appear while certain object select in microsoft one note

Toolbar name	Description about describe toolbar function
Add – ins tab	Add one note application additional add –ins tools and control in working one note digital document, like add command, toolbars, menu, and other add – ins features in working application.
Home (narrow) tab	Display home tab narrow one note digital document to display and add document clipboard, basic text, tags, and other control to making one note text more attractive.
Insert (narrow) tab	Insert one note digital document narrow control in shape of tables, files, images, manage links, creating meetings, manage recording and other control.
Draw (narrow) tab	Draw narrow option on working one note digital notebook, insert one note tools, touch tools, edit narrows ink tools.
View (narrow) tab	Display one note view narrow effect, change view, docked page, full page, change or modify one note digital page setup, zoom in zoom out page in digital document.
Pages tab	Setup one note digital document navigate note book, move pages, create new page, delete page, move page and other control.
Audio & video	Audio & video tools insert into a working one note digital document audio or video.
Playback tab	Record audio, record video, play, pause, stop, rewind 10 minutes or second, see playback, configure and customize audio & video settings,
Table tools	Insert table tools in working one note digital document configure and modify table.
Layout tab	Select table, column, row, cell, delete table, column, rows, insert row above, below, insert left, insert right, hide borders, shading, align left, center, align right, sort, convert to excel spreadsheet in current table.
Equation tools	Insert equation tools to insert and manipulate equation and related control.
Design tab	Insert equation tools, equation, ink equation, add equation basic math symbol, manually insert or deal with fraction, script, radical, integral, large operator, bracket, function, accent, limit & log, operator, matrix for adding or solving equation.
Other commands	Other command display information in working one note digital document.
Share tab	Insert and share one note digital document, share this notebook.

Menu of microsoft visio application

Menu name	Detail description about menu/tab
File menu/tab	Create new visio drawings, insert or download readymade new visio design, open, save, share, print, and export visio design in various format, view user account, configure visio option settings.
Home tab	Adding created visio design home tab clipboard controls, apply or add font dialog attributes, adjust design paragraph, apply tools, fill shape styles, arrange visio object, and editing visio tools shape layers option form its category.
Insert tab	Insert visio created design new pages category, illustrate visio drawings object with picture, chart, cad drawings, using or insert shape containers tools, create and manage visio links, insert text box, object, screen tip, field and symbol at working visio design.
Design tab	Setup page of visio drawings, change page orientation, size, and set auto size, apply page design themes with choice name professional, modern, trendy, hand drawn, this document, change apply these variants color, add design theme colors, effects, connectors, select and apply backgrounds, borders & titles, add re-layout page, or insert connectors in current design.
Data tab	Insert external data into visio design, select import data graphic, insert data legends, show and hide shape data check box options, include adding advance data linking dialog settings.
Process tab	Create new sub process in visio design, select or apply visio diagram validation check box and control on design, import, export, share point workflow elements in current design.
Review tab	Adding review tab proofing tools, language features, comments, insert ink tools, and shape reports control on working visio design or diagram effect.
View tab	Adding or show view of visio design, turn on/off check box effect on current window design, set zoom option or level, making enable or disable visio visual aids, arrange multiple visio open window, move or switch between multiple visio window, create macros and insert add – ons feature in working design.
Developer tab	Insert or create macros event code, set macro security configure open visual basic, insert com add- ins, drag and drop application controls, insert shape design tools and operations, create new stencils, show and hide document stencils check box option settings.
Org chart tab	Using and inserting a org chart layout to complete change structure and design of visio design, change complete layout, arrange chart shape, change current design shapes, insert picture, organize data and information.

Additional menu appear while certain object select in microsoft visio	
Toolbar name	**Description about describe toolbar function**
Add – ins tab	Insert add – ins control in visio application name menu, toolbars, and custom toolbars add – ins features in working application.
Stencils	Stencil tab enable visio user to create new stencil in metric or us units, view created stencils, use master shape in stencils, switch among stencils window, close stencils window.
Icon editor	Use icon editor window and apply clipboard control, select for icon selection, using paint tool with icon editor elements, and close icon editor window.
Picture tools	Any picture inserted in visio drawings then you picture adjustment tool name brightness, contrast, auto balance, and compress picture, use these tools to configure picture properties, select and apply picture styles, moving inserted picture in back or front, rotate picture, use crop tool to crop picture.
Ink tools	Insert ink tools features for selecting or using ballpoint pen, use ink highlighter, stroke eraser, using pointer tool, change pens color, weight, create ink check box selection, convert ink shape, close ink tool window.
Shape sheet tools	View visio created design in shape tools with formula, values, sections, and other, insert new section, delete row, using editing shape data, hyperlink, set shape action, apply formula tracing with trace precedent, or trace dependents.
Container tools	Set size, margin, fit to content, automatic resize, container shape, select drag and drop container styles from container styles, select and change heading style, select container membership control on working visio design.

Menu of microsoft project application

Menu name	Detail description about menu/tab
File menu/tab	Create new project, open existing project plan, save, save as new project, print existing project, export project, and finally configure project default options settings.
Task tab	Apply clip board control on current task, add task font, maintain task schedule, select and control task, insert task elements, get information & properties about current task, include apply editing related settings in working task.
Resource tab	Assign resource to the number of created task, view team planner, add task assignment, insert or add resources, view properties about task resources, create and maintain levels of task created resources elements.

(Contd.)

Menu name	Detail description about menu/tab
Report tab	Compare project, and project created report compare in menu angle or views, view created reports in new report, dashboards report, costs, in progress report, getting started report, custom report, and view recent reports, view visual report information.
Project tab	Insert subproject, insert add – ins features in project, view project properties and information, create and maintain schedule of project, view status about project, using proofing tools.
View tab	Change view of created projects in many task view, change project in resources views, manage project data information, zoom enlarge project information, split project views, arrange created multiple open window, create and maintain project schedule.
Developer tab	Insert project macros code, manage project developer elements, include manage or insert add – ins or com add – ins.

Additional menu appear while certain object select in microsoft project	
Toolbar name	**Description about describe toolbar function**
Gatt chart tools	Gatt chart tools used to explain gatt chart based project work data easier to explain with its default function and control.
Calendar tools	Using calendar tools to demonstrate project calendar based work and electronic task information.
Network diagram tools	Insert or format network diagram tools related project task with network diagram project tools options.
Task usage tools	Insert task usage tools to explain project task work.
Resources plan tools	Insert or operate resources plan tools to explain its related control or features.

Menu of microsoft skype for business application

Menu name	Detail description about menu/tab
File menu	File menu contain some important skype file menu category control to sign in, change sign – in address, view my skype status, get received files, display conversation history, close and exit skype form business instant messaging application.
Tools menu	Apply and configure skype for business tools and control settings, configure skype recording manager settings, view and edit audio/video device settings, dial in conference settings, include modify advance option setting of skype for business 2016 application.
Help menu	View help information about skype for business application basic guideline and control function, get application privacy statement, view quick tips, and know about skype for business application.

Version of microsoft office

Microsoft office version	Year
Microsoft office suite	1995
Microsoft office suite	1997
Microsoft office suite	2000
Microsoft office suite	Xp
Microsoft office suite	2003
Microsoft office suite	2007
Microsoft office suite	2010
Microsoft office suite	2013
Microsoft office suite	2016